Angels at the Table

Angels at the Table

A Practical Guide to Celebrating Shabbat

YVETTE ALT MILLER

continuum

Continuum International Publishing Group

The Tower Building
11 York Road
London SE1 7NX

80 Maiden Lane
Suite 704
New York NY 10038

www.continuumbooks.com

British Library Cataloguing-in-Publication Data
A catalogue record for this book is available from the British Library.

ISBN: 978-1441-12397-8 (HB)

Library of Congress Cataloging-in-Publication Data

A catalog record for this book is available from the Library of Congress.

Typeset by Pindar NZ, Auckland, NZ
Printed and bound in India

Contents

Contents

Dedicated to my children, Meir Yaakov, Sarah Raisel, Gidon Zvi Aaron, and Natan Sasson. Your purity of faith and trust in God add beauty and merit to the world. May all of your Shabbats be full of blessings and delight.

1

Greeting the angels:
an overview of Shabbat

More than the Jewish People has kept Shabbat, Shabbat has kept the Jewish people.
—Ahad HaAm

Congratulations. Just by opening this book — by expressing your curiosity — you have taken a first step on a journey to finding something precious: a gift that was once given to you, and which many of us have misplaced. This gift, the Torah, was given to you, to your timeless Jewish soul thousands of years ago, in a great ceremony, and for many years you guarded it and enjoyed it. Of all the commandments in our holy Torah, perhaps none has been identified as closely with the Jewish people as our weekly day of Shabbat.

"Shabbat" is usually translated into English as "rest," but in Hebrew the word has a different meaning. Shabbat is not a day for relaxation, but for living on a different plane. God made us a holy people, and the hallmark of our holiness and closeness to Him is our weekly moments of Shabbat, when we begin to emulate the angels, living closer than usual to God.

What is this experience like? I've read many descriptions, but none can convey it fully. Some things simply have to be experienced to be understood. What does a pear taste like, for instance? Try explaining it to someone who's never tried one. You could spend hours describing a pear, its grainy texture and sweet taste, but in the end, you'd probably cry, "Please taste it and you'll know!"

Well, this book is a cry to "Taste it!," but its goal is something much sweeter

than the ripest pear. It is about Shabbat, which the Torah tells us is a "taste of the World to Come." What Shabbat is; how to celebrate it; and ideas for making it relevant and easy and fun. But in the end, to really understand Shabbat, you have to just taste it. Spend one Shabbat observing it the way that Jews have for millennia. Shabbat is our greatest gift from God, and it is there for every Jew to simply reach out and take it for his or her own.

Shabbat is a sensory experience. It is all-encompassing. It dictates how we eat, how we dress, how we travel, how we spend our time, how we interact with others. For 25 hours each week, the Shabbat-observer lives in a parallel universe: part of this world, but also part of the Divine World to Come. Judaism teaches that, while we don't know much about the afterlife, we do know that Shabbat is a taste of it: to observe Shabbat is to live for 25 hours in a little bit of Heaven.

A different sense of time

Shabbat does not fit in easily with the modern world. My family and I observe Shabbat in the Orthodox manner, as an all-encompassing day of difference and holiness. Every element of our lives on Shabbat is governed by a holy schedule. We are used to the rhythms of the day, but every now and then we get a reminder of how differently most people experience Saturdays.

I remember once inviting a family who lives near us to walk with us to services one Shabbat morning; the family didn't observe Shabbat, but they wanted to try out our shul (synagogue). We met them, as arranged, at a corner between our houses and walked together to shul. It was a lovely day and as we strolled along, greeting other families similarly walking to shul, our friends remarked that the entire tempo of their day had just changed. They had had an "ordinary" early morning, full of noise from the radio and television, a hurried breakfast, and some very early errands. They then rushed back home, changed into nice clothes, put their young child in her stroller, and walked out their front door. As we met at the street corner and walked together through the sunlight, chatting, our friends kept marveling

how slow and sedate their day suddenly felt. This is the spirit of Shabbat.

I've had many conversations over the years with people who told me that although they were attracted by the idea of Shabbat, it was impossible for them to actually observe it. They were too busy, or had no other time during the week to go grocery shopping or run other errands, or they were sure their kids would hate it, or they had to work overtime, or couldn't miss a week of soccer practice. These obstacles are real, but they are not insurmountable.

People can surprise themselves at what they are, in fact, able to accomplish. If someone suddenly offered you, a very busy person, tickets to watch your absolute favorite television show — perhaps one with a celebrity presenter, a select studio audience, or a game show with the chance to win millions — being taped on a Saturday, you might choose to quickly rearrange your weekend schedule so you could attend. No time to grocery shop? I'll do it on Sunday. Can't miss soccer practice? Oh, yes I can! The kids have a birthday party? I'll drop off a present later; their friends won't mind. The excitement is understandable; people wait for years for the chance to be in the studio audience for the most popular programs. Yet, if we are willing to make so many sacrifices in order to be present at an exciting television show, how much more should we be willing to make similar arrangements so that we can bask in the presence of God and enjoy a day of complete holiness? Not every Jew is curious about celebrating Shabbat, but for those who are, no obstacle is insurmountable.

Here is something to keep in mind if you are curious about observing Shabbat but don't know how you'd pull it off: millions of people do. People who are busy, people who work, people who are sick, people who live alone, and people who have 12 kids. People who are rich and people who are poor. People who are partners in prestigious firms and must always appear pulled-together, and people who have to frantically work four jobs just to make ends meet. They've all come up with coping strategies and shortcuts to get ready each week, and they all usher in the spirit of Shabbat each Friday evening as they light two candles and wave the warmth of the flames towards themselves. This book will help you with many of the practical considerations about "making Shabbat." For the rest, please

make a leap of faith, and know that God Himself will help you along. For, as Judaism teaches, when you take one step towards God, He will rush to take many steps towards you.

All or nothing?

Here's a big question. Millions of people might celebrate Shabbat in an all-encompassing "Orthodox" manner, but millions more do just part of Shabbat, for instance lighting the Shabbat candles on Friday evening or going to synagogue on Saturday morning, but no more. Can one celebrate Shabbat by observing just some of its precepts?

This book will answer that question from a practical, not a theoretical, point of view. Certainly, some Jewish thinkers would encourage people to keep some of Shabbat because some is better than none. Others would disagree. This book is designed to help people celebrate Shabbat totally: to enjoy 25 uninterrupted hours of holiness. And instead of offering a theological argument why, I want instead to tell you a very personal story.

I have always been a Judaism junkie. I was raised in a Conservative home, where we kept "kosher-ish," lit Shabbat candles on Friday night (sometimes), drove to synagogue on Saturday morning (sometimes), and celebrated some of the holidays. Some of the time. It was a warm, loving home, but not intensely spiritual. And then there was me. The reason we lit the candles on Fridays and went to synagogue at all on Saturdays was because I loved it. My favorite record was *Fiddler on the Roof*. My favorite book was *The Chosen*. I can't say I liked Hebrew School, but I loved the fact that my teachers there seemed to have something that I didn't: a familiarity with Jewish texts and traditions about which I didn't even know how to ask. I wanted to learn about the Talmud, but I didn't even know what its volumes were called. I wanted to study Jewish philosophy, but couldn't name a single Jewish thinker.

And so I was left with a saccharine, ersatz Judaism. The Judaism of *Fiddler on the Roof* (which I still love) and *Yentle* (which I don't). The

Judaism of most American Jews, which seems to hint that there is a wealth of wisdom and beauty to be found in our religion and our tradition, but doesn't tell you just what it is. The Judaism that offers nuggets of beauty in rabbis' sermons and quotes displayed on the walls of Jewish museums and synagogues, but never educates its children to know the source of those quotes and aphorisms that we're given. There is a whole class of "professional Jews" in most Jewish communities today that acts as the gatekeeper to our own traditions, without educating or steeping their congregants in our own religion.

After years of yearning for an authentic Judaism that I never could understand or locate, I went away to college. After my freshman year, I transferred to Harvard University. I moved into my dorm room on a Saturday morning, and afterwards I walked around Harvard Square, exploring the campus. Mid-afternoon, I passed Harvard Hillel, and knocked on the door. I knew that Shabbat services would be long over, but I was homesick and yearned for a connection to Judaism that a center like Hillel might provide. I wanted to see a friendly face.

The door was answered by another sophomore — I'll never forget the moment, for it completely changed my life — and she answered that yes, indeed, I had missed services and Shabbat lunch, too. But, she said, I could come back at five o'clock for "Shalosh Seudos," and closed the door. Now, I didn't know she had said "Shalosh Seudos," which means the "third meal" one eats formally on Shabbat, because I'd never heard of such a thing. "Shalosh Seudos" sounded like gobbledegook to me, but I did understand the five o'clock part, and I returned to Hillel then.

There were about three dozen students at Hillel at five o'clock, and we sat down to eat a light meal of pita bread, hummus, and other snacks. Everyone was friendly and we chatted. Towards the end of the meal, the students started singing. First Yedid Nefesh, or "Beloved of my Soul," a song that compares the Jewish people to a deer running to do the will of its beloved God. (That song became so important to me at Harvard that, 12 years later, I chose it to be the song played as I walked down the aisle to get married!) Then, without breaking the same slow, plaintive, vaguely Oriental tune of Yedid Nefesh, the students segued into The 23rd Psalm,

the famous one that says "though I walk through the valley of the shadow of death I shall fear no evil." I'd never known where that line came from and I was captivated. As the song went on, building in intensity, one of the final lines moved me even more: the Psalm thanks God for "setting a table before me," for raising me up above my enemies, for anointing my head with oil, then exults "my cup overflows." As we sang that line, I felt choked up: not the emotion I'd expected to encounter on a late Saturday afternoon at my new college.

I was captivated. (And you will be, too; these are songs that are traditionally sung at the third meal on Saturday afternoon, and their words are contained in Chapter 12.) At the conclusion, we sang yet one more psalm, then the Grace after Meals. We ended Shabbat with Havdalah, the ceremony marking the end of Shabbat, together (described in Chapter 10), and then started making plans for the evening and going home.

The entire late afternoon meal had taken maybe an hour and a half, but I felt energized and refreshed. I couldn't wait until the next week. I went back again and again, Saturday after Saturday, until I, too, knew the songs and the blessings, not only of Shalosh Seudos but of the entire Shabbat experience, from Friday night through Saturday evening. Years later, as we were about to graduate, I talked with a fellow student about our college experiences. He, too, had become religiously observant, and I asked him if he had any regrets, for instance, not eating in any of the popular non-kosher student hangouts or not attending some activities on Friday nights. He said that yes, he had missed out on some experiences, but had more than made up for those losses with the intensity of emotional experiences he'd experienced as an observant Jew at college. I knew what he meant instantly: there were so many emotional highs in our time as undergraduates, and it was a given for both of us that most of those memorable experiences occurred on Shabbat.

Following college, I remained observant for a time, and then dropped out for a couple of years. I went to graduate school, travelled, and as I became friends with people who were not Jewish or religiously observant, my own observance lapsed for a time. As I became less and less observant, I told myself that I could still keep Shabbat: the kernel of my Jewish week. I could

discard most of Jewish observance, I reasoned with myself, but I could still keep the wonderful traditions of my weekly holiday.

In a narrow sense, I did, but in a greater sense, I did not. Sure, I still went to services some Friday nights and Saturday mornings, and I still had some festive meals. But the essence for me was gone. The magic had vanished. When I knew that I could take my observance or leave it, choose to attend Shabbat dinner or go out to a restaurant with friends, decide to go to synagogue or watch television, the observance that I did perform lost much of its specialness, much of its sparkle.

(I remember a turning point vividly: a friend was visiting and she dropped her contact lens in a dark room. Now, turning on an electric light is a violation of Shabbat, but as my guest fumbled for her lens, I switched on the overhead light — the first time I had done so on Shabbat in years. This was a well-meaning gesture, but as my hand flipped the switch, I felt as if I was breaking something precious and rare with it. For keeping Shabbat is a deliberate decision we make; once it is shattered it can only be put back together again through our own concentration and resolve.) Shabbat is in essence a magical, transformative experience, and if you do not imbue it with transformative meaning, you cannot fully accept its magic. The Torah teaches us that on Shabbat every Jew acquires an additional soul; in the years that I did not fully observe Shabbat, I felt that I never opened myself to fully accept that special Shabbat spirit, and felt unaccustomedly alone.

I remember one instance when I felt this lack particularly keenly. I had accepted an invitation to Shabbat dinner at the home of a religiously observant acquaintance who lived some distance from me. I was living in London at the time, and I took the "tube," or subway, to Golders Green, an Orthodox neighborhood in that city. There were lots of guests at the table, and we had a great time. The meal was ending and I was just thinking of what time I'd have to leave to make the last tube home, when in walked a group of people who'd had a meal elsewhere nearby and were stopping by for dessert.

There was one girl I recognized in the group, though as she walked in I didn't see her so clearly, but instead saw myself as I had been a few years previously in her. She was religiously observant, and had walked to dinner,

and was going to walk home. She was wearing a nice coat — her Shabbat coat, as I'm sure she thought of it — and was flushed from the cold. To this day I can't quite put my finger on it to describe, but she had the aura of Shabbat around her. She was happy and chatting with her friends and dressed nicely and relaxed. But there was more to it than that. As I struggle even now with the words to describe what I saw in her that night years ago, I can only say that it was Shabbat, and that in order to know what I mean, you have to celebrate Shabbat, too. How I envied that girl at that moment: envied her ease, and her Shabbat happiness, and her festive mood. I would have given anything to be her that night, and it was only many years later, once I'd become "shomer-Shabbat," or Shabbat-observant, again, that I once more felt the rich specialness of the day.

This book will help you to do that, from preparing beforehand to celebrating afterwards. There are tips and ideas and information and stories. But the only person who can really make Shabbat is you. It doesn't fit in with most people's schedules, and it seems daunting before you try, but the rewards are immense. I've tried to make this book a tool for you to claim what you already own, God's greatest gift to the Jews: Shabbat. Good luck in claiming it for yourself!

Shabbat: the focus of the week

When God created the world, he made the days of the week. Instead of being happy, however, one particular day — Saturday — complained to God. "Sunday has Monday," Saturday complained, "and Tuesday has Wednesday." "Thursday has Friday, but I have no one," Saturday said to God. God listened to Saturday's lament and then said, "Hush, don't be sad any more. I will give you a partner: the Jewish people will be your partner."

My children learned this story in school, and it captures the essential relationship between the Jewish people and Shabbat. We are married. As we usher in Shabbat on Friday night, Jews sing "Welcome the Shabbat bride." When we sit at the Shabbat table we sing about the ideal Jewish wife.

Shabbat is that wife and we, the Jewish people, are her groom. What does this mean? Theologically, it is a profound metaphor, but I've always thought about it practically. Just as one nurtures a marriage, a Jew nurtures one's relationship with Shabbat. And just as one is renewed by one's relationship with a spouse, one is renewed by Shabbat.

As a Shabbat-observant Jew, Shabbat means never being truly alone. God has prepared a special forum for us to connect to other people. When I was a single person (especially once I returned to being religiously observant), Shabbat was the focus of my week. Since it is so important to the Jewish community, I was rarely alone on that day. I might have met friends for meals and drinks during the week, but Shabbat was when I often had invitations for formal meals Friday night and Saturday lunch, or for weekends away. It was the one time all week when I entertained formally, inviting guests over for meals and long afternoons.

For many years, when I was younger, I had a "Shabbat partner": a girlfriend with whom I ate and spent time most weeks. (If you are just starting out in Shabbat observance, finding a friend to observe it with might help you to ease into the transition of celebrating Shabbat regularly.) We attended the same synagogue, but had different social circles, and we'd alternate, introducing each other to our friends and making and hosting meals. There was no pressure to go anywhere else or take care of anything or accomplish any tasks during those hours on Shabbat. We chatted and read and visited with people. So long as we were within the holy 25 hours of Shabbat, thinking, reading, resting, and connecting both with God and with other people were all that we were expected to do, and all that we could practically do.

I remember a vivid example of the way Shabbat cuts out all extraneous noise so that, once a week, we can connect with what matters in life. When I was a graduate student, a friend and I rented the house of a well-known professor who had a job teaching abroad. The professor came back a few times a year to attend conferences, and we thought he was odd. He was awkward and shy, and was rarely the first person to initiate a handshake or a conversation. In fact, my housemate and I made fun of him and told funny stories about him to our other friends. Though he was Jewish, he

was a staunch Communist, with no interest in religion. We had no point of connection. Our few conversations were strained, and we never bothered to get to know each other at all.

One Friday night, however, when my landlord was visiting, I had no invitations. I had just lit my Shabbat candles and was about to make Kiddush (blessing) over my wine. The landlord walked in and I invited him to join me. I made Kiddush, then the blessing over the challah (a rich braided loaf of bread), then ate. In fact, I remember, that I was doing the bare minimum for this meal. Instead of challah I had two pita loaves (a permissible substitute), and my meal consisted of wine, pita, and some spreads.

My landlord joined me for this modest Shabbat dinner and we had a long conversation. He was not odd at all during that meal, I remember, but really interesting and brilliant and great to talk with. He told me about his family and his job and his field. We ate the pita and spread and drank the wine and, after a long time, he excused himself to go. As he left, he told me he'd never done that before: this was the only time in his life he enjoyed this part of his heritage. I felt privileged to have been the catalyst for his one and only brief experience of Shabbat.

After that meal, my landlord and I were on very good terms, and after I returned to the United States, I kept in touch with him via e-mail. A year after I came back to the US, perhaps two years after he joined me for that Shabbat dinner, I heard from his wife that he'd had a sudden massive stroke and died. Looking back, I regret so much that that one Shabbat dinner was the only slice of Shabbat I ever shared with him. I also regret that I ignored the Jewish concept of "hiddur mitzvah" or beautifying a mitzvah (divine commandment), and had such a simple dinner. But I'm overwhelmed at the memory of the meal we did have, and how the spirit of Shabbat transcended the situation and allowed an older professor and a younger graduate student to connect for one meal.

Now that I'm older and have a husband and children, Shabbat is no less special. This is the one day of the week when my husband and I focus most on each other, when we play most intensely with our kids. Shabbat unites us as a family: we all work so hard to prepare and make it special, and then once it begins, we all feel bathed in a glow of leisure, of holiness,

of being caught up in something together, of striving to imbue our every meal, our every conversation with beauty and gratitude for the world God created for us.

This is the goal of Shabbat: transcending the ordinary. During the week, we run around and take care of business and our material needs. This is important, but what is it all for? As I look around my cluttered house these days and listen to my children's demands for ever more activities, lessons, and toys, I sometimes think of words of lament the poet William Wordsworth wrote 150 years ago:

> The world is too much with us; late and soon,
> Getting and spending, we lay waste our powers;
> Little we see in Nature that is ours;
> We have given our hearts away, a sordid boon!

What is it all for? Where is the connection? The human interaction? The time to think?

Shabbat provides the structure necessary for sitting quietly. For having over guests who don't need to run somewhere else after a given length of time. For having long conversations with our children. For finishing books. For taking walks outside. For talking to God. For studying the Torah. It gives the week a focus and a structure. Of all the gifts the Jews have given the world, the concept of a "weekend" is perhaps the most valuable. We all need time to rest and recharge, and a change of pace from the week.

On a more practical note, too, Shabbat offers us a measure of grace and formality in our increasingly hectic, informal world. I often read of the demise of the dining room in modern houses, yet in my family, the dining room is used every week, for dinner on Friday night, through to breakfast, lunch, and dinner on Saturday. (When my children were very young, they once followed the exterminator through the house as he sprayed each room; when they reached the dining room they all clamored and told him, "This is where we have Shabbat!") We set the dining room table each week with a white tablecloth, silver candlesticks and Kiddush cups, linen napkins,

and our formal china. Whereas during the week our dinners together last perhaps 20 minutes if we're lucky, on Shabbat, our meals are multi-course affairs, full of song and conversation.

Another important aspect of Shabbat is the time it affords to visit friends and to have guests to our home. Whereas the week can sometimes seem like a mad dash to get everything done, Shabbat is a time of enforced leisure. It can be difficult to coordinate schedules or book babysitters in order to see friends, but over Shabbat meals, visiting is a pleasure. When my husband and I sometimes invite friends over for Shabbat meals who don't usually observe Shabbat, we often hear that they don't want to burden us by coming to our home and forcing us to cook. "Please come," we always tell them, "we always make ourselves nice, festive meals anyway: sharing with friends is simply a way to make the holiday complete." Among our friends who do observe Shabbat, inviting each other over for a Shabbat meal is the accepted norm of visiting: we might not have time during the week to get together, but on Shabbat, spending time talking, eating or walking with friends is what we expect to do.

Preparing for Shabbat

The Talmud tells that as we light the Shabbat candles on Friday evening, two angels enter our home: a good angel and a bad angel. The good angel wants us to have a complete, meaningful Shabbat, and the bad angel wants the opposite for us.

As we light the candles, the angels look around our house and see whether we've prepared for the Shabbat. They ask themselves three questions. "Is the meal cooked?," "Are the Shabbat candles lit?," "Are the beds made?" If the answer is yes to all three questions, the household truly is ready for Shabbat and the good angel blesses it, saying, "May it be like this for them next week, too." The bad angel, much to his chagrin, is forced to reply, "Amen." But if the answer to these questions is no, it is the bad angel who pronounces, "May it be like this for them next week, too," and the good angel who is forced to agree, "Amen."

Why do the angels ask these three questions? And why is their blessing that whatever situation they find in our homes be repeated again next week?

I think the three questions are easier to understand than the blessing they lead to: these questions really get to the heart of all the practical preparations for Shabbat. We have to cook festive meals, clean (or at least tidy up!) our homes, and dress ourselves for the holiday. This formula also provides an upper limit to our preparations; there is no need to drive yourself crazy making every single thing in your home perfect for Shabbat. You should just focus on making sure you've prepared food to eat, and both your home and the people in it are fairly neat and tidy.

The nature of the blessing is more complex. Why not just bless or curse the household to have a good or bad Shabbat that week? Perhaps it is self-evident to the angels that only with a prepared table and house can there be true Shabbat joy, so at the time of candle lighting the nature of this Shabbat is already set. As for next week, there is a Jewish concept that "mitzvah goreret mitzvah": a mitzvah (fulfilling a commandment) leads to another mitzvah. Likewise, forgetting one mitzvah leads us to forget others.

For those of you who are starting from scratch, then, the decision to make Shabbat is a wrenching one, requiring you to break the curse of the bad angel that all your future Shabbats be unobserved, like your past ones. For those who do prepare for Shabbat already, this blessing is a warning to keep striving ever upward, to imbue each Shabbat with new holiness, never to coast or take things for granted. And as you strive to observe Shabbat, remember the concept of "mitzvah goreret mitzvah": your observance will get easier with every passing week.

So, how does a busy person make sure their house, their candles and their food are all ready and festive for the weekly holiday of Shabbat? There are two answers to this question, both equally correct. One answer is that people don't ever get to do everything they'd like to, and that Fridays are a little crazy for most people who observe Shabbat! Keeping Shabbat for years has taught me that jobs expand to fill every second of the time available for them. In the winter, when Shabbat begins as early as four o'clock in the afternoon, it is a race to tidy up the house, put away laundry, cook dinner, and make sure everyone showers by the appointed moment. But in the

summer, when Shabbat doesn't begin until eight o'clock at night, the task somehow is hardly easier!

The other answer, however, is that it is not too difficult. Millions of people do manage to make it to the Shabbat deadline each week with some semblance of cleanliness and preparation. They simply structure their weeks around the holiday, building towards the climax of Shabbat each Friday night. Doing laundry? Make sure everything's put away by Friday. Planning to clean the house? Try to do it later in the week so things are still neat by the time Shabbat starts. Shopping? Cooking? Make some dishes in advance so you have Shabbat meals ready. There's usually a bit of a rush right before candle lighting, as everyone makes last-minute preparations, but, with planning and practice, people soon fall into routines that work for them.

Making Shabbat your cornerstone

When I was newly married, I used to make large, elaborate Shabbat meals, clean the house, polish the silver, and get everything in order — all on Fridays. Consequently, when Friday evening rolled around, I was always stressed and grumpy. Sure, the house looked and smelled wonderful, but I was so miserable, it was no way to greet Shabbat. One weekend my mother (who is wise and very calm) visited and, observing my manic Friday, told me about the Shabbats of her childhood, when her Bubbe (Grandmother) Yitta would prepare everything each week.

My mother's Bubbe Yitta grew up in a shtetl (a small Jewish town) in Poland, and lived in a Yiddish-speaking environment for her entire life, even after she moved to London and raised her family. Many American Jews get nostalgic at thoughts of the rich Jewish life of our ancestors in Eastern Europe's shtetls; my mother was describing the real thing when she told me about her bubbe's strategies. Shabbat dominated Bubbe Yitta's week, my mother told me. She started preparing as early as Tuesday, and each day would cook and bake something to eat on the holiday. Once Friday rolled around, my Bubbe Yitta was busy, but never frenzied.

As the years have gone by, I've taken that advice, and added some of my own coping strategies. I soon realized that cooking new dishes each week was too time-consuming. Instead, I developed a limited menu that I make week after week. It is easy for me to cook the familiar dishes, and an added benefit is my children love our Shabbat menu: they now associate gefilte fish, chicken soup with matzah balls and other classic Jewish dishes with Shabbat's happiness.

More profoundly, observing Shabbat is easier once you get used to setting it aside as a special day, the best day of the week. Individuals and families who observe Shabbat routinely do this without thinking about it, and those who want to make the transition to observing Shabbat can ease their paths by designating Shabbat the time to enjoy the best of what they have. Thus, in my home, for example, we rarely eat dessert after dinner during the week, but we always have lots of dessert after dinner on Friday night and lunch on Saturdays. During the week, I insist on my kids eating healthy breakfasts, but on Shabbat we make special "surprise sandwiches" (which feature chocolate as a primary ingredient). During the week, my husband and I are often too busy to play games or read to the kids, but on Shabbat we spend hours playing board games and reading out loud. Try saving special things for Shabbat: by designating Shabbat your special day to enjoy the best material things your life has to offer, you guarantee their weekly use, as well as enhancing the special quality of your Shabbat.

It isn't just children's activities that can be indulged on Shabbat. Once people begin integrating Shabbat into their lives, it becomes natural to reserve all the best things for that day. Here are two small examples that show how unconscious this reflex to honor Shabbat becomes. I once bought a book for my kids in a sale, and it quickly became a favorite: it is an amazing, magical, beautifully illustrated picture book about a child spending a summer with his grandmother exploring a river. The book is not Jewish or Shabbat-oriented in any way, but it is lovely, and my oldest son told me it really ought to be a "Shabbat book" that we take out only on Shabbat. Nobody ever told my son we had to restrict our book selections in this way, but to this boy who has grown up observing Shabbat, it seemed natural that beautiful, special things would be especially reserved for this special day.

When my son suggested this, I thought it was quaint. But then I uncon-sciously did the same thing some years later. When my grandmother, of blessed memory, died, I inherited her very large, very ornate engagement ring. The ring is too large and too grand to fit at all into my lifestyle. (My own husband proposed to me with a wrist watch, to give a sense of how unusual it would be for me to wear a large diamond ring.) I would never wear my grandmother's ring normally, but it was natural for me to start wearing it on Shabbat, my weekly time to become a subtly different person, and enjoy the finest things in my life.

To many people, the concept of keeping one's best things for Shabbat seems restrictive. Why shouldn't we enjoy our good clothes, our good china, our favorite foods any time we want? Why horde them all for one weekly 25-hour period? In many years of observing Shabbat, I've found that the answer to this question is deeply counterintuitive: by saving our best things for Shabbat, we actually use them more than we would otherwise.

For instance, when was the last time you used your good china? Ate in your dining room? Wore your best jewelry? Invited over lots of guests? For many people I know, the answer is months or even years ago. Take one of my relatives: he and his family live in a house with a beautiful dining room — which they have used exactly once in five years of residence. I'm sure that when this relative and his wife bought their house, they looked in the pretty dining room and envisioned lovely family meals there. Yet busy life intervenes, and so often we never get out of "everyday" mode. My relatives mean to set aside time for special meals and other times, but like everybody else, they are very busy people, and that special time gets shunted aside. Shabbat might only come once a week, but it comes every week. It gives us a regular date when we are commanded to make everything in our homes and lives special.

This was brought home to me dramatically some years ago when a syna-gogue friend and I signed up for an activity that brought us together several times during the week. I had met my friend at synagogue, and for many years saw her almost exclusively on Shabbat. We chatted after services, and sometimes we would invite each other's families over for Shabbat and other holiday meals. And what was the impression I had of this friend? She was

elegant. Gorgeous. Gracious and attractive and always beautifully turned out. Week after week I saw her wearing beautiful, feminine outfits with long skirts, high heels, and lovely jewelry. She always wore attractive hats that suited her face. She was a wonderful cook and presided over magnificent feasts in her lovely clean and tidy home. Her kids are well-behaved and would eat and play and help clean up after meals nicely and graciously. Everything about my friend exudes beauty, refinement, and elegance.

It was a shock, therefore, once our activity started, to see this friend during the week! She wore ordinary clothes that were completely utilitarian, if not downright dowdy. Boring shoes, dumpy handbags, flat hair. When I ran into her, she was often harried. I visited her house during the week and it was messy with clutter. Her kids were loud. I hardly recognized the majestic, elegant friend I still saw weekly at synagogue. No contrast could have been greater. For my friend is successful and competent during the ordinary work week, but on Shabbat she glows. I had become acquainted with a woman when she was accompanied by her extra Shabbat soul, and was startled to see the weekday woman, going about her business without the extra spark of Shabbat holiness that transforms her into a queen.

This book is full of tips and ideas to help you make this profound change in your own life and your own home. It will help you change the way you live and do things on Shabbat, and also help you to prioritize your time outside of Shabbat. In a Hebrew-speaking environment, it is easy to always keep in mind the primacy and imminence of Shabbat. The days of the week are numbered towards it: Monday is called "Day One" in Hebrew, Tuesday is "Day Two," Wednesday is "Day Three," and so on. The only day to possess an actual name in Hebrew is the last one, *Shabbat*. In our English-speaking world, it is easy to lose sight of the recurrence of Shabbat week after week. In order to keep Shabbat in the center of our plans, we have to remind ourselves to work towards it each time. As we do so, we begin to recognize the holiness this holiday brings to us weekly, to live a life that is enriched by this weekly gift from God.

Each person will come up with their own individual way of planning for Shabbat; the ideas in this book can help you get started on your own personal journey. Good luck!

2

Rules and laws of Shabbat

When I was a child, my family often enjoyed festive Shabbat meals on Friday nights. They were lots of fun, and my mother's roast chicken and chicken soup were delicious. For a period of a few years, we even drove to synagogue on Saturday mornings; we enjoyed the morning service and social hour that followed, then we often went someplace else; for instance, to a nearby shopping mall to eat lunch in the food court. Shabbat was undemanding: friendly, nice, and familiar — but had only a shadow of the magic and transformative feeling that has always made it central to Jewish life.

Many Jewish people today celebrate some elements of Shabbat, and even in a watered-down form the sanctity of this towering day manages to enrich their lives a little. It is as if a starving person were presented with a feast prepared by their loving parent, and all they ate was just a little crust of bread. Even that tiny crust of bread would sustain them for a while and make them feel better. Of course, if one would sit down to enjoy their parent's feast in its entirety, they would know joy measures beyond that afforded by their crust of bread.

Shabbat is our enormous feast prepared by God, who is like our loving parent. When we neglect our relationship with Him, our souls begin to starve, just as our bodies would were we to go without food. This spiritual starvation has become the norm in much of modern society, so we do not often notice it, even though its symptoms — materialism, shallowness, a sense of always searching for a greater purpose that we can never quite find — are all around us. Because we are so cut off from our spiritual tradition and our religious past, we modern, secular Jews don't even think to turn to God to provide us

with the meaning and peace that is missing from our lives and our families. The very thought of praying seems laughable to many Jews, and indeed most Western Jews think of Protestant Christian prayer — hands together, head bowed, which might seem awkward to Jews — as the ideal of prayer, instead of the many Jewish ways of communing with God.

Likewise, many contemporary Jews would never think of observing a traditional Shabbat, even though their very souls are crying out for this God-given nourishment. Often families do light two candles on Friday night and eat a loaf of challah with their meal, and find meaning and beauty in this. But these are but crumbs compared with the joyful feast of following an entire Shabbat. It seems daunting to take on an entire Shabbat of traditional, Orthodox-style engagement. We have all seen pictures of old-fashioned Jews wearing black hats and coats, and they seem so foreign to us modern Jews. The thought of mimicking *any* of their strange behaviors might be off-putting or bizarre.

Yet I am telling you to do exactly that. Not to dress very differently, nor to speak very differently, nor to change much about yourself or the way you do things. Just to alter the way you act for one day a week. Allow yourself to eat the feast that God has prepared for you, and for every other Jew. Return to your roots for just one day. Many modern Jews enjoy some of the foods of their ancestors: lox and bagels, latkes, matzah balls, rugelach. Your great-grandparents ate them, but they didn't eat them in a vacuum. Chances are, if you go back more than two or three generations, you'll find that all of your great-grandparents and beyond knew the joys of Shabbat. It was likely the highlight of their weeks, the times they longed for and looked forward to, the times they enjoyed the company of their friends and the peace of this holy day. You can feel closer to them by eating the foods they enjoyed and singing the songs they sang, but you can get even closer to them by setting aside one Shabbat to experience what they felt as the highlight of their weeks, their taste of God's World to Come.

When embarking on Shabbat observance, the rules can seem strange and scary. Yet they quickly become second nature. And at the same time, the beautiful benefits of Shabbat quickly transform our lives.

Researchers at many universities, particularly at the University of Minnesota School of Public Health, have recently done some ground-breaking studies on the effects on adolescents of eating together with their families. Studies show that children who eat together with their families enjoy higher grades, are less likely to smoke or take drugs, eat healthier food, and have higher self-esteem than children who do not partake of family meals. Some researchers have found a direct correlation between the frequency of family meals and these positive effects. While it seems to be optimal to eat together as a family as frequently as possible, the weekly nature of Shabbat is a very good place to start scheduling regular, leisurely meals together as a family. Shabbat meals offer families the chance to get to know each other again: to reconnect after the hustle and bustle of each hectic week.

Indeed, Shabbat is a day for all members of the Jewish community — single and married, young and old — to seek out and enjoy companionship on this day. My husband and I benefited particularly from the social nature of Shabbat in the traditional Jewish community: we (like countless other couples) first met each other at a Shabbat lunch table! I was visiting my friend Ruthie in New York for a few days. Ruthie and her sister were living together in a little apartment on West End Avenue at the time, and each week they made lovely Shabbat meals, and invited lots of friends over to share in the holiday. Ruthie and my husband had some mutual acquaint-ances, and sometimes saw each other around the Upper West Side. Ruthie invited him to Shabbat lunch, along with lots of other people. The crowd was gregarious, and we all had a lovely time. It was a beautiful day and, after lunch, we all decided to take a Shabbat walk in Central Park. My hus-band and I continued our conversation throughout the Shabbat afternoon, and by the time Shabbat was over, we knew we were meant for each other. I have since met many other couples who first met as guests at a Shabbat meal. The special nature of this day ensures that we reach out to others to eat together, pray together, and learn Torah together; we are meant to enjoy Shabbat as part of our community.

The benefits of Shabbat go even further. Following the many rules of Shabbat forces us to be introspective, and also to have fun. There is time

to be alone, during prayer, and also together, during meals and following synagogue services. We are not allowed to physically create things on Shabbat, so we turn inward and create emotionally and spiritually instead. And, perhaps most importantly for modern Jews, on Shabbat we are prohibited from engaging in the world electronically. That filter is denied to us for 25 hours each week, and we are forced instead to relate to people one on one, as individuals, without the filters of texting, e-mail, telephones, beepers, television, fax, headphones, iPods and the like.

What are these rules? This is a strange aspect of Shabbat observance to many people who do not yet observe Shabbat in the traditional way. In part, many Jews are misled by the old Christian concept that the Sabbath is a "day of rest." If Shabbat were merely a day of rest, however, a great way of spending it would be to stay in our pajamas, watch TV all day, and eat our meals off of trays on the couch. Yet that would be anathema to the spirit of Shabbat! Certain things are demanded of us, and other things are prohibited.

In fact, Judaism teaches that Shabbat creates a metaphysical relationship between us and God. The basis of Shabbat is that God created the universe and everything in it in six days of labor, and then on the seventh, He ceased. This is a profound concept, and very difficult for us to fully understand. (Many people particularly dislike the literalism of God creating the entire universe in six days; surely, they say, it took many billions of years instead. To address this, I'd refer readers to the fascinating book *Genesis and the Big Bang* by former MIT professor and Orthodox Jew Gerald Schroeder, which discusses the concept of what "day" meant in the early moments of our universe.) Yet by observing Shabbat, by also ceasing creative work on this holy day, we are somehow emulating God. This draws us closer to him, but Judaism goes even further: it asserts that by keeping Shabbat, by following this example of God Himself, we become partners with God, too. By observing a traditional Shabbat, we can elevate ourselves to be partners with God in Creation.

Also beautifully, this partnership heralds the future Messianic era, in which men and women will be united with God in perfect harmony. There are many ways in which Shabbat is seen as a foretaste

of the World to Come: this is perhaps one of the most majestic, and most profound.

The 39 prohibited activities on Shabbat

Every Sunday school student knows that when God led us out of slavery in Egypt, we wandered in the desert for 40 years before He led us into Israel. What is usually not taught is that we worshipped God for those 40 years in the "Mishkan," a beautiful, portable structure that we assembled and disassembled as we struck camp at different places in the desert.

> And God spoke to Moses, saying, "Speak to the children of Israel, that they make an offering for Me. From every man whose heart makes him willing you shall take My offering. And this is the offering which you shall take from them: gold, and silver and brass, and blue cloth, and purple cloth, and red cloth, and fine cloth, and goats' hair cloth, and rams' skins that are dyed red, and sealskins, and acacia wood. Oil for the light, spices to scent the anointing oil, and for the sweet incense. Onyx, and gems to be set in the crown, and in the breastplate (that the Temple workers wore). And let them make me a mishkan (sanctuary), that I may live among them." (Exod. 25.1–8)

The actions that are prohibited on Shabbat are the 39 activities that were required to set up and conduct services in this "Mishkan," this travelling synagogue in which we housed the stone tablets that God gave to Moses on top of Mount Sinai. In Hebrew they are called the 39 "Melachot," or "projects." During the 40 years the Jewish people travelled in the desert after leaving Egypt, and for many years in Israel before we built our holy Temple in Jerusalem, our people's spiritual center was the portable Mishkan that we carried with us and erected whenever we made camp. That is where we prayed and sacrificed to God, and its activities form the basis of our Shabbat observance today.

In the course of setting up and praying in the Mishkan, our ancestors built (1), dismantled (2), carried objects through the outdoors (3), and completed

the building or setting up of things (4). In order to make the curtains that hung in the Mishkan and acted as walls and doors, our ancestors had to shear sheep (5), wash (6), mix raw materials (7), dye (8), spin (9), set up looms (10), weave (11), remove materials from a loom (12), untangle (13), knot (14), untie knots (15), sew (16), and tear (17). In order to grow the food that was sacrifice in the Mishkan, our ancestors had to sow (18), plow (19), reap (20), bind grain into bales (21), thresh (22), separate things into different categories (23), sift (24), grind (25), knead (26), and cook (27). In order to prepare the meats that were sacrificed, our ancestors had to trap (28), slaughter (29), skin (30), tan (31), scrape (32), mark (33), tear (34), and cut (35). During the course of conducting sacrifices, our ancestors lit fires (36), put out fires (37), wrote (38), and erased (39).

Let's look at what these prohibitions mean today.

The "Melachot" of creating

On Shabbat, we refrain from physically changing our environment. This is a day of spiritual, emotional, and intellectual activity. It is not a day for molding the world around us. In the traditional Jewish world, there is a stark difference between the six days of the week, when we engage in business, creating and shaping things, and Shabbat, when we cease from physical creativity.

Melachot that come under the rubric of creating include: building objects, dismantling objects, tearing things, completing projects, mixing objects to create something new, writing, and erasing. Even carrying objects outdoors between buildings comes under the heading of creating, and is not done by Shabbat-observant Jews on Shabbat.

The prohibition of not carrying things outside, particularly, has strong ramifications today. Jews are allowed to carry things inside private property (such as a house or a fenced yard), but not outside, in public space. This means that we cannot carry prayer books, keys or even strollers or wheelchairs outside our homes on Shabbat.

One obvious difficulty this prohibition implies is carrying children: how are we to take children with us to friends' houses or to synagogue on Shabbat without strollers? There is one leniency regarding children:

if a child is old enough to be able to walk, but requires assistance on a particular journey on Shabbat, it is permissible to carry him or her for part of the way.

Another difficulty presented by this prohibition is carrying keys: how can we leave our homes on Shabbat if we cannot even take our house key with us? Some people place keys near their door; some people who live in apartments leave their keys with their doorman. Others "wear" their keys. Many men wear a "Shabbat belt": a strip of elastic with metal clips on either end. These clip onto a key, so that the key becomes the buckle of the belt. Since the key is part of a Shabbat belt, it is considered clothing (which we are allowed to wear), rather than something to be carried on Shabbat. Many women have jewelry fashioned that can hold a key: when it is incorporated into a brooch or a bracelet, a house key becomes part of a woman's jewelry, and can be worn, rather than carried.

Because this prohibition is so onerous, the Talmud provides a way to soften the restriction on carrying objects in a public place. Many Jewish communities erect an "eruv": a special fence around their community, which designates the entire area inside it a communal space. Many established Jewish communities have eruvs, allowing residents to push strollers and wheelchairs, and to carry necessary items.

If you are lucky enough to live within a large Jewish community, check with a local rabbi whether or not you reside within an eruv. If you do not, take comfort from that fact that more Jews probably reside outside an eruv than within one, and even some Jewish communities whose members observe Shabbat choose not to use eruvs anyway. They simply forgo carrying items outside of their homes. With practice, so will you.

(For the more serious issues of mobility presented to those in wheelchairs, or with canes, it is possible that alternate arrangements for Shabbat — such as erecting a small or temporary eruv, or spending Shabbat with a host inside an eruv — are possible; one should check with a local rabbi or Jewish organization.)

Cooking

Another major difference between Shabbat and the six ordinary days of the week is that cooking also comes under the umbrella of creating, and it is not done on Shabbat. Entire books have been written about the rules of food preparation on Shabbat, and when you are ready to fully observe Shabbat you might like to consult them. (A very detailed classic is *The Shabbos Kitchen* by Rabbi Simcha Bunim Cohen. A shorter choice is *The Laws of Cooking on the Sabbath and Festivals* by Rabbi Ehud Rosenberg.)

While cooking is prohibited on Shabbat, it is also considered especially nice on Shabbat to enjoy hot food. I, like many Shabbat-observant people, usually plug in an electric warming plate before Shabbat, and put my food on that. Many people also use slow cookers. In fact, the classic Shabbat lunch stew, a delicious dish similar to a French cassoulet, called *cholent*, is traditionally kept warm overnight in a slow cooker and served after services on Saturday. In order to have hot liquids on Shabbat, Shabbat-observant Jews plug in hot water urns before Shabbat and leave them on throughout Shabbat.

Foods that don't need to be cooked are easy to assemble on Shabbat: one can make salads and mix salad dressings on Shabbat, so long as the salad and dressing will be eaten on Shabbat.

Primeval acts of creation: lighting fires

This (along with extinguishing fires, which is also not done on Shabbat) is one of the most far-reaching prohibitions that shapes Shabbat observance in the modern age. For most forms of electricity use involve lighting and extinguishing fires, and so are not used on Shabbat. (Much electricity use is also prohibited on the grounds of not completing a structure, which applies to completing circuits as electric items are turned on.)

This means that Shabbat-observant Jews do not drive or ride in cars on Shabbat. Before Shabbat, they turn on those lights they wish to use during Shabbat before Shabbat begins, but then don't flip lights on or off once Shabbat begins. Some people use timers to program lights to go on and off during Shabbat. (In my own home, we often put a strip of masking tape over light switches before Shabbat, so that none of us — particularly

the kids — accidentally turns on or off lights once Shabbat starts; when you reflexively reach up to flip a switch, feeling the masking tape over it reminds you not to touch it on Shabbat.)

Using radios, telephones, televisions, computers, pagers, CD players, doorbells, and any other electric item is also avoided on Shabbat. Counterintuitively, I have found that rather than making one feel hemmed in on Shabbat, not using modern electrical gadgets is deeply liberating, as it frees us from the tyranny of telephones, computers, television, and the like.

Live and let live: the right of life on Shabbat:

On Shabbat, all living creatures have the right not to be harmed. On Shabbat, we are prohibited from trapping or killing animals, even from drawing blood from any living creature: human or animal. This is our day to move through the world without causing harm, to enjoy the world that God has created for us without altering it or depriving others (even animals or insects) of their own capacity to enjoy it as well.

Also, even though growing plants is an affirmation, not destruction, of life, we also do not do any agricultural activities on Shabbat. Beyond feeding pets and other animals (which is certainly allowed on Shabbat), other forms of agricultural work are stopped on Shabbat. Again, this is a day to leave our physical environment undisturbed: to allow other living things to grow and live without our interference.

Other rules

There are a few other rules that Shabbat-observant Jews follow on Shabbat. In addition to not changing the physical world around them, traditional Shabbat-observers also do not engage in business: they don't carry money, and don't buy or sell. Related to this, the Talmud prohibits people from walking long distances between towns. Shabbat is meant to be a day of stopping, rather than a day of progressing towards a physical goal.

Finally, ever since the destruction of our ancient Temple in Jerusalem (and until its restoration in Messianic times), Shabbat-observant Jews refrain from playing musical instruments on Shabbat. People might drum a beat on a dining room table to accompany the many rousing songs sung

after Shabbat meals, but that's generally as far as instrument playing on Shabbat goes.

"Pikuach nefesh": saving a life

These rules and prohibitions shape every aspect of life on Shabbat, but it is important to note that they can — indeed, must be — suspended if ever, God forbid, there is a risk to human life. In Judaism, almost every rule has to be broken if doing so will save a life. (The three exceptions to this are idolatry, incest/adultery, and murder.) In any case where there is even a question that a person's life might be at risk, it is a mitzvah — a commandment — to do what is necessary to save it. Thus, even the most observant Jew will call for a taxi or ambulance to take a pregnant woman to the hospital when she is in labor (and will even pay for the taxi on Shabbat, too, ideally with money that was already set aside for the job). The most Orthodox Jew will never hesitate to call for the police, fire department or ambulance, or to rush someone to the hospital, when they even suspect that somebody's life is at stake. Likewise, Shabbat-observant doctors are permitted to drive to the hospital if they are needed on Shabbat.

Here is an illustration of the practice of "saving a life" ("pikuach nefesh" in Hebrew) on Shabbat. I once spent a Shabbat evening in the home of a family in Mea Shaarim, a celebrated Orthodox neighborhood in Jerusalem that has become shorthand for being the most Orthodox a person can be. Mea Shaarim is probably the most famous, religiously observant Jewish community on the planet. To walk through its narrow streets is like being transported back in time to a religious Jewish shtetl in nineteenth-century Eastern Europe. The men wear long black coats and black hats; the women wear long-sleeved dresses and kerchiefs over their hair. Boys walk down Mea Shaarim's sidewalks with their long earlocks bouncing, and the little girls are all neatly attired in old-fashioned dresses and long braided pigtails. Many people speak Yiddish. The walls of buildings are festooned with signs requesting that visitors to the neighborhood please dress modestly.

At the time, I was young and single and visiting Israel, and a rabbi had arranged for me to have Shabbat dinner with a Mea Shaarim family, so I

could see what their lifestyle was like. I arrived at their modest apartment. They had set up two tables in their small living room: one for the women of the family and their female guests, and one for the men. Everyone was very friendly, though there was a language barrier. My Hebrew was terrible. The lady of the house did not speak English or French, and was not able to pronounce my (French) first name. Finally, she asked me my Jewish name. I replied it was Yitta, and my hostess beamed with recognition. For that whole evening, I enjoyed being Yitta; I truly felt as if I had stepped back in time and was dining with my Yiddish-speaking Orthodox ancestors in Poland; I felt a kinship with my great-grandmother Yitta, for whom I am named, and who surely would have felt more at home with these hosts than I did.

What does this story have to do with saving a life and the rules of Shabbat? The family's apartment was cramped, and the lady of the house had lit her many Shabbat candles on the women's table. A guest requested a napkin, and as I passed it to her, it caught on fire. As I watched, horrified, it flared up, the flames reaching higher and higher, soon almost to the ceiling. Mortified, I desperately tried to extinguish the flame. Instead of going out, my waving and blowing of course caused the fire to grow to enormous heights. There I was, in Mea Shaarim, having lit a fire on Shabbat, and about to do serious damage to a family's home — possibly the entire apartment building.

Without further ado, a woman at the table scooped up the napkin in a plate and poured water over it to put it out. This was extinguishing a flame, a major no-no on Shabbat, performed by one of the most Orthodox women imaginable. But there was no hesitation, no discussion, and no recrimination: if one perceives a possible danger to life, one is required to address it, even on Shabbat.

Changing to a Shabbat-observant lifestyle

There was once a young man who was so inspired by God that he worked very hard to make those around him follow God's commandments, too. He

encouraged his fellows to keep Shabbat, to be strict in eating only kosher food, to be zealous in giving to charity, never to gossip. . . . After some time, however, he realized that his progress was slow; the people he encountered rarely listened to him. The young man decided that he couldn't possibly change the whole world. So he settled on changing his town instead.

In middle age, this man entreated his neighbors to live a God-fearing life, to be scrupulous in observing Passover and Rosh Hashana, Yom Kippur and Purim, to be kind to their animals and never to harm another person. But as much as he remonstrated with his friends, he eventually saw that he was not able to change the behavior of his fellow townspeople. Instead, the man eventually decided, he would have to settle for changing the people in his family.

So in his old age, this man told his wife to be careful when she went to the ritual bath.

He told his daughters to learn Torah daily, his sons to be scrupulous in their prayers. He made sure to warn his grandchildren never to taunt or bully their playmates. And yet, after many years, the man concluded that he wasn't really changing his family members as he'd hoped.

In the final years of his life, this man gave up on his lifelong habits of trying to influence others. One day, when he was very, very old, another old man, a friend from his childhood, came to visit. "I remember when you once wanted to change the world," said the friend; "tell me, have you succeeded?" The man had to reply no. "And did you ever succeed in changing your town?" his friend asked. Again, no, the man replied. "Surely, you must have been able to change your family, though?" asked the friend.

"No," the man sighed. "I never was able to change the world, nor the town, nor even, I must admit, was I able to change my own family." He sighed. "However, after many, many years of effort, all is not lost." His friend was puzzled; who was changed by this man's intense devotion to God? The old man smiled. "I think, at last, I might have been able to change myself."

This story, attributed to the eighteenth-century Chassidic Rabbi Meshulam Zushia, seems immediately familiar. Of course we cannot alter other people's behavior; in fact, we are lucky if we can even succeed in changing

ourselves! This story — and common sense — suggests that as you embark upon a personal journey towards Shabbat observance, it will remain just that: an intensely personal quest. Does this mean that people who are embedded in marriages or families are doomed to travel this road alone? Not at all.

It has been said that every Jewish marriage is a "mixed marriage"; even among observant couples, there is usually one partner who is more enthusiastic about religious observance. While it won't always be possible to inspire your spouse or children to be as excited as you are about keeping Shabbat, it is likely that your sincerity, combined with the lovely sights, smells, music, and food of the holiday, will begin to sway your family as well. Even if your family doesn't share your same drive to keep the holiday, you can always tell them you expect them to keep certain basic ground rules to allow you to do so: say, for instance, being there for Shabbat dinner and lunch with you, accompanying you to shul (synagogue), or not watching TV or playing video games in the living room or anywhere else you expect to be on Shabbat.

For parents of young children, there is less of a problem in instituting Shabbat observance as a family; when children are very young it is easy to define the new "normal" of your family life to include celebrating Shabbat. For older children, sharing your learning about Jewish tradition can help them to internalize their heritage and religious observance for themselves. People (children included) crave authenticity, and there is nothing more intellectually or spiritually authentic than the Torah. You can explore Jewish bookstores for meaningful religious texts to study with your children; a suggested reading guide for people of different ages is included at the end of this book. You can also consult an Orthodox rabbi, your local Chabad House (www.chabad.org for the nearest location), or websites such as the Orhodox Union (www.ou.org), Aish HaTorah (www.aish.com) or Or Sameach Yeshiva (http://ohr.edu) for personalized guidance on topics to study.

One final note on bringing your family with you as you embark on Shabbat observance: in every family, there is usually one member who does the most to set the tone in the home. This is often, but not always, the wife

or mother. Keep in mind that it is possible to create a warm, welcoming atmosphere that includes Shabbat in your home. This takes planning, and the exact formula will be different for every family. It takes time and effort to prepare inviting Shabbat meals. It takes study to know about Shabbat and to be prepared to discuss Torah concepts on the day. It takes the courage and effort to invite guests to be a part of your Shabbat. It takes great initiative to reach out to other Jews who observe Shabbat as well, and to gradually build for yourself a community of like-minded friends who also keep this weekly holiday.

I once knew a young woman who was concerned that her fiancé was not as interested in or committed to religious observance as she was. She even wondered briefly if she should pursue the relationship, or if the religious differences between them were too vast. During this time, as they weighed the possibility of getting married, I shared with her a fascinating story that is found in the Talmud, which was told to me long ago when I was engaged, and which has influenced me greatly over the years. In this story, a righteous man and a righteous woman were once married to each other. Alas, they found themselves unable to have children, and so decided to divorce and each try their luck with a new spouse. Each of these God-fearing people then married a wicked person. Lo and behold, however, they had very different fates. For the righteous man in time was influenced by his wicked wife to become wicked, while the righteous woman prevailed over her wicked husband and, in time, transformed him into a good man.

My friend pondered this story a great deal. Of course, it didn't apply literally to her or her fiancé; her fiancé might not have been as eager to embrace traditional Jewish practice as she was, but he wasn't "wicked." Nevertheless, this Talmudic story gave her courage. They did marry, and — as in the story — my Shabbat-observant friend in time succeeded in helping her husband to see the beauty of a traditional Shabbat. They still have very different personalities and different approaches to Jewish tradition, but today they are united in their observance of Shabbat, and are raising their children in a beautiful Shabbat-observant home.

I think the Talmudic story has such an impact because it reminds us that people do change all the time, and often they change because they are

influenced by the example of those nearest to them. Shabbat, especially, is such a powerful force for good in the world. When people are exposed to authentic Shabbats, particularly in their own homes, they often find themselves turning towards it as flowers turn towards the sun. There is so much joy, and so much opportunity for real communication and meaningful activity on Shabbat, that in time family members will appreciate it, even if they don't always choose to follow it as stringently as you would wish.

In the most religious households, there is often a maxim that children never be berated for making a mistake in their Shabbat observance; it is recognized that if religious observance is coerced, it quickly becomes sour. Shabbat-observant families instead seek to instill a love for Shabbat and mitzvot in their children by making Shabbat and mitzvot as sweet as possible. If you make your home on Shabbat as warm and as welcoming as you can, if you are certain and unapologetic in your own commitment to Shabbat, and if you maintain a welcoming demeanor, your spouse and children might not plunge into Shabbat as quickly as you'd like, but they will edge towards it as they learn to recognize its beauty.

3

Shabbat evening

When you are embarking on Shabbat observance for the first time, it can help to wrangle invitations for meals — or even a complete Shabbat — from families or individuals who are used to observing the holiday. An Orthodox Rabbi or Jewish outreach organization should be able to set you up with an invitation.

The ease with which Shabbat-observant people invite others, even strangers, into their homes on Shabbat can seem startling at first. But such is the centrality of Shabbat in traditional Jewish life that opening one's home to others on this day is the norm. Most Shabbat-observant individuals have numerous stories of being put up by selfless hosts. I can recall times that I've slept on a mattress on the floor of a crowded, tiny house in the Jewish Quarter of Jerusalem's Old City, along with a dozen other guests, times that I've eaten Shabbat meals in the communal dining hall of a religious kibbutz with hundreds of others, times that I was hosted by people — often near-strangers — when I was far from home in their houses, in apartments, even in dorm rooms. Here is one story that is typical of the hospitality inherent in Shabbat-observant communities.

A few years ago, my husband and I spent several wonderful days in London. We planned on being in London over Shabbat, so we researched the city and booked a hotel near a synagogue. We knew we'd be able to walk to shul, but the thought of buying ready-made kosher food for our Shabbat meals and eating them in a cramped hotel room depressed us. A few weeks before our trip, I called up the synagogue we planned to attend and explained our predicament. The lady who answered the synagogue's phone couldn't

have been nicer. Don't worry, she assured us, she would arrange something for us. A few days later, she called me back and proudly announced that we were taken care of: the shul was hosting a communal lunch and Shalosh Seudos on the Saturday we'd be there. We could eat those meals with the wider community. As for Friday night, the receptionist told us, a family who lived near the shul had invited us over for Shabbat dinner.

My husband and I went on our trip, and when Friday rolled around, we made our way to the apartment of the couple — complete strangers — who'd invited us. They were lovely, and we enjoyed our evening with them and their other guests. As the evening drew to a close and we thanked them for their hospitality, for opening up their home to strangers whose only bond was a desire to observe Shabbat, they graciously told us that the only thanks they required was that we, too, one day open our home to other Jews. Our hosts had been invited in by local people on Shabbat on their travels, they explained, and they were glad to be able to do the same to us. The same will be true for you; for once you take a step towards keeping Shabbat, an entire welcoming community of like-minded Jews will join you in supporting your Shabbat observance.

But what does this observance look like? What does a traditional Shabbat look like in the home of a Shabbat-observant family or individual? Here is a description of Shabbat in my own home.

Friday afternoon

In a sense, I am always preparing for Shabbat. I try to invite guests to my family's meals a couple weeks in advance, and to respond to friends' invitations to "eat out" at their homes for various meals as well. I try to go shopping for all the food I'll need by Thursday, and start cooking and cleaning my house on Thursday as well.

After many years, I've got it down to an art: I do my shopping and start cooking for Shabbat on Thursday. And I never make just one portion of anything: each time I bake cakes, make matzah balls, kugels, or other dishes, I try to double or even triple the recipe so I have something to stow

in my freezer and ease my Shabbat preparations another week. On Fridays, I also try to tidy up my house before candle lighting time. When my kids come home from school on Friday afternoon, they know the drill: each one tidies their room, they all clean up the toys in the playroom (well, that's our goal anyway, and once in a blue moon all the toys might actually make it onto their shelves!), and then I help them shower and change for Shabbat. It doesn't always go smoothly, and with several kids the house isn't always as neat as I'd like it to be, but we each know what's expected of us when it is time to light candles.

"Candle lighting"

Five thousand years ago, in the city of Ur, in present-day Iraq, lived a boy named Avram. Avram's father was an idol-maker by profession, but even as a child Avram turned away from idols; he realized it was not idols, but God, who was responsible for creating the world and everything in it. As Avram grew up, he shared his beliefs, introducing everyone around him to the concept of God. Avram eventually found and married his soul-mate, a woman named Sarai, and together Avram and Sarai converted everyone they came across to monotheism.

One day, God Himself spoke to Avram. He told Avram and Sarai to leave Ur, to leave all that they knew, and to embark on a journey. God did not tell Avram where they were going; "You will go to the land that I will show you" was all that God revealed. After a long journey, God led Avram and Sarai to the Land of Israel, where He renamed them Abraham and Sarah.

Once in Israel, Abraham and Sarah pitched their tent at a busy crossroads, and spent their time greeting everyone who passed by, telling each traveler about God. Abraham and Sarah urged every passer-by to come into their tent and be their guest, and gave them food and drink and rest from the hot sun.

Each Friday afternoon, Sarah would light two Shabbat candles. Now, the Torah had not yet been revealed on Earth, but such was Sarah's devotion to God that He revealed the existence of Shabbat to her. Week after week, year after year, a miracle occurred: Sarah would light her candles, and the candles

would not extinguish, but instead miraculously burned for an entire week. Everyone who entered Sarah and Abraham's tent thus was immediately enveloped in a powerful aura of holiness and Shabbat, and saw Sarah's precious candles glowing steadily. Abraham and Sarah eventually had a son, Isaac, who joined with them in spreading the word of monotheism. Isaac grew up steeped in his parents' holiness, enjoying life in their tent, with its ever-burning Shabbat candles.

Eventually, Sarah died, and when her holy presence left her tent, her miraculous Shabbat candles went out. The constant spirit of Shabbat that had suffused Abraham and Sarah's tent was gone.

After Sarah's death, Abraham turned to his trusted servant Eliezer and asked him to go and search for a bride for Isaac. Eliezer wondered: how will I know which woman will be an appropriate match for the holy Isaac? Eliezer therefore asked God for a sign. God supplied a sign to Eliezer indicating that a girl named Rebecca was Issac's bashert, or intended one. When Eliezer asked the maiden Rebecca if she would like to return with him to Abraham's tent to be a wife for Isaac, Rebecca recognized at once that here was the opportunity for a life full of the sanctity and holiness for which she had always longed. Overjoyed, Rebecca said yes to Eliezer, quickly bade goodbye to her murderous, uncouth family, and left with Eliezer to return to Israel and meet her husband Isaac. When Rebecca first laid eyes on Isaac, he was immersed in prayer. Rebecca had long craved a spiritual environment, and she was overjoyed. For the first time in her short life, she felt at home.

Rebecca and Isaac were a holy couple, steeped in appreciation for God and the beautiful world He created. On Rebecca's first Friday in her new home, she took Sarah's Shabbat candles and lit them. Behold, a miracle occurred: Rebecca's candles, like Sarah's, did not go out, but instead burned steadily from one Friday to the next, suffusing her tent and her family with Shabbat holiness all week long, as long as she lived.

Many Jews light candles on Friday night, but not everyone realizes that the time to light candles varies throughout the year. The Jewish calendar is closely tied to the rhythms of the world that God created: the rising and setting of the sun dictate the times of day that we pray, and the hours in

which Shabbat begins and ends. "Candle Lighting" time is 18 minutes before sunset. (It is technically permissible to light Shabbat candles exactly at sunset; many Shabbat-observant Jews aim to be ready to light at the appropriate time — 18 minutes before — but use those final 18 minutes as a cushion in case they need to finish any last-minute preparations.) This means that in summer, when the sun sets late in the day, Shabbat begins correspondingly late. In winter, when the sun sets very early, Shabbat begins in the late afternoon.

Like most Shabbat-observant Jews, I have a list of the candle-lighting times for each Friday handy so as I rush about on Friday afternoon I can check when that week's deadline for my particular city is. (Many Jewish calendars, newspapers and websites contain weekly candle-lighting information. The website of the Chabad-Lubavitch movement, www.chabad.org, will give you candle-lighting times for any location worldwide.)

In my home, Friday afternoons usually find me on the phone with my good friend Chani, in New York, as we vie to outdo each other in pre-Shabbat desperation. "Shabbat begins in three hours for me and I still haven't started cooking," one will challenge. "Oh yeah," the other will say, "I have two and a half hours; all I've cooked is my green beans, and I'm having 30 guests!" "How did you make that kugel?" we'll call and ask, as we trade recipes and tips over the phone. Sometimes I call up other Shabbat-observant friends to compare notes; it is a weekly marathon to get everything ready, and it can be fun to know I'm not alone but instead am part of a vast network of Shabbat-observant people, each laboring to ensure a beautiful atmosphere in their homes come sundown.

(It is all a bit different from when I was single; I remember arriving once years ago at another single friend's house for dinner a few minutes before candle lighting, to see her just come in from work, and madly dash around her apartment for 18 minutes, frenziedly boiling eggs and noodles, heating water, cooking potatoes, and taking the fastest shower ever! She was a whirlwind of frantic activity — and wound up making a lovely Shabbat!)

A note: we can often learn so much from our children, and I once learned something touching and wonderful from my daughter when she was five years old. She has a lovely, calm disposition, and one day as we prepared

to light the Shabbat candles, she confided in me that before Shabbat arrives she likes to "relax." In her Jewish school, at Friday lunchtimes the students would stage a mock Shabbat meal. The teacher encouraged the children to sit and relax on the rug before their faux Shabbat preparations. "And at home," my daughter confided, "after I take a shower and get dressed for Shabbat, I sit on the rug of my room, and just relax and think about Shabbat." Like any mother, I just burst with pride at these wise words, and I try to take my little daughter's advice and similarly relax for a moment before candle lighting. She is right: pre-Shabbat preparations are often so hectic that it can be difficult to segue into the calm of Shabbat and focus on daavening ("praying") over the candles without a moment of mental relaxation and refocusing beforehand. On those Friday evenings when I can follow my daughter's example, it is always much easier to get into a spiritual feeling and truly concentrate on what I'm doing as I light the candles.

Finally, as the daylight winds down and candle lighting approaches, my husband and I call our kids into the dining room. (A note about husbands: many of my female friends are more interested in beginning to keep Shabbat than their husbands are, and have asked me advice about going ahead ushering in Shabbat before their husbands are home from work. Even though my husband is also Shabbat-observant, he is a physician and Friday evening sometimes finds him stuck at the hospital with a patient, a form of work that, since it falls under the category of saving a life, is permitted on Shabbat. I, too, know how it feels to bring Shabbat into one's home without one's spouse. Even though this is not ideal, the partner who is home should still make Shabbat for himself or herself; as Jews, we each have an obligation to observe Shabbat.)

With minutes to go before candle lighting, my family gathers together. If we are hosting guests, we make sure all the men and boys are wearing kippot, and we offer hats to the married women. We bring out our tzedakah boxes, or "pushkies" as they're traditionally called. It is customary to give money to charity right before Shabbat, and we each have our own pushkies to put our money in. My husband and I have a pretty silver one that we were given at our wedding. Each of my kids, however, has made their own very homely pushkies at school out of empty food containers with slits cut

into the lids. My personal favorite is the pushkie on which somebody has written the famous Talmudic saying that the world rests on three things — prayer, good deeds and tzedakah — complete with lovely illustrations.

Tzedakah is not "charity" in the sense of the English word. Unlike charity, tzedakah is not optional. The amount given to tzedakah is also fixed: according to Jewish law, we must give between 10 and 20 percent of our income to the poor. For that reason, our own personal family ritual is for us first to give our kids their allowance money. The kids then take the amount prescribed by Jewish law — between 10 and 20 percent of their "income" — and put it in their pushkies. It takes some planning to get the appropriate change, so the kids can easily take the 10–20 percent of their money, but doing it this way gives the kids a real feeling that they are giving what they should, and teaches them in a very personal, visceral way the obligation of tzedakah.

After we place coins in our pushkies, we put the pushkies away, as they will become "muktzah" (not something we can touch on Shabbat) as soon as the Shabbat candles are lit. I set up a tray with four candlesticks on it: two ornate, silver candlesticks that I inherited from my great-aunt for myself to light, and two candlesticks made out of glass bottles covered with tissue paper and varnish that my daughter made in nursery school, for her to light.

Jewish law dictates that if there are any girls or women in the home, they must light the Shabbat candles. Only in a household with no girls or women should men light them. Technically, one must only light a minimum of one candle, though most people in practice light at least two. Each family and individual is different. In many families, the female head of the house is the only one to light, and she lights two candles. In other families, there are different permutations: the head of the house lights three, or she lights one candle for each member of her household, or each daughter lights one candle while their mother lights two. . . . Unusually, in the prescribed context of Jewish ritual, there is no one rule! Where should one light the candles? It is customary to light them either in the place where one eats or one sleeps. Most people light their candles on a shelf or sideboard in their dining rooms.

When we have guests for Shabbat dinner, I usually set out two inexpensive tea lights for each female guest, and then give my guests the option of lighting their own candles or of being included in the aura of my household as I light mine. On evenings when we are invited out to friends for Shabbat dinner, I sometimes light candles beforehand in my own home, or else light tea lights at our hosts' home.

A word on timing: during the summer when Shabbat starts very late in the day, I often light my Shabbat candles early, and thus bring in a few extra hours of Shabbat for my household. The Talmud divides the daylight hours into four periods. On Fridays, it is permissible to light the Shabbat candles up to a quarter of the daylight period "early." You should check with a rabbi about the exact timing of this, but in practical terms, it means that if candle lighting is, say, 8 p.m., I can light the candles at 6 p.m. My kids are young and eat dinner early; this way, even though we cannot make Kiddush over the wine before the actual candle-lighting time, they can at least enjoy their early dinner while it is technically Shabbat in our home. That might not seem like an important goal but, believe me, once you start to observe Shabbat, the prospect of a couple hours extra of this holy day will suddenly sound appealing!

At 18 minutes before sunset, my daughter and I stand in front of our candlesticks. We've tidied up and, for once, the house is spotless. Our Shabbat dinner stands ready on an electric hot plate, Shabbat lunch is gurgling away in the slow cooker, and the hot water we use for coffee and tea is ready in an electric urn on the counter. Our dining room table is set for dinner. Everyone is freshly showered and wearing good Shabbat clothes, and often we are joined by guests.

We strike a match and light our candles. Once lit, we wave out our matches, close our eyes, and motion the light of the Shabbat candles towards us. Many Jews have strong memories of watching their mothers or grandmothers wave the light of Shabbat candles towards them. It is a beautiful custom, and seems to capture the warmth and holiness that our Shabbat candles represent.

When I was a child, and my mother lit the Shabbat candles, she would gesture the light towards herself, while reciting a phrase that her grandmother,

who grew up in a shtetl in Poland, used to say. We weren't exactly sure what each word meant, but saying these words, maybe more than anything else connected to Shabbat, connected my mother to this ritual and gave her the same warm, comfortable feeling she had had as a child watching her Bubbe bring in Shabbat. Many years later, after I'd studied Hebrew as an adult, my mother and I finally realized what the original words were that my great-grandmother had been saying: "Baruch Hu, U'varuch Shemo": "Blessed is He, and Blessed is His Name." My daughter and I now join my mother in saying these timeless words three times softly as we motion the light in towards us.

We then stand still and, still closing our eyes, incant the blessing that renders it Shabbat in our home:

Baruch Atah Adonoi, Eloheinu Melech Ha-Olam, Asher Kidishanu Bemitzvotav
Vetzivanu Lehadlik Ner Shel Shabbat. (Those present say: Amen.)

Blessed Are You, My Lord Our God, King of the Universe, Who Made us holy with His "Mitzvah" (Commandment) to light lights of Shabbat. (Those present say: Amen.)

There is a curious inconsistency in Shabbat I've always noticed. Generally, Shabbat is the one day that we do not make personal requests of God. We are not supposed to pray for specific things that we would like on this day. Sure, there are lots of prayers on Shabbat — even more than on weekdays — but they are all general in nature. Even the centerpiece of Orthodox Jewish services, the prayer called the "Shemoneh Esrei," which is usually full of requests for personal favors from God (we ask for health, for livelihood, for peace, etc.) is amended on Shabbat to make it more general, without all the special favors we usually ask for ourselves.

Nevertheless, right after we light the Shabbat candles is considered an optimal time for women to pray intently to God and, yes, make personal requests galore. After I say the blessing over lighting Shabbat candles, I stand there, eyes still closed, and pour out my heart (quietly) to God. I ask

him for help in raising my kids, in blessing the Jewish people, for help with specific problems and goals I might have.

After many years of making up my own prayers each week, I discovered that many prayers have been written over the years for women to say at this time. Some are in Hebrew, and some are in Yiddish, the vernacular that Jewish women for centuries were most comfortable in. The Yiddish prayers are called "techines" and lately there has been renewed attention of them by feminist writers. The prayer that is most commonly included in Orthodox prayer books today, and the one that I say most weeks, is this. It is a Hebrew prayer I find it soothing, and it really helps me prioritize all the things I want to ask of God at this important time.

> May it be Your will, my God and God of my forefathers, that You show mercy to me (and to my husband, my sons, my daughters, my father, my mother) and to all those who are close to me. And to us and to all of Israel, grant a good life and healing. And may we be remembered and counted for redemption and compassion, and make your presence dwell among us. And may I raise to adulthood wise and perceptive children and grandchildren: (children) who love God, who fear the Lord, truthful people, holy descendants, who cling to God and who light up the universe through Torah and good deeds, and in every way work to further (God's) creations. Please hear my "techina" (women's prayer) in this season, in the merit of Sarah and Rebecca and Rachel and Leah, our matriarchs, and light our lights so that they will never go out, and illuminate Your face to us and redeem us. Amen.

Many women who prefer not to say this prayer instead recite another popular prayer after lighting their candles, requesting that God restore the Temple in Jerusalem to its glory, and thus usher in a Messianic era of perfect peace.

> May it be Your will, Lord our God and God of our ancestors, that the Temple be quickly rebuilt in our days, and give us our measure in Your Torah. And there we will serve You with love as in days of old and as in ancient times.

And may the offerings of Judah and Jerusalem be as pleasing to You as ever and as in ancient times.

Following these prayers, my daughter and I uncover our eyes. Everyone in the room then says either "Shabbat Shalom" ("Complete Shabbat" in Hebrew) or "Gut Shabbos" ("Good Shabbat" in Yiddish) to each other. Some parents bless their children at this point. (We give our children the traditional Shabbat blessings at our Shabbat dinner table, and the traditional texts are included in the discussion about dinner, below.)

Kabbalat Shabbat

In the world of traditional Jewish Shabbat observance, there are two services after sundown on Friday night, and each of them takes about 20 minutes to complete. In fact, many people "daaven" ("pray") them quickly, so that they can get back in time for a leisurely Shabbat dinner. The traditional arrangement for many Orthodox families is for the men of the house to go to shul (synagogue) for services about 20 minutes before candle lighting to daaven the afternoon service (which also takes about 20 minutes), while the women of the family stay home and light candles. (Again, this is just one arrangement; many women also attend services, and men sometimes stay home.) Once the sun sets, Orthodox shuls will hold a brief service to welcome the Shabbat, called "Kabbalat Shabbat," and then the Shabbat evening service.

In good weather I often go to shul to daaven these services. When I stay home, I daaven them alone or with my kids in the living room. In the height of summer, sundown is very late, and it can take a while before we are ready to sit down for dinner. Most of the year, though, sundown is early enough that after daavening these quick services, we can enjoy lots of time for a long, leisurely Shabbat dinner.

"Kabbalat Shabbat" means welcoming the Shabbat, and it is probably the most beautiful service in the entire Jewish week. This service to welcome the Shabbat was created during the Renaissance in the Israeli town of Safed.

Safed had always been a center of Jewish mysticism. The Talmud (the compilation of the oral teachings given by God to Moses at Mount Sinai) instructs us to go and greet the "Shabbat bride" on Fridays. For years, this was not taken literally — except in Safed. There, for centuries, residents had been dressing up, walking out into the fields at the edge of town at sundown on Fridays, and reciting psalms in order to welcome Shabbat. In Jewish literature, Shabbat is often compared to a bride, but the mystics in Safed sought to make this image more vivid by pretending to greet an actual person as Shabbat was ushered in by going outside into the dusk and singing psalms to welcome her.

Then, in the 1500s, a Safed Rabbi named Shlomo Alkabetz wrote the evocative prayer called "Lecha Dodi," or "Come, my Beloved," which calls on Jews to come and greet the Shabbat bride as she enters our shuls and homes. "Lecha Dodi" became the centerpiece of the Safed Kabbalat Shabbat service, and it eventually spread throughout the Jewish world. Today, this brief service is recited after candle lighting, before the Shabbat evening service on Friday evenings.

Kabbalat Shabbat is comprised of eight psalms and two prayers. I once visited the famous Ari shul in Safed, where Rabbi Aklabetz used to pray. Modern-day followers of Alkabetz's mystical tradition told me that they review their own past weeks as they daaven this service. Typically for Safed, it had a mystical flavor. I was entranced, and ever since then I, too, have thought about my own past week when daavening Kabbalat Shabbat. While I recite the first psalm, Psalm 95, I visualize last Sunday; while reciting the second psalm, Psalm 96, I visualize last Monday, and so on, through the week. The service climaxes with the rousing prayer written by Rabbi Alkabetz. At its end, we stand up, turn to the back of the room and bow, as if to a real person who has just walked in, singing, "Come my Beloved to greet the bride — The Shabbat presence, let us welcome!" It is always a beautiful, transformative moment.

This and other prayers can be found in any number of Orthodox prayer books. As you embark on keeping the rituals of Shabbat, it will help enormously to have your own traditional siddur (prayer book) to use and refer to. My own particular favorite is published by the Jewish publishing company

Artscroll; this "Artscroll Siddur" is ubiquitous in shuls the world over, and its clear layout and print make it lovely to daaven from. (It can be found in Jewish bookstores or ordered from www.artscroll.com.) Other popular Jewish prayer books include the "Koren Sacks Siddur," edited by Britain's Chief Rabbi Lord Jonathan Sacks and published in conjunction with the American Orthodox Union (available in bookstores or at www.korensiddur.com), the "Burnbaum Siddur," a classic first translated in the 1950s and available in Jewish bookstores and on-line, and the "Hirsh Siddur," with a translation and commentary by the nineteenth-century Rabbi Samson Rafael Hirsh (available at Jewish bookstores or at www.feldheim.com).

The Shabbat evening service

Immediately following the short "Kabbalat Service" we recite another brief set of prayers: the Shabbat evening service, called "Maariv," or "Evening" in Hebrew.

"Maariv" begins with some short blessings recognizing God's role in the passage of time, and in the permanence of His love for us and His Torah. These are followed by the "Shema" prayer: the instantly recognizable Jewish declaration of God's existence and His Oneness. Following the "Shema" prayer, we say some brief transitory prayers, and then recite the "Shemoneh Esrei" prayer.

The "Shemoneh Esrei" prayer is the heart of Orthodox Jewish prayer, the core of the traditional Jewish services, and is recited three times a day. "Shemoneh Esrei" means 18 in Hebrew, and it is so called because during the week it contains 18 separate blessings. On Shabbat, however, we have a tradition of not making personal pleas, so the Shabbat "Shemoneh Esrei" is shortened to only seven blessings, which do not ask God for anything specific for us as individuals. (The weekday "Shemoneh Esrei," for instance, contains blessings asking God to grant us a good livelihood and good health; these are omitted on Shabbat.)

Maariv continues with a prayer blessing Shabbat. We then recite "Aleinu," or "Our Duty," which proclaims our fealty to God. After this, if

we are daavening in a shul with a minyan (ten or more men), we recite the mourner's "Kaddish," the prayer that people in mourning say blessing God, and then conclude with a joyous song, "Adon Olam," which again elucidates our closeness to and trust in God.

Why have a minyan? Many non-Orthodox Jews become very upset when told that traditional Jewish services require a minyan of at least ten men to say the full complement of prayers. (Without a minyan, some prayers are omitted.) In fact, in many years of hosting individuals and families for Shabbat, I would say this is one of the primary stumbling blocks for many people as they consider embracing Jewish traditions.

I find it very difficult to answer these questions, for two reasons. For most Jews who are not Orthodox, Saturday morning worship in a synagogue is a fundamental part of their Jewish observance, perhaps even the central part. Most non-Orthodox Jews go to synagogue expecting to find religious experience, or even transcendence, there. The thought that there would be "second-class citizens" in this setting, who do not count towards the quorum necessary for Jewish prayer, seems offensive in the extreme. Yet this experience is completely foreign to an Orthodox Jewish way of living. For millennia, the synagogue was never the central place that Jews expected to find their spirituality, and in Orthodox circles it still is not.

The home is our new Beit Hamikdash, our new Temple, not our synagogue. (This concept is discussed further in Chapter 4.) Our homes are where we daaven, where we learn Torah. It is home to the most spiritual moments of our days: where we say our first, personal morning blessings after we wake up, where we make the blessings before and after eating, where we allocate our tzedakah, do acts of kindness for others, refrain from gossiping, study religious books, kiss our mezuzahs, host guests, and enjoy our Shabbat. When every aspect of your day is infused with mitzvot (commandments) and religious intent, spending a few hours in shul on Shabbat morning is minor.

Yes, Jewish men are obligated to pray with a minyan, a group of at least ten bar-mitzvahs (males over the age of 12), but Jewish women are not. Observant Jewish men do attend minyanim (the plural of minyan), either in a synagogue or elsewhere, three times a day, but Jewish women

generally just daaven at home. This brings me to the second difficulty I often have in discussing the concepts of minyan and different gender roles with my non-Orthodox friends and guests. In modern-day secular society, we have gone a long way towards erasing gender distinctions. This has been, of course, the result of long-fought battles, and our present (near) gender equality has abolished the horrendous sexism that marred the lives of previous generations of women. Most people — including virtually all Orthodox Jewish women — applaud the strides women have made in the past several decades. Even in Orthodox Jewish society, there are more opportunities for women than ever before, and this is regarded (virtually) everywhere as a good thing.

Yet traditional Judaism does very strongly believe that men and women have differing natures. It regards women as more nurturing than men, and more responsible. It regards men as a bit of a wild card: as something that has to be reined in. As we might say today, men are from Mars and women are from Venus. I always find it ironic that non-Orthodox critics of traditional, Orthodox Judaism see it as sexist against women, when, if anything, it is sexist against men. It is assumed that women will be responsible enough to wake up and daaven properly on their own. Orthodox Judasim, however, assumes that men will not: without the discipline of being obligated to daaven with a minyan, it assumes, men will oversleep or forget. So men are required to daaven together: it is discipline that women are assumed to already posses. In practice, Orthodox Jewish men attend shul (or often minyans in offices or homes) three times a day for hasty daavening, before they go off to work and then home at the end of the day. This was never meant to be the central experience of their religious life, and in Orthodox homes it never is.

4

Drawing close to God: blessings at the Shabbat dinner table

Shabbat dinner is possibly the most famous Jewish event in our tradition. Even Jews with minimal connection to traditional Jewish observance have usually experienced some form of Shabbat dinner at some point in their lives. When rabbis and other Jews involved in outreach seek to connect with unaffiliated Jews, Shabbat dinner is the place they usually start. Why? Perhaps it is because the beautiful songs, the wonderful smells of the delicious Shabbat food, the lovely set table with its tablecloth and sparkling kiddish cups, the fragrant challah, all tap into something deep inside of us: the very essence of what it means to be a Jew.

In the year 70 of the Common Era, or 3940 of the Jewish calendar, the mighty army of the great Roman Empire approached Jerusalem. Roman soldiers attacked the city walls with catapults and battering rams, and on the ninth day of the Jewish month of Tammuz, Romans breached the outer walls of the city.

For three weeks, Roman forces fought Jerusalem's Jewish residents in fierce, hand-to-hand combat. For three weeks, the ancient Jews resisted the Roman invaders, fighting them in the streets, in the courtyards, in the alleys, even in the houses of Jerusalem. Despite their heroic resistance, Jerusalem's citizens were beginning to lose the battle. Daily, the Roman forces advanced closer to the "House of Holiness," called the Beit Hamikdash in Hebrew: the Temple where God's presence dwelt in the heart of Jerusalem. Jewish life revolved

around this holy building; it was where Jews brought weekly sacrifices of food and animals to dedicate to God, where every Jew communed with their creator, and where all of Israel's Jews enjoyed one another's company at the three annual festivals.

The valiant residents of Jerusalem fought with one heart to keep the marauders away from this holy place. Yet the Romans were beginning to triumph. Jewish blood flowed freely in the streets, and soon Roman soldiers could see their prize: the heart of the Jewish people, the holy Beit Hamikdash.

Finally, on the ninth day of the Jewish month of Av, Roman soldiers entered the Holy of Holies of the Jewish people, the Beit Hamikdash. Soldiers tore the Temple's woven curtains from their rods and smashed the Temple's ornately carved wooden furniture. They marched into the building's inner sanctums and raided the treasures that were housed there: the gold and silver vessels, the golden seven-branched menorah that God Himself had commanded the Jews to make, the Ark containing the stone tablets brought down by Moses from Mount Sinai. To this very day, the Arch of Titus, erected in the imperial heart of Rome, stands in modern-day Rome and depicts, carved into its side, that day when Roman soldiers destroyed the Beit Hamikdash, showing Roman soldiers carrying the golden menorah home to Rome in triumph.

The marauding soldiers destroyed the Beit Hamikdash utterly. After they had carted away its treasure, they burned the building so that almost no trace remained. From that day to this, two thousand years later, the only remaining remnant of the great Beit Hamikdash is one outer Western Wall, today revered by Jews all over the world as the last remnant of our Temple.

The Roman invaders then turned on the defeated populace, and forced many of the Jews of Israel into exile. And the defeated Jews turned to their teachers, their rabbis, and asked, "What shall we do now? How shall we worship God without His holy Beit Hamikdash to congregate in? Where can His holiness — his 'Mikdash' — now exist?"

The answers our ancient Jewish ancestors received set the direction of Judaism for the next two millennia. "Our House of Holiness — our Temple in Jerusalem — may be destroyed, but God's holiness has not disappeared from the earth with it. Instead, our own homes will have to become little Temples,

called in Hebrew 'Mikdash Me'at.'" Each Jewish householder now has to create his or her own Mikdash Me'at, his or her own holy Temple. "And," the Rabbis decreed, "the altar of this Temple will be our own ordinary dining room table. Through our own actions we will henceforth have to elevate each meal to be an occasion to serve God. We can no longer sacrifice in the Temple, but instead we will recall the Shabbat sacrifices at our own Shabbat tables from now on; we will worship God with every meal we eat."

How can we bring this lovely setting into our own homes? How can we transform our Shabbat table into a Mikdash Me'at, the successor to the Temple in Jerusalem, and a place where we worship God? The time-tested formula of Shabbat meals really can bring the holiness of the ancient Temple into our homes. Here is how one practitioner goes about setting up a traditional Shabbat experience.

Setting the table

Before Shabbat begins, I set our dining room table for the holiday. There is no rule about how to do this, but I usually start with a white tablecloth because in many Jewish communities this is considered the most formal. In many Judaica or kosher stores, you can buy clear plastic table covers that go on top of the fabric, because kids of all ages spill their drinks, and nobody wants to buy a new fabric tablecloth each week. (However, I use one of the new generation of "spill proof" cloths, purchased in an ordinary housewares store; it looks like normal material, but drinks just bead up on it instead of being absorbed.)

If we're having loads of company I might use fancy paper plates and napkins but, generally, we'll use our best china, glasses, and cloth napkins. I don't trust my young children with our good china yet, so over the years they have decorated special Shabbat plates for themselves at craft stores and at craft-themed birthday parties. Sometimes, to keep my children occupied as I get dinner ready, I'll have them fold the napkins in fancy shapes or make place-cards for us and our guests.

In addition to our formal place settings, we also include several ritual items on the table, whose use will be explained below. Each member of our family has their own kiddish cup for wine or grape juice. This is a special cup, often silver, to hold wine or grape juice as we bless Shabbat. If you do not have dedicated kiddish cups, however, it is perfectly acceptable to use an ordinary wine glass or cup instead. I also set the table with a tray containing two loaves of challah, covered with a cloth. Next to this I place a shaker of salt. I place a bottle of wine (for the adults) and a bottle of grape juice (for the children or any adults who do not drink wine) on the table. Since we seek to beautify everything we use on Shabbat, I also place an embroidered cover reading "Kiddush Shabbat" around the wine bottle for decoration, flowers on the table for decoration, and beautiful silver trays on the table to hold the kiddish cups and wine bottles.

Ritual items required for the Shabbat meal

➤ Wine or grape juice
➤ At least one cup for wine or grape juice
➤ A plate with two loaves of challah
➤ A cloth or napkin to cover the challah loaves
➤ Salt
➤ A separate cup to ritually wash hands (in bathroom or kitchen, not on the table)

"Shalom Aleichem"

Shalom means "peace" and Aleichem means "to you." The first thing we do when seated around our Shabbat table on Friday night is sing a song called "Shalom Aleichem" to greet the extra "malachim" (messengers from God, or angels) who accompany every Jew on Shabbat. The traditional tune (you can find it on CDs or the Internet) is catchy; it can be nice to get into the rhythm of this song and tap your feet or the table or clap your hands as you sing.

Shalom Aleichem	Peace to you
Malachei ha shareit	Angels who serve
Malachei Elyon	Angels (of) God
Mimelech	from the King
Malachei ha Malachim	Who reigns over kings
Ha Kadosh Baruch Hu.	The Holy One, Blessed is He.
Boachem L'shalom	(May) your coming (be) for peace
Malachei haShalom	Angels of Peace
Malachei Elyon	Angels (of) God
Mimelech	from the King
Malachei ha Malachim	Who reigns over kings
Ha Kadosh Baruch Hu.	The Holy One, Blessed is He.
Barchuni L'Shalom	Bless me for peace
Malachei haShalom	Angels of Peace
Malachei Elyon	Angels (of) God
Mimelech	from the King
Malachei ha Malachim	Who reigns over kings
Ha Kadosh Baruch Hu.	The Holy One, Blessed is He.
Tseitchem L'Shalom	(May you) depart towards peace
Malachei haShalom	Angels of Peace
Malachei Elyon	Angels (of) God
Mimelech	from the King
Malachei ha Malachim	Who reigns over kings
Ha Kadosh Baruch Hu.	The Holy One, Blessed is He.

Blessing the children

After singing "Shalom Aleichem," we bless our children. This is a powerful moment, as we prepare to act like God, bestowing blessings on our "creations": our children. Though the formula differs for girls and boys, both blessings incorporate the holy words that God revealed to Moses 3,000 years ago, as the Jewish people prepared to leave the desert and enter the Land of Israel.

And the God spoke to Moses, saying: "Speak to Aaron and to his sons, and say: in this way you shall bless the children of Israel. You will say to them: God bless you, and keep you. God make His face to light up on you, and be gracious unto you; God lift up His face to you, and grant you peace. So shall they put My name upon the children of Israel and I will bless them." (Num. 6.22–27)

We bless each child separately. In our home, my husband goes in order from oldest to youngest, though you can bless your kids in any order you choose. To bless a child, stand, place your hands on the child's head, and pronounce the blessing out loud. The blessings are different for girls and boys.

Blessing the daughters

For girls, we bless them with the hope that they be like our matriarchs, Sarah, Rebecca, Rachel, and Leah. We also repeat the threefold blessing with which God told Aaron to bless the Children of Israel in Numbers 6.22.

> *Y'simcha Elohim K'Sarah, Rivkah, Ruchel v'Leah.*
> May God make you like Sarah, Rebecca, Rachel and Leah.
>
> *Yivarechecha Adonoi v'Yishmarecha.*
> May God bless you and guard you.
>
> *Ya'air Adonoi Panav Eleicha vi'chunecha.*
> May God light up His Face on you and Show mercy to you.
>
> *Yisay Adonoi Panav Eleicha v'Yisem lecha shalom.*
> May God turn His Face to you and Make you complete.

Blessing sons

The blessing for boys is more surprising. Why not emulate the girls' blessing, and wish our boys blessings like our patriarchs, much like we wish upon our girls blessings like our matriarchs? Why do we wish our boys will be like the relatively obscure Ephraim and Menasha? Who were these men, anyway?

The Jewish Patriarchs are Abraham, his son Isaac, and Issac's son Jacob, who was also known as Israel. Jacob had 12 sons and one daughter. Jacob's favorite child was probably Joseph, of the many-colored coat fame. Joseph's brothers were very jealous of him, and one day they ambushed Joseph and threw him into a pit. Joseph was rescued later, however, by a caravan of traders, and these traders sold him into slavery in Egypt. In Egypt, Joseph rose to become the vizier of Egypt, second in power only to Pharaoh himself. After many years, a drought occurred in the Land of Israel, and Jacob gathered together all of his clan — 70 people — and journeyed down to Egypt, where Joseph had taken the precaution of storing grain against just such a drought. Jacob's other sons had long ago told Jacob that a wild animal killed Joseph, but now Jacob found out this was not true, and at last could embrace his darling son again. Joseph forgave his brothers their treachery and lies, and the family was reunited.

Now, after this all transpired, Jacob was very old, and he knew that he would die soon, in Egypt. Before he died, Jacob called his son Joseph to him and asked Joseph to make sure that one day Jacob's coffin would be carried out of Egypt and reburied in Israel. Joseph promised this and then, knowing his father's death was near, Joseph brought his own sons — Ephraim and Menasha — to Jacob for a blessing. Jacob told Joseph that Ephraim and Menasha, Jacob's grandsons, were like children to him, on a par with Jacob's biological sons. Jacob hugged and kissed the boys. He then placed his hands on Ephraim and Menasha's heads and pronounced this blessing: "The God before whom my fathers Abraham and Isaac did walk, the God who has been my shepherd all my life long until this day, the angel who has redeemed me from all evil, bless the boys, and let my name be named in them, and the name of my fathers Abraham and Isaac, and let them grow into a multitude in the midst of the earth" (Gen. 68.15–16). Jacob then turned to Joseph and told him this blessing should be used throughout the generations of Israel "By you shall Israel bless, saying: God make you as Ephraim and as Menasha." (Gen. 68.20).

Jacob also bequeathed an extra portion of his estate to Joseph and to Joseph's sons Ephraim and Menasha. The famous Rabbi Joseph Hertz, who served as Chief Rabbi of the British Empire in the first half of the twentieth

century, wrote a widely used commentary on the Bible. On this verse, he draws on traditional Jewish commentary on the characters of Ephraim and Menasha:

> To this day, every pious Jewish father on Sabbath eve places his hands on the head of his son, and blesses him in the words: "God make thee as Ephraim and Manasseh." Ephraim and Manasseh would not barter away their "Jewishness" for the most exalted social position, or the most enviable political career, in the Egyptian state. They voluntarily gave up their place in the higher Egyptian aristocracy and openly identified themselves with their "alien" kinsmen, the despised shepherd-immigrants. Every Jewish parent may well pray that his children show the same loyalty to their father and their father's God as did Ephraim and Manasseh.

Now, in biblical times, the eldest sons received a special blessing, reserved for the firstborn, and Menasha was older than Ephraim, and thus expected the dominant blessing. These blessings from their father determined not only the spiritual future of sons but also their inheritance of land and property. Yet when Jacob blessed Ephraim and Menasha, he deliberately crossed his arms, so that with his right hand (which conferred the better blessing), he touched Ephraim, and with his left hand, Menasha.

Ephraim, particularly, has the power to move God Himself, and in blessing our sons that they become like Ephraim, we are conveying a powerful ability to sway God. The prophet Jeremiah, who foretold the end of the world and the dawn of the Messianic period, singled out Ephraim as the symbol of the Jewish people. In an incredibly beautiful and famous passage, Jeremiah envisions Ephraim's grandmother Rachel pleading from the grave to God to stop punishing her children with exile from their Land, and then Ephraim himself turning back to God. God finally relents, and allowing the Jewish people to return to their homeland of Israel, grants them the Messianic period:

> Thus says the Lord: A voice is heard in Ramah, lamentation and bitter weeping, Rachel weeping for her children. She refuses to be comforted for her children,

because they are not. Thus says the Lord: Refrain your voice from weeping, and your eyes from tears, for your work shall be rewarded, says the Lord, and they shall come back from the land of the enemy. And there is hope for your future, says the Lord, and your children shall return to their own border.

I have surely heard Ephraim bemoaning himself: "You have punished me, and I was punished, as a calf untrained; turn to me, and I shall be turned, for You are the Lord my God. Surely after that I was turned, I repented, and after that I was instructed, I struck upon my thigh; I was ashamed, yea, even confounded, because I did bear the reproach of my youth."

Is Ephraim a darling son unto Me? Is he a child that is dandled? For as often as I speak of him, I do earnestly remember him still; therefore My heart yearns for him. I will surely have compassion upon him, says the Lord. (Jer. 31.15–20)

Thus, the blessing for boys is:

> *Y'Simcha Elohim ki'Ephraim v'ki'Menasha.*
> May God make you like Ephraim and Menasha.
>
> *Yivarechecha Adonoi v'Yishmarecha.*
> May God bless you and guard you.
>
> *Ya'air Adonoi Panav Eleicha vi'chunecha.*
> May God light up His Face on you and Show mercy to you.
>
> *Yisay Adonoi Panav Eleicha v'Yisem lecha shalom.*
> May God turn His Face to you and Make you complete.

"A Woman of Valor"

After blessing the children, we recite "Aishet Chail," or "A Woman of Valor." This text comes from the last 21 verses of the biblical Book of Proverbs (Prov. 31.10–31). "Chail" (it rhymes with "smile" and the first "ch" sounds like gargling in the back of the throat) is the same word for "soldier" in Hebrew. It connotes toughness and strength. This beautiful text describes

the qualities of an ideal woman. She is a businesswoman. She takes care of her husband and children. She works tirelessly to build wealth. She is charitable. She is God-fearing. She is loved.

Now, I'd always learned that reciting "Aishet Chail" had nothing to do with singing the praises of the lady of the house. In fact, I remember one teacher in my seminary in Jerusalem thundering, "Aishet Chail isn't meant to be recited by the husband to his wife, as she sits looking all demure and blushing down at her end of the table . . ." No, my teacher asserted: the ideal woman being sung about is not the particular lady of a particular house. It is the very people of Israel! And the husband of this "woman," who is really the people of Israel, is none other than God Himself! Thus, everyone sings "Aishet Chail," whether they are man or woman, married or not. This is not a song about an earthly woman or an earthly family. It is a song about all of us, about the entire Jewish people and our relationship with God, which is as close as that of husband and wife! Many commentators have shared this view. Indeed, "Aishet Chail" is a standard part of Shabbat dinner, and people of all ages, both men and women, and in all states of life sing it.

However, to my great surprise, when I married my husband I found that he very firmly sees "Aishet Chail" as an ode sung by a husband to his wife. At first I tried to reason with him, to convince him otherwise, to make it about the wider Jewish people. But over the years I gradually gave in. I mention this because my husband instituted a very personal tradition in our house that I've come to adore. This is completely his invention, but some families might want to adopt it or try it sometime. After blessing the children, before reciting "Aishet Chail," my husband asks each of our children to "name three nice things Mommy did for you this week." The answers are often rote, and the younger children usually copy what the older kids have said, but every now and then they throw out something original and touching.

When we have guests at our table, my husband gives visiting children the option to "play this game too" if they want to, as he puts it. When guests take him up on his offer, it is interesting to note that visiting kids often can't think of anything they appreciate from their mother for a while. They hem and haw and eventually — with prodding — come up with one

or maybe two nice things their mother has done. It is not that these kids are ungrateful, or don't appreciate all that their mother does. Most of the children we have over as guests are fantastic kids. But they're not used to being asked to appreciate their moms, and so it takes them a few minutes to formulate a thought of appreciation. This, more than anything else, has made me a convert to my husband's way of approaching the "Aishet Chail." I like how he brings this very profound metaphysical relationship down to the very practical level of our family. As my kids go around the table listing things they appreciate, my heart swells with pride that they are exercising their ability to have gratitude.

We then recite "Aishet Chail." We sing it in Hebrew, but if you don't understand the text in Hebrew, you might want to consider reading it in English. One final note: one of my favorite Jewish books is a commentary on this prayer written by the famous Jerusalem-based teacher and author Rebbetzin Tziporah Heller. Rebbetzin (the title means wife of a rabbi) Heller goes through this prayer line by line, commenting on the deeper meanings of each verse. (If you are interested in Rebbetzin Heller's commentary it has been published as "More Precious than Pearls." Rebbetzin Heller maintains her own interesting website at http://tziporahheller.com.)

"Aishet Chail" is an acrostic: the first letter of each line goes through the Hebrew alphabet, from aleph to tav:

An accomplished woman, who can find? — Far beyond pearls is her value.
Her husband's heart relies on her and he shall lack no fortune.
She repays his good, but never his harm, all the days of her life.
She seeks out wool and linen, and her hands work willingly.
She is like a merchant's ships, from afar she brings her sustenance.
She arises while it is yet nighttime, and gives food to her household and a ration to her maidens.
She envisions a field and buys it, from the fruit of her handiwork she plants a vineyard.
With strength she girds her loins, and invigorates her arms.
She discerns that her enterprise is good — so that her lamp is not snuffed out by night.

Her hands she stretches out to the distaff, and her palms support the
  spindle.

She spreads out her palm to the poor, and extends her hands to the
  destitute.

She fears not snow for her household, for her entire household is clothed
  with scarlet wool.

Luxurious bedspreads she made herself, linen and purple wool are her
  clothing.

Distinctive in the councils is her husband, when he sits with the elders of
  the land.

She makes a cloak to sell, and delivers a belt to the peddler.

Strength and majesty are her raiment, she joyfully awaits the last day.

She opens her mouth with wisdom, and a lesson of kindness is on her
  tongue.

She anticipates the ways of her household, and partakes not of the bread of
  laziness.

Her children arise and praise her, her husband, and he lauds her:
  "Many daughters have amassed achievement, but you surpassed them all."

False is grace and vain is beauty, a God-fearing woman — she should be
  praised.

Give her the fruits of her hand and let her be praised in the gates by her very
  own deeds.

Kiddush

After concluding these blessings, it is time to make a Kiddush or blessing
over wine or grape juice. "Kiddush" means "Made Holy," and reciting this
prayer is one of the central features of Shabbat observance.

Kiddush is more than just the blessing one makes over an ordinary glass
of wine. It is the sanctification of the entire Shabbat. The Torah states that
we must "Shamor" (Guard) and "Zachor" (Remember) the Shabbat. What
does this mean? What is the difference between guarding and remembering? The Talmud explains that "Guard" refers to guarding against the

39 types of work prohibited on Shabbat. "Remember" means to take one moment each Shabbat to remember what Shabbat is all about. We do this during the holy moment of Kiddush, when we remember that God Himself rested on Shabbat, and that He has given this day to the Jewish people as a gift for all eternity.

Kiddush is actually recited twice on Shabbat: before dinner on Friday evening, and before lunch on Saturday afternoon. All Jews — men and women — are obligated to hear it. In our own home, my husband recites Kiddush. This is an honor usually reserved for the man of the house, though each household has its own customs. Since women are obligated to hear Kiddush just like men, women can also recite it. Some households might offer this honor to a guest or visiting parent. The person reciting Kiddush must be obligated in the mitzvah: they have to be Jewish, and be a bar mitzvah or bat mitzvah (that is, is at least 12 years old if a girl and 13 if a boy).

My husband gathers together Kiddush cups for everyone present. A long time ago, my husband's parents started a beautiful family tradition: whenever a child is born, they buy him or her a beautiful silver Kiddush cup for their very own. Thus, each of our children has their own Kiddush cup that will, we hope, follow them in the future as they build their own homes one day. We also have many extra cups for guests to use. My husband places these on a tray, then fills his own Kiddush cup (bought for him by his parents when he was a baby) with wine or grape juice to the very rim. (We make Kiddush over a full cup to symbolize that God's gifts to us on Shabbat are overflowing.) Technically, we can make Kiddush over any food or drink, but it is traditional to use either wine or grape juice. These share the same blessing and are used in many important Jewish rituals.

Holding his overflowing Kiddush cup, my husband recites the Friday evening Kiddush:

(Recite silently: "And there was evening and there was morning the Sixth Day.")

And the Heavens and the Earth and all their multitudes were completed. And God completed on the seventh day His work that He had done, and He refrained on the seventh day from His work that he had done. And God

Blessed the seventh day and made it holy, because on it He refrained from all His work that God created to make.

Blessed are You God, our Lord, King of the world, Who Creates the fruit of the vine.

(Everyone present says "Amen.")

Blessed are You, God, our Lord, King of the world, Who has made us holy with His commandments, took pleasure in us, and with love and favor gave us His holy Shabbat as a heritage, a remembrance of creation. For that day is the prologue to the holy Jewish holidays, a memorial of the Exodus from Egypt. For us did You choose and us did You make holy from all the nations. And Your holy Shabbat, with love and favor did You give us as a heritage. Blessed are You, God, Who sanctifies Shabbat.

(Everyone present says "Amen.")

At this point, my husband pours a little wine or juice from his cup into each of the empty Kiddush cups before him. If you like, you can top up the cups with a little juice or wine from the bottle so they're full before distributing them. The important thing is that each person has at least a drop of the wine or grape juice over which Kiddush was recited in their cups.

Because in Judaism we do not do anything extraneous between the time we say a blessing and the time we do the action the blessing was for, we do not talk or leave the table while my husband fills the cups. (If you need to say something directly related to the mitzvah — for instance, "You've forgotten your mother's cup!" or "Use grape juice for the kids!" — you can.) We pass out the filled Kiddush cups, and everybody takes a sip.

Hamotzi

At this point we all turn our attention to the two loaves of challah sitting on the table, covered by a cloth or napkin. Why bread? In Jewish law, a meal is only considered a meal when bread is served; anything else is a snack. Consequently, there are all sorts of rules that pertain to the consumption of bread in Jewish law that are absent when eating other foods. Before we

eat bread, we have to first ritually wash and dry our hands and say a bless-ing. The rabbis of the Talmud strongly encouraged people not to eat bread while walking or standing; we ought to sit at a table when we eat a meal involving bread. During a meal that includes bread, we also are strongly encouraged to talk about Torah. Following consumption of bread, we sing a praise-giving psalm to God. Then, there is a lengthy prayer that concludes a meal at which bread was partaken. It doesn't matter if all we eat is a hot dog in a bun: in Jewish law, since bread is eaten, that hot dog counts as a meal, with all the attendant rituals. Conversely (and counterintuitively), if we enjoy an elaborate meal where no bread is served, Jewish law merely requires one quick blessing before and another after this food. In Judaism, bread makes the meal.

Among other activities, we are commanded to eat festive meals on Shabbat. In the Jewish view, of course, this includes bread. (In fact, if we were to eat only bread on Shabbat, we would still fulfill the mitzvah of eating Shabbat meals.) But why use two loaves?

When the Jews left slavery in Egypt, God led them deep into the desert. At first, the Jews were euphoric, but soon their euphoria turned to worry, then panic. They surveyed the arid landscape around them. Nothing grew; no water flowed. "Did you lead us out of Egypt, God, only to let us die in the empty desert?" they cried. Many of the Jews demanded to go back. "Yes, we were slaves," they reasoned, "but in Egypt we did not starve." Still other Jews rhapsodized about the delicious foods they enjoyed in Egypt: the cucumbers, radishes, and onions. Surely, they would never taste anything half as good again!

Yet God took care of the Jews as he led them through the desert. He miraculously provided streams of clear water everywhere they camped. And every morning, a special food called Manna dropped from the sky. This Manna was unlike any food the Jews had seen before: it was a special gift, provided directly by God. Each morning the Jews would go out to seek that day's portion, and there was always enough for each person's needs. The Manna tasted of those foods that each Jew most loved; for one person Manna might taste of rich milk and cheese; for another, it might be the flavor of apples or of lemons. The Jews ate each day's Manna and relished it.

At first, some of the Jews decided to stockpile excess Manna. They did not trust in God's continuing goodness, and thought that He might some day decide to stop the Manna. So they gathered extra of the food, and secreted it away. But lo and behold, the following day the Manna they had hidden was rancid and full of maggots. For it was not God's intention for the Jews to store their Manna; He wished to show them that they must trust in him every day, and rely on their Heavenly Father for each day's food while in the desert.

There was one exception to this rule against storing Manna, however. Each Friday, God would distribute a double portion of Manna to the Jews: one portion for Friday's meals and one portion for Saturday. This way, nobody would have to gather food on the holy Shabbat. This extra portion would not spoil, but remained fresh and sweet for consumption on Shabbat. Thus, the Jews got their first taste of Shabbat's holiness and plenty in the desert, even before God revealed the Torah and the many laws and practices of Shabbat.

We use two entire loaves at our evening and midday meals on Shabbat to represent the double portion of Manna that God gave us before Shabbat. It is reminder of His unwavering generosity to us. This generosity is easy to forget when we are safe in our strong, modern, heated, and air-conditioned homes. It is easy to forget as we shop in the supermarket for ready-grown, packed and shipped food, or go to restaurants for dinner for meals prepared and cleared by others. The hand of God seems very remote indeed from our modern, busy lives.

Of course, we know that were God not to grant the earth rain, the farmers who grow our food would not be able to coax crops from the ground. But that is so far away. We recognize that our health, our luck, our very existence which allows us to provide for ourselves and our families comes from God. But that is so very abstract. It is much easier to see ourselves as responsible for our own success: we work for our money, and we spend that money to provide for our loved ones. Where is God in that? Remembering the Manna helps us answer this question. God is everywhere in our lives. Just as God gave us Manna, so too today He gives us the sustenance we take for granted. Just as God decided when we could gather Manna for an extra day and when we had to rely on His generosity daily, so also today

it is God who ultimately decides if our labors will be successful or not. We have come a long way from living in the desert, and being acutely aware with each passing breeze that it is God who sustains us and provides for us, just as a loving parent carefully nurtures a child. It is so easy to believe that we provide for ourselves, that we make our own security. Gazing on the challah loaves and remembering the Manna our ancestors ate in the desert helps us recall that we are no less dependent on God's aid and His love today.

Before we eat bread, Jewish law states we must first ritually wash our hands. Just as there is physical dirt, there is also spiritual pollution. There is an expectation that we have come to the Shabbat table physically clean; at this point in the evening, it is time to wash our hands spiritually, as well. "Soiled" can be translated into Hebrew in two ways. The common English sense would be "m'luch'lach" from the Hebrew word for dirt or soil. But in Hebrew there is a keen sense that people inhabit two worlds: the physical and the spiritual. Thus, soiled can also be translated into Hebrew as "tamay," or spiritually soiled. Thus, before partaking of bread, we all are required to ritually wash our hands.

In our house, we sometimes do this in the dining room, and sometimes in the kitchen or bathroom. For our wedding, some relatives gave us a special washing cup (these are large cups with two handles, and are ubiquitous in religious Jewish homes, though you can use any sort of cup for ritual washing) with a matching large bowl. When we have lots of little kids or anybody for whom getting up from the table is difficult, we come around with this washing cup set and a towel; people can wash their hands into the bowl right at the table. Otherwise, we all get up from the table and file into the kitchen or bathroom.

To wash, we fill a cup with water and pour some over each hand three times. You are supposed to make sure your whole hand is wet up to the wrist. After pouring water three times over your right hand and three times over your left hand, you pick up a towel and say a blessing while you dry your hands. (Note: if you have washed your hands in the bathroom, you must step out of the bathroom to dry your hands and say the blessing. In Judaism, we are not allowed to pray anywhere where we can see a toilet.)

The blessing is:

Baruch	=	Blessed
Atah	=	(are) You
Adonoy	=	My Lord
Eloheinu	=	Our God
Melech	=	King
Ha	=	(of) the
'Olam	=	World
Asher	=	That
Kidshanu	=	Made us holy
b'mitzva'otav	=	in (through) His commandments
vetzivanu	=	(and) Commanded us
al	=	to
natilat	=	wash
yadaim	=	both hands.

In our home, we have a special towel that says "al natilat yadaim," or "to wash both hands" on it, and we use special, ornate washing cups on Shabbat. There is a strong idea in Judaism both that we beautify the mitzvot (commandments), and also that we beautify Shabbat. Much of what we use on Shabbat is ornate and decorated, and set aside just for Shabbat and holidays. But it is perfectly acceptable to use ordinary objects, too. As you grow in Shabbat observance, you might decide to acquire more ornate Judaica items. Particularly if you know young children, it can be especially fun and meaningful to have them make home-made versions of these items.

As mentioned, in Judaism, the blessing over an action and the action itself are linked. We are supposed to say blessings right before doing what is being blessed; we are not meant to take detours or do extraneous things between saying a blessing and completing the action the blessing is over. Thus, after we wash our hands, we are not allowed to talk or do any other activities before eating the challah.

Kids love this; it becomes a sort of juvenile game. Since it usually takes

a few minutes before everyone present has washed and dried their hands and resumed their seats in the dining room, kids love goofing off, knowing that nobody can say anything to them until after eating some challah. Even my husband gets in on the act. If one of our kids has washed before my husband (and thus cannot speak while my husband can), he'll say something goofy to them, knowing they'll giggle but not respond. One exception to this no-talking rule is anything that is directly related to the process of getting ready to bless and eat the challah; if there is any sort of problem or question about the challah or people's readiness to eat it, you can speak on this issue. (Even many Orthodox Jews are ignorant of this loophole; it can be comic to see people resort to extensive, improvised sign language to communicate things about their challah.) Many people hum a little tune after washing their hands, before blessing and eating challah. One of my children's teachers taught her that even humming is an interruption and should not be done, though many families do it, and it can be a lovely way of passing the few minutes until everyone is ready and in their seats once more. (I also do try to minimize the goofiness that can arise around this ritual, because this is an important moment when we are fulfilling a mitzvah, after all.)

Until this point, the challah has been covered on the table by a napkin or special decorated challah cover; we now remove the cover. Why do we cover the challah? The reason is picturesque and touching. We cover the challah so that it won't see us bless the wine before we bless it, and therefore won't be jealous. Why do we bother anthropomorphizing the bread in this way? Some people find it sweet; to others it might seem odd. A beautiful story about the Rabbi Reb Yisroel Salanter illustrates perfectly the sensitivity inherent in this Shabbat ritual.

Lithuania in the eighteenth and nineteenth centuries was a land of giants of Torah. At few other times in our history has one country been so full of the most towering Jewish scholarship. Among the great rabbis of nineteenth-century Lithuania, one of the most superb was Reb Yisroel Salanter. Reb Salanter emphasized the Jewish tradition of "mussar," or ethical teaching, and wrote profound guides to ethical dilemmas and behavior that have deeply affected the lives of Jews throughout the world for the

past 150 years, and continue to do so today. (An excellent series of lectures on mussar is provided on-line by the well-known Israeli rabbinical training school, Yeshivat Har Etzion at www.vbm-torah.org if you are interested in learning more about this movement.)

One week, when Rabbi Yisroel Salanter was travelling, he went to stay with a family for Shabbat. The father of this family was immensely impressed that the great Reb Salanter was his guest, and wanted everything to be absolutely perfect. Before Shabbat, the host gave instructions that all the silver was to be polished, the house was to be cleaned, and the most wonderful delicacies were to be cooked for the Shabbat meals. Everything was done according to his instructions, and the family with their esteemed guest sat down to a magnificent Shabbat table on Friday night.

With great relish, the host went through the Shabbat rituals, and soon it was time to eat the challah. Everybody rose to wash their hands, then reassembled at the table. The host grandly removed the challah covering, and all eyes took in the two perfect, golden-brown loaves. With great pomp, the host recited the blessing over the challah, cut the slices, and then looked for the salt which is to be sprinkled on top of the challah before it is eaten. However, to his great consternation, it appeared that his wife had forgotten the salt when she had set the table.

The host turned on his hapless wife and roared at her: "You fool! The great Reb Salanter is our guest, and you have forgotten this crucial detail of the Shabbat meal!" Tearfully, his humiliated wife hurried into the kitchen to retrieve the salt.

After she returned and everyone present had eaten of her delicious challah, Reb Salanter turned to his host. "Excuse me, but can you tell me why we cover the challah on the table?" Reb Salanter asked the man. Confused as to why he was being asked such a simple question, the host replied, "Of course. We cover the challah so that it will not be jealous when we bless the wine before it!"

Reb Salanter explained: "And if we take such pains to protect the feelings of the challah — which, after all is an inanimate object — how much more should we trouble ourselves to be sensitive to the very real feelings of an actual

person! You have upset and embarrassed your wife here tonight! You have treated her as lower than the inanimate challah loaves on your table. Have you learned nothing from the Shabbat rituals? You must take the lesson you learn from treating the challah on your Shabbat table with respect, and use it to elevate the feelings and honor of all people — especially your wife's!"

After we uncover the challah, we hold up the two loaves and say "Birshut," then put them back on their plate or cutting board. "Birshut" means "with permission," and this is an old-fashioned way of showing respect for the others at your table; before you do anything for them, such as bless the bread on their behalf, you first ask if this is acceptable.

Take the loaves in your hands; one loaf should be resting on top of the other. Make the blessing over bread:

Baruch	=	Blessed
Atah	=	(are) You
Adonoy	=	My Lord
Eloheinu	=	Our God
Melech	=	King
Ha	=	(of) the
'Olam	=	World
Hamotzei	=	The (one who) brings out
Lechem	=	Bread
Min	=	From
Ha	=	the
Aretz	=	Land

Take the bottom loaf. (For Shabbat lunch, you will use the top loaf.) Some people at this point use a knife to slice the loaf into enough slices for each guest. In my own home we have the custom of tearing the challah; both are acceptable. Those who tear the challah do so to recall the building of the Beit Hamikdash, the holy Temple in Jerusalem. Because the Beit Hamikdash's purpose — its very essence — was entirely peaceful, no sharp tools that could have doubled as war instruments (such as knives or axes)

were used in its construction. Since our Shabbat tables are like mini Temples ("mikdash me'at"), some people recall this aspect of the Beit Hamikdash by tearing, instead of cutting, the challah.

After the challah has been sliced or torn into the appropriate number of pieces, we sprinkle them with a little salt. This also recalls the Beit Hamikdash, where salt was sprinkled over the sacrifices made to God. The Jewish people are also sometimes compared to salt; both are hardy and rugged. Neither one ever spoils, but instead remains true and pure. After sprinkling a little salt over the challah, distribute it to everyone. (The person who made the Hamotzi blessing usually eats the first piece, and gives the second to their spouse.)

My husband's family has incorporated a ritual that they say is Sephardi (non-Ashkenazi, or from the Middle Eastern or southern European Jewish tradition) in origin. They do not hand each other challah, but instead toss it to them. As each person catches their piece of challah as it falls gently into their hand, they are meant to be reminded that God similarly causes our sustenance to be "dropped" into our hands. This is fun, but we don't always do it. Some weeks, the kids like this tossing of challah just a bit too much. And as nice as it is to recall God's blessings for us at this moment, maintaining decorum at the Shabbat table is more important. When our kids or guests' kids threaten to get too rambunctious, we pass the challah around calmly!

One final question about challah: does the bread we eat at the Shabbat table have to be this traditional delicacy? Not at all. In fact, though challah has become ubiquitous in the Jewish world, traditionally non-European communities used two loaves of pita bread at Shabbat. (Some people still do.) While challah is traditional, you can use any two loaves of unbroken or unsliced bread or bread rolls. My great-aunt of blessed memory loved matzah, and always made hamotzi on Shabbat over two slices of matzah. (This would be acceptable for Ashkenazi — or Northern European — Jews; Sephardi Jews cannot make the hamotzi blessing on matzah when it is not Passover.)

The only rules about the two loaves of bread on the Shabbat table are these:

➤ We must use two loaves.

➤ The loaves must be whole.

➤ We must to be able to say the "hamotzi" blessing over them. (For instance, using crackers would be unacceptable, as we say a different blessing before eating them.)

➤ The loaves must be edible. (How do we define edible? The Talmud says: if a dog would eat it, it is edible.)

Thus the loaves on our Shabbat table echo the double Shabbat sacrifices offered by our ancestors in the Beit Hamikdash, our Holy Temple, and, before that, the manna that we received directly from God. For hundreds of generations, we have enjoyed the bounteous double portion that our challah loaves represent on Shabbat. It is amazing that the chain continues, unbroken and whole, each week to the present day, at our Shabbat tables, in Israel, and all over the world.

5

An evening of holiness: Shabbat dinner and after

After everyone eats a piece of challah, we move on to the rest of the Shabbat meal. There is no need to make any other blessings over food; the Hamotzi blessing over bread covers all the other food. It is traditional to enjoy a multi-course meal on Shabbat. A typical meal might include a fish course, followed by soup, then a main course, then dessert. There are no rules for how or what you should eat. Only keep in mind that Shabbat is the day to go beyond the ordinary: it is the day to use our good china, to eat in our dining room if we have one, to use a tablecloth, to eat something formal. We are not specifically commanded to have this or that food at our meals, but we are expected to serve something nicer than we usually eat when it is not Shabbat. (I have included some very easy, simple versions of a number of traditional Jewish recipes in Chapter 14.)

Years ago, while visiting Jerusalem, I attended a lecture given by a former "refusenik" named Yosef Mendelovich. Refuseniks were Jews in the former Soviet Union who applied for permission to leave the USSR and move to Israel. Discrimination against Jews in the Soviet Union was unrelenting, Jewish holy books were strictly forbidden, and many of the over a million Russian Jews yearned to leave to be able to practice their religion in freedom. Yet almost all of the many Jews who applied to leave were refused permission. Not only that, these refuseniks frequently lost their jobs and even their homes after applying to emigrate. They and their families were ostracized. Many refuseniks were even imprisoned.

This particular refusenik, Mr. Mendelovich, had been part of a group of similarly persecuted refuseniks who planned to hijack a plane and force it to fly them to freedom in Israel. They were discovered, and Mr. Mendelvovich was sent to prison in Siberia. I'll never forget the words he spoke, many years after his ordeal, when he was a free man in Jerusalem.

In prison, there were many other Jews, and for the first time I was able to learn about our tradition, about Jewish laws, Torah, and mitzvot. One prisoner taught me the aleph-bet, the Hebrew alphabet, and another prisoner taught me about Shabbat. It was the first time I knew about Shabbat. We learned that this day was supposed to be special, and so I tried to make it special, even in prison. Each day, we were given a small amount of bread. We were so hungry, that it was very difficult to save any of it, but I managed not to eat a small morsel each day, to save it for Shabbat. Then, each Friday afternoon, as Shabbat approached, I would take an old nail, and use it to scratch a picture of two candles onto the wall of my cell. I looked at these two candles, and then I would take out all the bread I had saved during the week. In this way, on Shabbat, at least, I always had extra food to eat. I tried to make my Shabbat special and holy, even in prison.

When I tell people this story, they often ask how Yosef Mendelovich made it out, to Israel. While in prison, his case attracted the attention of high-ranking Jewish communal activists, particularly in the World Jewish Congress, who lobbied ceaselessly for his release and, eventually, in 1981, after over a decade in his Siberian jail, Mr. Mendelovich received permission to leave the Soviet Union. He flew to Israel, and when he landed went straight to the Kotel (the Western Wall) in Jerusalem, and daavened there to God: his first prayer as a free man. He eventually enrolled in a Yeshiva (rabbinical training school), became religiously observant, married, and started speaking out about his experiences in the Soviet Union.

I often think of Mr. Mendelovich, and the many other refuseniks like him who embraced Shabbat and Jewish practice even when it was so difficult and dangerous. I sometimes think of Mr. Mendelovich's hoarded breadcrumbs as I prepare my own Shabbat meals. We take so much for

granted today. It is easy to overlook the abundance of food and other comforts we have. At times it takes a story such as this to remind us to appreciate the food, the homes, the ease we possess. For, of course, no matter how many obstacles we face in preparing for Shabbat, these seem puny when compared to the trials many of our ancestors and fellow Jews have overcome.

Menus

This is not to say that you have to spend all day — or even a great portion of your day — in the kitchen preparing your Shabbat meals. I have eaten (and served) amazing meals that were purchased, that were cooked all day in a slow cooker, or that were assembled once Shabbat began. Here are a few sample menus to get you started as you think about your Shabbat meal strategy. (The recipes for these dishes and more can be found in Chapter 14.)

Scenario one: lots of time to prepare
A typical Shabbat meal might look like this:
1 Challah
2 Gefilte fish
3 Chicken soup with matzah balls
4 Roast chicken, noodle kugel, carrot tzimmes, and tossed salad
5 Chocolate cake

Scenario two: one hour to prepare
This menu assumes you haven't had time to do any prep work during the week, and you come home from work with enough time to spend an hour cooking:
1 Challah (purchased)
2 Chopped herring and apple salad
3 Roast chicken with carrot and potato, plus tossed salad
4 Baked apples and cookies (purchased)

Scenario three: 20 minutes to prepare

This menu assumes you have ten minutes in the morning to assemble a meal in your slow cooker, and another ten in the afternoon before Shabbat begins:

1 Challah (purchased)
2 Sliced carrots and celery, hummus (purchased)
3 Tossed salad
4 Slow-cooked chicken, plus noodles or instant rice
5 Fresh fruit and cookies (purchased)

One friend of mine who works long hours serves delicious wraps on Shabbat: she buys tortillas, ready-washed bags of salad and cold cuts, then rolls up the greens and meat along with mayonnaise and mustard in the tortillas and slices them. This particular preparation can even be done once Shabbat begins. Whatever your budget, tastes or time constraints, Shabbat is the time to make an extra effort to have a beautiful meal.

Conversation

Just as we dress up on Shabbat, and set our table nicely and prepare a beautiful meal, so we also must prepare for our conversation on Shabbat. Shabbat is certainly a time to simply catch up with family and friends and enjoy pleasant conversation. But it is also more than that. It is a time to be holy, to exist on a higher plane. We do this through externalities such as our dress and demeanor, and also through our speech.

Most Orthodox Jews have the custom of not talking about "ordinary" topics on Shabbat. These topics are not considered "Shabbosdich" (Shabbat-like), and include money, work, and shopping. Many Jews extend the prohibition against talking about un-Shabbosdich things further. I remember when I first became observant, for instance, I never read novels on Shabbat, but instead spent my Shabbat hours reading books on Torah or Jewish philosophy. This was my own personal "chumra," or stricture, but it is typical of the holy atmosphere that traditional Jews try to create for themselves on

Shabbat. I have known people who had the personal custom of not wearing wrist watches on Shabbat (so they could enjoy themselves without worrying about time or appointments), who didn't read the newspaper on Shabbat (because they wanted to think about more important things than current events), and people who made an effort to learn and talk about Torah on Shabbat, even when they didn't do so during the week.

These are personal views, and one shouldn't lose sight of the fact that Shabbat is meant to be a pleasure, not a burden. Making rules about what we discuss on Shabbat is meant to uplift us, not make us grumpy or bored. Every person has to find their own way of making Shabbat special. What you consider special and holy will evolve over the years as you get more used to keeping Shabbat and integrating traditional Judaism into your lifestyle.

Whether this is our first Shabbat, however, or our thousandth, there are several ways we can distinguish our speech on Shabbat from our ordinary way of conversing during the week.

Jewish names

One powerful way to distinguish our speech is by using Jewish names. In Judaism, names are important. They signify something about the bearer, and there is an idea that names even bestow certain characteristics. Among Ashkenazi Jews, Jewish babies are usually named after relatives who have passed away. Among Sephardi Jews, it is common to name children after living relatives. In all these cases, parents hope implicitly to bestow certain characteristics of the namesake on their children, and to create a bond between them. In Jewish tradition, when a child is sick, God forbid, we sometimes give them an extra name, such as Chaim or Chaya (meaning "life"). When people convert to Judaism, they often take Jewish names that sound like their original name, or else use the Jewish patriarchs' or matriarchs' names.

Not all modern Jews use these Jewish names every day, but they are nonetheless crucially important to our identities. They speak to our very essence, and are a way to identify our innermost, Jewish selves.

When we Jews were slaves long ago in ancient Egypt, we abandoned almost all of our traditions. We ate the foods of the Egyptians, we celebrated the festivals of the Egyptians, we loved the art and the music of the Egyptians. Yet, somehow, we remained worthy of God's remembrance; God still recognized us as his special people. How? Because we Jews kept three of our traditions: we continued to dress as Jews. We still spoke in Hebrew. And we kept our Jewish names. Thus did God continue to know us.

In modern times, many Jews barely use their Jewish names. We go by Michael instead of Micah, Dean instead of David, or Anna instead of Ayelet. I myself go by Yvette instead of my Yiddish name Yitta. We blend in with wider, non-Jewish society, but often at the cost of forgetting who we really are. How many of us maintain even as much of our Jewish identity as our ancient slave ancestors? Few of us dress differently any more. Few Jews outside of Israel speak Hebrew. For most of us, possessing a special Jewish name (typically bestowed on boys at their brit milah, or circumcision, and on girls at a naming ceremony within their first year of life) is our last solid link to the Jewish people.

Yet there is a powerful idea in Jewish tradition that the name we use every day also shapes our identity. If we use a certain name for long enough — even if it is not what we were formally named as a young baby — then if begins to become ours. Likewise, if we neglect the Jewish name that was bestowed upon us by our parents, its hold on us loosens. (This is something to think of when we or our kids are tempted to use light-hearted or irrever-ent nicknames in our daily interactions!)

Shabbat is an ideal time to renew our connection to our Jewish names. One idea to make Shabbat more special and meaningful might be to use our Hebrew names for those holy 25 hours. This is not Jewish law — you don't have to use your Hebrew name on Shabbat — but for families and individuals embarking on Shabbat observance, using Hebrew names can be a fun way of making the day more special, and reminding ourselves of our deep-seated Jewish identity. As you call your family or even guests by their Hebrew names, you can forge a separate identity for yourselves as links in a chain stretching back to Sinai and beyond: as direct descendants of our

ancient Israelite ancestors, and proud members of the Jewish people. Try addressing your spouse, your kids, parents, or even your friends by their Hebrew names. To be sure, you'll be self-conscious at first, but by doing so you'll be tapping into a deep part of their identity. It is one way to remind yourself and those around you that you are holy people, on a holy day.

If you choose to do this, one fun way to get started is to check out some books on Jewish baby naming from the library. Set these aside for Shabbat, and then sit with your guests or family and look up the meanings of your Jewish names. Find out where your names come from and what they mean. Then spend a few minutes talking about the relatives for whom you are named. If you have more than one generation at your table, perhaps you can hear stories about your namesakes and learn more about their lives. If you have children, tell them whom you named them for, and why. Encourage them to ask questions. Try to make this connection feel real to them; help them to understand their name has deeper meanings than simply something to answer to. If anyone at your table was not named after a relative or does not possess a Jewish name, then look up their English names and try to find the closest Hebrew version to it. Sherrie can begin to think of herself as Shira ("Song"); Bruce might begin to think of himself as Baruch ("Blessed") instead. Remember that, in Judaism, being known by a name makes it yours; if you do not have a separate Jewish name, adopting one with a special meaning or significance for you on Shabbat can be the first step to making it your own.

A "bad tongue": "lashon ha'ra"

Besides calling each other by our Jewish names, are there any other ways our conversation can distinguish Shabbat from ordinary days? Of course; the more ambitious we are in our speech and conversations on this day, the more special Shabbat will feel.

First, a note about Jewish speech in general. I have found over the years that one feature sets apart conversation among religiously observant Jews from conversation in the general community. Yes, everyone talks about

books and music, weekend plans and current events, clothes, food, our kids, our jobs, our classes. But observant Jews live with the reminder — constantly repeated — not to speak "lashon ha'ra." Literally, "lashon ha'ra" means "the bad language" or "the bad tongue," and it refers to gossip. But not gossip as it is usually understood in English. Lashon ha'ra refers to any idle speech about another person, even if the speech is ostensibly good. Thus, it is not only "ussar" (or "forbidden") to say, for instance, "That Sylvia's such a slob — I saw her desk at work yesterday, and it was so messy!" We're also forbidden from saying, "That Sylvia's so neat — I saw her desk yesterday, and it was all orderly and tidied up!"

For who knows the effects our speech will have on others? Perhaps our listener was thinking of hiring Sylvia for a new project, but now she won't because it is obvious that Sylvia's a slob — or maybe she won't because Sylvia's desk is so neat she must not be busy or sought-after! The point is that we can never know where our words will ultimately have an effect, so we are forbidden from speaking idly at all.

There is a famous story that illustrates the powerful effects of our lashon ha'ra.

There was once a woman who spoke much lashon ha'ra. After many, many years, she began to regret her loose tongue. Eventually, so burdened was she by the guilt of all she had spoken about other people, she went to her rabbi. "Rabbi," she said, "I feel terrible. For years, I have spoken lashon ha'ra about my friends, my neighbors, my family. I would like to make amends. Tell me, rabbi, is there anything I can do?" "Certainly," replied the rabbi. "Go home and fetch me a feather pillow from your house." Overjoyed that the rabbi was going to help her with her problem, the woman rushed away and returned with a large feather pillow.

"Excellent," said the rabbi. "Now, take this feather pillow outside. It is a windy day today. Undo the stitches, and watch what happens!" Excitedly, the woman took her pillow outside. There was a strong breeze. She undid the stitches of the pillow, and soon the wind blew the pillow's feathers around in a thick swirl. While the woman watched, every feather was soon airborne, carried far, far away on the day's strong gusts.

Once all the feathers were gone, the woman rushed back inside to the rabbi. "Rabbi," she cried breathlessly, "I did as you asked. I went outside, opened the stitches on the feather pillow, and watched as the wind blew away all of the feathers. Now what shall I do?" The rabbi turned to the woman. "Go back outside," he instructed her, "and now gather together all of the feathers. Put them back inside your pillow, and when you've finished, come back to me, and I will tell you exactly how to make amends for all the lashon ha'ra you have spoken."

Crestfallen, the woman exclaimed, "But I cannot possibly gather together all of the feathers! By now, the wind has blown them to the four corners of the earth!" The rabbi nodded, his eyes full of sadness. "So, too, with your words," he began gently. "Your words, too, have been blown far and wide."

Just as we cannot tell where the wind blows a feather, so we cannot tell where our words might penetrate.

It is an awesome responsibility to guard our tongues. The laws of lashon ha'ra are remarkably complex. We are not only forbidden from speaking idly of others, for instance, but we are also forbidden from hearing idle chatter about another person. While there are instances when conveying information about another person is allowed (even mandated), they are regulated in Judaism, to prevent any extraneous gossip from occurring.

Many Orthodox Jewish families keep stickers on their telephones reminding them not to gossip, so uppermost in people's minds are the laws of lashon ha'ra. Many people also regularly review the Jewish laws of proper speech, either alone or with a study partner. One wonderful source of information on the laws of lashon ha'ra is the New York-based organization Chofetz Chaim Heritage Foundation, named after the monumental work of Rabbi Yisrael Meir Kagan, the nineteenth-century rabbi who did most to catalogue and publicize the laws of proper speech. This foundation sends out a wealth of information, including daily e-mails on different aspects of these important Jewish laws that you can review in a few short minutes each day when you have the chance. The Chofetz Chaim Heritage Foundation's website is www.chofetzchaimusa.org.

On Shabbat, an ambitious way to make the day special might be to be diligent about refraining from gossiping and idle chatter about other people. It can present an exciting challenge to see if you can go for 25 hours without this conversational crutch. If you embark on this challenge, it would help to first establish some ground rules with your family and guests. You might want to learn the laws of lashon ha'ra formally. Two excellent books on the subject are Rabbi Kagan's original work, *Chofetz Chaim* (literally "Desire Life"), which has been translated into English by Shimon Finkelman and Yitzchak Berkowitz, and *Guard Your Tongue* by Zelig Pliskin.

If you wish to simply get started on this challenge without formal study, however, try to incorporate these ten guidelines into your conversation on Shabbat:

➤ Do not repeat anything negative about other people in general conversation.

➤ Do not idly talk about others, even if you regard the story or anecdote you wish to convey as neutral or positive. A comment like "Dave has a really short temper" might be true, but it will also predispose people to think of him in a certain way. Even a comment like "Dave's a great guy; he'll give you the shirt off his back" is lashon ha'ra: who knows where the "feather" of that comment will be blown by the wind of gossip?

➤ Give other people the benefit of the doubt: just assume there are mitigating factors to their behavior you don't know about.

➤ When you hear something negative about other people, remind yourself the speaker might be misinformed.

➤ If someone begins to repeat stories or gossip about another person, change the subject or walk away; listening to lashon ha'ra is just as bad as speaking it.

➤ Be careful not to talk idly about institutions or groups of people.

➤ Remember that lashon ha'ra applies to children as well as adults; it is natural to want to talk about our kids, but avoid any idle speech that portrays children in a negative light.

➤ Refrain from characterizing your or other children. Don't say anything

like "Well, you know what little Caitlin is like . . .," or "little Sarah is such a joker" or even "our little Jacob is the serious one in the family . . ." Comments such as these place children in boxes, and might influence how other people see them for years to come. Besides being unfair, this speech can constitute lashon ha'ra.

➤ There are occasions when it is necessary to convey information about another person, for instance when giving employment references, or when there is (God forbid) a threat to somebody's well-being. When you feel you must convey crucial information about a third person, do so privately.

➤ Resist the temptation to justify comments about other people as being "for the common good." Your boss, for instance, might be a bitter, petty jerk, but telling other people that almost always qualifies as lashon ha'ra. Little Cameron might be a terror on the playground, but do you really have to tell that to all the other moms at preschool?

It is difficult to follow these and the other detailed guidelines the Torah maintains for proper speech. There are times when we all over-speak and say things that we regret. When this happens, try to resolve to do better next time. With practice, I have found that it does get easier to refrain from — or at least minimize — speaking lashon ha'ra. It becomes an ingrained habit to be circumspect about other people. After you become sensitized to the Jewish rules of proper speech, it will begin to feel jarring when other people start to gossip.

One of the most helpful ways in which I try to tackle my yearning to speak lashon ha'ra is by trying not to make other people my primary topic of conversation. Instead, I try to talk with my friends and relatives about books, movies, current affairs, and ideas. These topics are often more interesting, anyway, and I have found that by shifting the focus of conversation away from other people I often wind up elevating the level of our conversation and communicating more deeply with others.

"Divrei Torah": words of Torah

What is there left to talk about? It might seem at first that there is very little left. Yet I have always thought of conversation as a sort of pyramid. If the bottom level is gossip, then the level just above is the concrete: discussing vacation plans, for instance, or projects at work, shopping, etc. A step above that is a more abstract realm: ideas, current events, books, and movies. It can be lovely on Shabbat to attempt to move up this scale from the concrete to the abstract. The highest level of conversation, however, on Shabbat and every day, is "Torah ideas": thoughts, lessons, and conversation grounded in Torah.

There is a Jewish idea that learning Torah brings holiness into the world. The Torah is like a telephone, through which we can access God and bring his presence into our lives, our homes, our communities. Many modern Jews are familiar with the old-fashioned stereotype of the "Yeshiva Bucher": the student who spends all day studying Torah full-time in a Jewish school, or Yeshiva. Many other modern Jews are familiar with the political debate in Israel over exemptions from military service for some full-time Yeshiva students. These ideas reflect the centrality in traditional Jewish communities of Torah study. Simply put, studying Torah is one of the most crucial things you can do, not only for yourself but also for your community. Jewish tradition teaches that the world stands on three things: Prayer, Acts of Loving-kindness, and Torah. Learning Torah provides a foundation for the continued existence of the entire world; it benefits not only the one doing the learning, but, in a profoundly mystical way, also the world as a whole.

Luckily for the person learning Torah, it is also an extremely rewarding intellectual exercise, with room to address all sorts of issues and questions. The Talmud refers to the Torah as the "Sea of Torah": the implication being that just as there are myriad countries, each with their own cultures and flavors, so too are there countless texts to study and issues to ponder within the Torah. The second-century CE Israeli Rabbi Yochanan ben Bag Bag famously said of the Torah: "Delve into it and continue to delve into it, for everything is in it. Look deeply into it; grow old and gray over it, and do not

stir from it, for you can have no better portion than it." His contemporary, Rabbi ben Hei Hei, added to this statement: "The reward is in proportion to the exertion."

No matter what your interest or inclination, there will be something within the Torah that you will enjoy learning and discussing.

While Torah learning is ideally done every day, it has a particular sweetness on Shabbat. As you approach your own personal Shabbat observance, learning and speaking words of Torah are a powerful way to transform the day into one of holiness and elevation.

Like Rabbis ben Bag Bag and ben Hei Hei (It is possible their comic-sounding names might have been pseudonyms invented to fool the occupying Roman authorities who ruled Israel at the time and forbade the learning of Torah), Rabbi Chanina ben Tradyon also lived in Israel in the second century of the Common Era. (Since the denotation "AD" refers to the Christian deity, many Jews prefer to measure the secular date with these terms: "BCE" — before the Common Era — and "CE" — Common Era, instead of using BC and AD.)

Rabbi Tradyon is well remembered for the horrible way he died. After defying the Roman ban on teaching Torah, Rabbi Tradyon was discovered and put to death by the Roman authorities, who wrapped him in a wet Torah scroll and then set him on fire, burning him alive. At the moment of his death, Rabbi Tradyon called out to his sobbing students, who stood by helplessly watching his execution: "The parchment on which the Torah is written is burning, my students, but the letters of the Torah — the letters are flying up to Heaven!"

Rabbi Tradyon is also remembered for pithily summing up the Jewish view of conversation, which places Torah learning and Torah thoughts in a central position:

Rabbi Chanina ben Tradyon says: If two sit together and there are no words of Torah between them, it is a session of buffoons, as it is said, "In the session of buffoons he does not sit" (Psalms 1.1). But if two sit together and words of Torah are between them, then God rests between them, as it is said: "Then those who fear God spoke to one another, and God listened and heard, and

a book of remembrance was written before Him for those who fear God and give thought to His name" (Malachi 3.16). From this verse we would know this only about two people; how do we know that if even one person sits and occupies himself with Torah the Holy One, Blessed is He, determines a reward for him? For it is said: "Let one sit in solitude and be still, for he will have received (a Heavenly reward) for it (Lamentations 3.28). (Pirkei Avot 3:3)

Thus, by speaking words of Torah at the dinner table (even, if we are alone, by thinking about Torah), we are able to literally bring God's presence into our midst. The Hebrew word used in this verse is "Shechina." This is a feminine word (Hebrew, like French or Spanish, has "genders" for all of its nouns) with many mystical connotations. It is also the word for God's presence that the Torah uses to describe the holy Temple in Jerusalem, where God dwelt. By speaking words of Torah at our Shabbat table, we are able to transform our own table into a Mikdash Me'at — a little Temple — in a very effective way.

It is typical in Orthodox Jewish households for the parents to quiz their children about all they have learned in school that week on Shabbat. Shabbat is the culmination of the week, so it is the natural day on which to examine that which has transpired over the course of the previous few days. At my own children's Jewish school, their teachers send home lists of questions to quiz them with at the Shabbat table each Friday. It is not only children who bring words of Torah into their homes on Shabbat. Adults (and older children) typically prepare short "divrei Torah," literally "words of Torah" to speak at the Shabbat table. A "devar Torah" ("Word of Torah": the singular form of the phrase) usually lasts only a couple of minutes. They are easy to prepare, and are a wonderful way to bring some Torah thoughts into our homes and elevate our Shabbat table to become the Mikdash Me'at it is meant to be.

Just as we have to prepare to ensure that our homes and meals are as splendid as they ought to be on Shabbat, so too we have to prepare this aspect of our Shabbats. It is typical for the divrei Torah of Shabbat mealtimes to center on the weekly Torah portion that is read in synagogue on Shabbat. (The Five Books of Moses — Genesis, Exodus, Leviticus, Numbers, and

Deuteronomy — are divided into 49 portions; one is read in synagogue each week, resulting, once you add in the special holiday readings, too, in a yearly cycle of Torah reading.) While it may seem onerous to have to spend time reading the weekly Torah portion in order to have some brief words of Torah to share at your Shabbat table, the effort is worth the reward. Chapter 11 contains some questions to help formulate divrei Torah from the weekly Torah portions, and the Appendix: Ideas for Further Reading gives some suggestions for learning other Jewish texts.

"Zemirot"

Possibly the most distinctive aspect of a traditional Shabbat meal is the singing afterwards. A "zemir" in Hebrew is a song, and after each Shabbat meal, we sing "zemirot," or songs, together. If you ever went to overnight summer camp, you know how much fun singing together can be. In Israel today, group sing-alongs are one of the most popular communal activities, even among people who are not particularly religious. Perhaps they have simply learned from the religious community: there is nothing as much fun as singing good songs together!

There is nothing more magical than strolling through Jerusalem's neighborhoods on Shabbat. The weather in Israel is often warm, air conditioning is rare, and most buildings feature large balconies. Families open their windows or often sit down to Shabbat meals on their balconies, and once they are finished eating they begin to sing. It is lovely to walk through the streets and alleyways, catching snatches of lilting Shabbat melodies from thousands of Shabbat tables. Singing transforms the Shabbat table into something other than merely a place to eat. It appeals to our other senses, and to our very souls. It reminds us that there can be so much beauty in our day: beauty that we never normally even think to bring out. At least once a week we can tap into it.

It is typical on Shabbat to sing several traditional songs. If you are just starting out your Shabbat observance, they might not be familiar to you. The texts and translations of some customary Shabbat songs are contained

in Chapter 12. But there are no hard and fast rules about what you can or cannot sing! In addition to the texts of some traditional Shabbat songs in Chapter 12, you will also find words to some simple Jewish songs, as well as some traditional songs in English you might know already. It might at first sound odd to end a meal with a song, but this is one of those things you just have to try: sing with your family and friends, and you'll see why Jews have concluded their Shabbat meals with singing for thousands of years!

Blessings after the meal

Following any meal at which we eat bread, we say "Birkat HaMazon," literally "Blessing the Bread." The text of this beautiful prayer is found in all Orthodox siddurs (prayer books); an English version is contained in Chapter 15.

After dinner

I'll always remember the moment I knew my husband was truly "shomer Shabbat," or observant of Shabbat. One Friday night we had finished Shabbat dinner. After clearing the table, he sauntered into the living room (which was actually nice and neat and cleaned up for a change, for Shabbat). He picked up the newspaper, sat down on the couch, sighed deeply and said, "Ah, I'm so glad it's Shabbat!" The relief on his face was profound; he looked completely relaxed and relieved not to be in the thick of the week. I gazed at him and wondered what was different. For on other days, when it is not Shabbat, my husband often sits down with the newspaper after dinner. Yet I realized at that moment his feelings and outlook on Shabbat were completely altered from the weekday grind. I wondered for a moment: what did he sense? What felt changed for him?

If I could bottle the atmosphere in our home on that Friday night and hand it out to readers along with this book, I would. Alas, however, all I can offer is the recipe: guidance to help you make the same Shabbat atmosphere

in your own home, instead. Everyone's individual Shabbat will be personal and have different nuances, but the goal of each traditional Shabbat is the same: to transcend the ordinary week, to move closer to God, and for 25 hours each week, to live on a higher level, to experience life that is in some measure a taste of the World to Come.

Now, there are two ways to experience Shabbat and, indeed, all Jewish ritual. We can, God forbid, see it as a burden, or we can choose to see it as a pleasure. Obviously, if we wish to enjoy Shabbat (and for our families to enjoy Shabbat and want to celebrate it with us), the pleasure route is desirable. If we wish our children, families, and friends to see the joy that Shabbat brings, again, we have to actively seek out the joy in it, and emphasize the wonderful things that Shabbat brings to us. If we view Shabbat simply as 25 hours during which we cannot watch TV, cannot drive, cannot write, cannot play a CD, cannot, cannot, cannot, we'll succeed in turning everyone away from the day. If we see Shabbat as a burden, our children, spouses, and other intimates will see it as a burden, as well. It is up to each of us, to everyone who wishes to experience a traditional Shabbat for themselves, as well as those who wish to create an atmosphere conducive to Shabbat observance for those around us, to seek out that which makes Shabbat pleasurable, and to emphasize the benefits of the day over its limitations.

Receiving Shabbat with joy

One of the greatest rabbis ever to live in the United States of America was Rav Moshe Feinstein, who was born in Russia, but lived and worked in New York for most of his life, until his death in 1986. Much of what we know as modern Orthodox Judaism is thanks to Rav Feinstein, who reconciled many of the modern mores and inventions that we take for granted today with Orthodox Jewish law.

I have always found one of Rav Feinstein's most interesting comments to be one that concerned child-rearing. In the days when most Ashkenazi Jews spoke Yiddish as their daily language, there was a common saying:

"*Shver tzu zein a Yid*," or "It's hard to be a Jew." This meant different things to different people, but often referred to the anti-Semitism that Jews faced, or the difficulty of adapting to modern, secular society while remaining true to traditional Judaism.

Rav Feinstein is said to have vehemently objected to the saying *Shver tzu zein a Yid*. Do not tell your children it is hard to be a Jew, Rav Feinstein said, lest they come to associate Judaism with bitterness and Jewish practice with loss and regret. Instead, Rav Feinstein insisted, we should say it is joyful to be a Jew, that Jewish practice brings us happiness, for in this way children will come to associate Jewish belief and practice with intense happiness and pride.

Sometimes all it takes is putting a smile on our face and suggesting a Shabbat-appropriate activity to put everyone at ease and make us excited about the opportunities for personal growth that Shabbat offers. At other times, getting everyone to enjoy Shabbat requires as much planning and preparation as it took us to prepare the Shabbat meals or divrei Torah.

One sure-fire way to elevate "Erev Shabbat," or the Shabbat evening of Friday night, is to turn to the time-tested Jewish activity of learning Torah. After dinner each Friday night, one friend of mine clears the table, changes the tablecloth, and puts out books on Torah and other Jewish themes. Her entire family then sits down and studies Torah together. Often, friends and neighbors come over, too, to study in partnership with her, her husband, and kids. This immediately gives my friend's family an aura of holiness and purpose, as they use their precious Shabbat hours to contemplate Jewish texts and philosophy.

In my own home, Friday evenings after dinner are usually much less rarified, but equally distinct and special. My own children are young, and often my husband or I will read them stories before bed on Shabbat. In order to foster a feeling of holiness and separateness from the rest of the week, we choose books and stories from a special Shabbat collection of Jewish-themed or particularly beautiful books. We don't need to buy all of these books; we often borrow books from the library and from friends just for Shabbat. You can also download Shabbat stories from the Internet; some good websites are www.aish.com, www.ou.org and www.chabad.org.

Another "rule" in our house on Friday nights is that everything is special. We try to invite friends over for dinner often so our kids have friends to play with. Even when we do not have guests, we make things special for ourselves. My kids, for instance, have special Shabbat pajamas. They can sleep in each other's rooms, or in the guest room on Shabbat. They stay up later than usual. On Shabbat (but not during the week) I'll open up our sleeper sofa so they can load it up with toys and play on it. Everything we use on Shabbat is the nicest we have; every toy, every book, every activity is a special treat that we reserve only for this day.

It is the same for my husband and me, too. On Shabbat, there is no phone to pick up, no e-mail to check, no bills to pay. I find that without these distractions, we talk much more on Shabbat than during the rest of the week. We play card games and read books. The house looks neater than usual, and we are dressed nicer than usual too. This creates a gracious atmosphere in which things seem more formal, more welcoming. If we have guests, I find that our conversations are often longer and more fulfilling in this setting than they are during the week when we grab a few minutes to chat on the phone or during car-pool pick-ups. On Shabbat, we slow things down and take much more care with our appearances and surroundings. We cut out all extraneous distractions so we can concentrate on other people, in person, without electronic filters. It creates a lovely, holy atmosphere. Anyone experiencing this can see right away why it is our homes that are now our Mikdash Me'at, our little Beit Hamikdashes, our own present-day Temples. For in biblical times, God's actual, physical presence (the "Shechina" in Hebrew) dwelt in the Beit Hamikdash. Today, this Shechina can be found in our very own homes. And Shabbat is the moment when we most perfectly make the Shechina welcome.

"Oneg Shabbat"

When I was in college, one popular activity among the Shabbat-observant Jewish students was holding "Oneg Shabbats" after dinner. "Oneg" means pleasure or delight in Hebrew, and these "Onegs" were a way to socialize

within the sanctity of Shabbat. An "Oneg" is a party, and some shuls or people sometimes hold them after dinner on Shabbat. An "Oneg" can include singing, divrei Torah, and conversation; they always include appetizing foods and drinks. (I will forever associate Entenmann's brand Danishes with Shabbat thanks to those college gatherings.) This is one more way to enjoy the power of the day of Shabbat, and delight in being with other people on it.

Before bed

As we make our way to bed on "Erev Shabbat," or "Shabbat Evening," we leave our lights on. Some lights we've affixed to timers, but others (like bathroom lights) burn throughout Shabbat. In our bedrooms, the situation is reversed: the lights are off, and we cannot use electricity to turn them on. This is a little inconvenient, but it also adds to the overall atmosphere of Shabbat specialness. There are some things that are bigger than us, we are reminded; there are times when we do not have the power to alter our surroundings with the flick of a switch or at a moment's whim. Everyone will come up with their own routines and a system that works best for them. We use a system of night lights and timers. (Each of our children has their own night light and Shabbat timer; they love figuring out where and how their Shabbat lights should be arranged.)

Before going to sleep on Shabbat, as on every day, we say the "Shema" prayer again. It is a beautiful, familiar ritual for both children and adults to end their day on a profound note of holiness. The first, commanding line is well-known to virtually every Jew:

Shema Yisrael, Adonoi Eloheinu, Adonoi Echad
Hear Israel: My Lord is Our God, My Lord is One.

The "Shema" prayer continues with a beautiful discourse about the centrality of God's law: we are meant to dwell on it constantly, and never to lose sight of it:

Blessed is the Honored Name of His Kingdom Everywhere Forever.

And you shall love God your Lord with all your heart, and with all your soul and with all your strength. And all these words that I command you today, shall be on your heart, and you shall teach to your children. And you shall speak of them while you rest in your house, and while you walk on the road, and when you go to sleep and when you awake. And you shall place them on your hand and between your eyes. And write them on the doorposts of your house, and upon your gates.

(The full "Shema" prayer then continues with excerpts from Deuteronomy (11.13–21) and Numbers (15.37–41). If you would like to enrich your Shabbat night, or indeed any night, by saying the full version of the "Shema," these paragraphs can be found in any Orthodox prayerbook, or in a copy of the "*Chumash,*" as the Jewish Bible is known.)

When I tuck my children into bed, I listen to them recite the "Shema," and then whisper them a beautiful blessing that generations of Jewish parents have said over their children before they go to sleep. It is taken from Genesis 48.16, when our Patriarch Jacob is about to die, and he blesses each of his children one last time. When he comes to his favorite son, Joseph, Jacob tells Joseph that he is blessing not only Joseph, but Joseph's children too. It is through this blessing of Jacob's that all the people of Israel are blessed today. For, as the prayer says, because of Jacob, all our names today incorporate the names (and the memory of) our patriarchs, who were directly blessed by God. This is a lovely ritual to follow if you have children to tuck into bed. It is common to recite this blessing every night, but if you are not used to it Shabbat is a wonderful night to begin.

Hamalach	=	The Angel
Hagoel	=	that redeemed
Oti	=	me
Mikol	=	from all
Ra	=	evil
Yivarech	=	will bless
Et Ha'n'arim	=	the youths

V'Yikarei	=	and will call (/name)
Ba-hem	=	in them
Shemi	=	my name. (i.e. Jacob's name will be incorporated in their names)
V'Shaim	=	And (also) the name
Avotai	=	of my fathers
Avraham	=	Abraham
V'Yitzhak	=	and Isaac
V'Yidgu	=	and they will grow
Larov	=	to greatness
B'Kerev	=	in the midst (of)
Ha'Aretz	=	the Land (Israel)

Many Jews today do not think of ending their day with these timeless prayers. Shabbat, however, offers us the perfect opportunity to begin incorporating these beautiful words into our night-time rituals. Even if we do not say the "Shema" ourselves during the week, do not instruct our children in how to say it, and do not formally bless our children before they go to sleep each night, we can perform these eternal rituals on Shabbat. On this holy day, these magnificent words and prayers can help elevate us and infuse our Shabbat with holiness.

6

Shabbat early morning

I love waking up on Shabbat morning. Whereas other mornings I know I have a million things that have to get done, every Saturday morning, I wake to the certainty that my entire day will be devoted to pleasure. No chores, no cleaning, no laundry, no work, no bills, no cooking, no trips to the grocery store, no carpools, no deadlines, no stress, no expectations. Even when I know I'm having guests later on, the work is already done: because of the rules of Shabbat, I'll have cooked it already. The most I'll have to do is toss a salad or arrange some already-cooked food in serving dishes. From the moment I wake up until sundown, I know my day will be devoted to grace and beauty. I look forward to a day spent visiting and talking with other people face-to-face, not via texts or e-mails. I look forward to a day in which my conversations with others will be about more than the mundane. I know that my quiet time will be devoted, if I choose, to learning fascinating new things and thinking about interesting new concepts. On Shabbat mornings, I wake to the certainty that my entire day will be the sort of day we all long to have: burden-free, filled with beauty, and shared with other people. The sort of day, in short, that the Torah tells us we can expect in Heaven, or (as it is known in Hebrew), the World to Come.

Not that there aren't still things to do and people to take care of on Shabbat. Most Saturdays my day starts at dawn, when the youngest of my children wakes and cries to be picked up. As soon as I open my eyes, though, I first thank God for waking me up: for reuniting my soul with my body this morning. I find it very profound to do this. In Judaism, we wake up and

immediately thank God for not having let us die in our sleep, for letting us exist. It is an obvious source of gratitude, but one that we have lost sight of in our hectic, secular world. How often do we get the chance to stop and thank God for the miracle of our own existence?

> There was once a great rabbi who had many students who hung on his every word. One morning, the students were surprised to find their rabbi was not at breakfast. Later on, they were shocked to discover he did not come to the classrooms, either. All day long, the students missed their rabbi and wondered where he was. Finally, as night fell, they knocked on his door, wondering what had befallen their beloved teacher. There was no answer. The students opened the door, and were astounded to find their rabbi, still in his night clothes, sitting up in his bed, a dazed expression on his face. "Rabbi," cried his students, "are you ill! Where have you been this whole day?" The rabbi gazed at his students and explained. "This morning, as every morning, I awoke and immediately said the prayer upon arising: I thank you, Eternal King . . . And then I stopped as the words hit me. I thank God? Students, do you realize what a privilege this is, to commune with the Almighty in this way? I realized the power of this statement! And I have been sitting here pondering the greatness of this ever since!"

This is an old fable that hints at the power of prayer. Most of the time, prayers are rote, maybe even a little boring. But every so often, their power hits us, and transforms an ordinary moment into a magical instance of complete clarity and connection to God.

Many Jews today are not in the habit of prayer. Many of us say we don't find it meaningful to mumble a bunch of rote words. The Jewish view is that while we always try to make our prayers meaningful (this is called having "kavanah," or being "directed" in prayer), we will not always succeed. We nonetheless have an obligation to say an extensive array of fixed prayers, however, in the knowledge that these kinds of spiritual moments will eventually ensue. We cannot know exactly when we'll have those sudden moments when we say "Aha!" and feel our connection to God, but in a lifetime of praying to God, there will be many.

My own affection for the first prayer of the morning goes further. Years ago, when I first began to say the traditional Jewish prayers each day, my mother mused to me that her bubbe ("grandmother") used to say these traditional prayers each day, as well. "She used to say a prayer as soon as she woke up in the mornings," my mother recalled one day, "it went *Moidey Anee Lifanecha . . .*" My mother said it in the very strong, sing-song-ey Yiddish accent that marked her childhood, and I had such a jolt. Here were the words of the morning "Modeh Ani" prayer (text below), as it was said by the last member of my family to live the timeless Torah-observant life-style of our ancestors: my last relative to speak Yiddish as her first language, and to pray these timeless words in the same thick Yiddish pronunciation of millions of our ancestors! Hearing my wonderful mother repeat them was like a message delivered directly to me across the generations.

> *Modah* (men say *Modeh*) *Ani Lifanecha, Melech Chai Vikayam, She-he-chezarta bi nishmati be-chemla — Raba emunatecha!*
>
> I thank You, Eternal King of Life, for You returned into me my soul with compassion — Great is Your faithfulness!

I am named after that great-grandmother, and often as I say this beautiful prayer early in the morning, I think of her, of her devotion, of her faith in God, and of the beautiful, traditional Jewish life that she led. Our ancestors have been reciting this early-morning prayer for thousands of years. For thousands of years, saying, "Modeh Ani," "I thank," to God as soon as we open our eyes in the morning has defined who we are as Jewish people. It is a profound statement of faith, of self-awareness, and a beautiful way to be the next link in the chain of Jews who have said this prayer for millennia.

This one-line prayer is said every morning, not just on Shabbat, but I am including it here because Shabbat can be a day of heightened holiness: a day to explore saying different prayers, even if you don't yet make a habit of saying them every day.

After saying the "Modeh Ani" prayer, I get up and get my children. I

make sure each of them says "Modeh Ani" as well. (It is such a short prayer, even very young kids have no trouble memorizing it, and it gives them an important feeling to know they are obligated to thank God for waking them up each day.) We then go to into the bathroom or kitchen together to ritually wash our hands.

Just as we ritually wash our hands before eating bread, we also wash them after waking up in the morning. There is again an idea that just as we can become physically dirty in the course of our day, so too we can become spiritually dirty as well. I've always thought it seemed natural to wash off this spiritual "dirt" (called "tamay" in Hebrew) after waking up: in Judaism, anything having to do with death makes us tamay, and sleep always seemed to remind me enough of death for this connection to seem clear. (Again, this is something that is meant to be done daily. However, for those just starting out in their observance, Shabbat provides an ideal time to try out this beautiful ritual.)

Many people who wash ritually buy special washing cups at Judaica stores; plain plastic ones can cost as little as a dollar. They have two handles for easy handling, but any cup or bowl is acceptable to use. We fill the washing cup, then pour it over our right hand three times, wetting both sides of our hand, up to the wrist, and then switch and pour water over our left hand three times, again wetting up to the wrist. After washing, we step out of the bathroom, take a towel, and dry our hands, reciting the blessing after washing hands:

Baruch	=	Blessed
Atah	=	(are) You
Adonoy	=	My Lord
Eloheinu	=	Our God
Melech	=	King
Ha	=	(of) the
'Olam	=	World
Asher	=	That
Kidshanu	=	Made us holy
b'mitzva'otav	=	in (through) His commandments

vetzivanu	=	(and) Commanded us
al	=	to
natilat	=	wash
yadaim	=	both hands.

There is one final blessing that is usually said almost immediately after waking up. You might laugh when you hear what it is. (I laughed the first time I heard of it.) But this very laughter shows us the great gulf between our modern, secular world and the world of traditional Judaism.

The next blessing we make is the prayer that Jews say after going to the bathroom. Did you snicker? Were you surprised? The first time I giggled at this made me realize that whereas the contemporary world hides bodily functions and considers them disgusting, Judaism considers them holy. What the present-day world considers low, Judaism elevates. Here's one example: in the secular world, sex is sometimes considered dirty; it is rarely talked about in polite circles. Yet Judaism celebrates it. Our sages were not squeamish about discussing it, but recognized its awesome power and saw it as a crucial gift from God. (In fact, our sages have even written that married couples ought to enjoy this aspect of their relationship on Shabbat as a way of elevating the day!)

Similarly, Judaism celebrates God's obvious mastery over our bodies. For as the prayer after going to the bathroom says, if any part of our body "were to be ruptured or . . . blocked it would be impossible to survive and to stand before you." Our bodies are so complex; the more we learn about the complex biology that keeps us alive, the more we stand in wonder at God's immense presence in our lives. For on one hand, as we learn more about the genes, the DNA, the cells, the very molecules that make up our bodies, we of course understand more about ourselves, about medicine. But, on the other hand, the more we understand the infinitely complicated building blocks that produce our bodies, the more we stand in awe before our Creator, who made such a complex system.

This is a powerful, profound prayer that you might start to incorporate into your life; if so, Shabbat can provide a perfect time to begin. After going to the bathroom and washing your hands, wash your hands again, ritually.

(Pour water three times over each hand again.) As you dry your hands, step out of the bathroom (because Jews are not allowed to daaven, or pray, where a toilet is visible), and say:

Baruch Atah Adonoi, Eloheinu, Melech Ha'Olam, Asher Yatzar Et Ha'Adam B'Chachmo, U'vara Vo Nikavim Nikavim, Chalulim Chalulim. Galuey V'Yadua Lifney Kisay Kavodecha She'im Yipateach Echad May-hem Oh Yisatem Echad Ma-hem, Ee Efshar L'hitkayam V'La'amod L'fanecha. Baruch Atah Adonoy, Rofay Kol Basar U'mafli La'asot.

Blessed are You, our Lord, our God, King of the World, Who Made mankind in His Image, and Formed in him(/her) many openings, many cavities. It is obvious and known before Your Throne of Honor that if one of them is ruptured or one of them is blocked, it would not be possible to be upright and stand before You. Blessed are You, our Lord, (who) Heals all flesh and Does all acts.

At this point, it is usually 6:05 for me on a Shabbat morning, I've been up for five minutes, and already I've thanked God for the miracle of my existence, considered the distinction between pure and impure, and pondered the incredible complexity of physical life! It is a far way away from the mornings of my childhood before I became religiously observant, when I would complain about having to wake up, and thought about nothing except getting dressed, or perhaps the various activities I was planning to do that day. Of course, many mornings now I'm similarly focused on the mundane. However, I've been shocked over the years at how effective saying these brief blessings, however rote, at the start of my day have been in reframing my mind, allowing me to focus on the bigger picture, and helping me to begin each day with gratitude. It is much different to be dragged out of bed at the crack of dawn by needy kids (or by an alarm clock and the promise of a dreary day at work), and say, "Wow, I'm alive! God, thank you for making me, and for being with me here throughout my day," rather than "Oh, another day, another set of burdens . . ." Saying these prayers starts the day off with holiness, and imbues my entire day with an awareness of my special relationship with God.

A grateful frame of mind

Years ago, during the second century CE, Rabbi Shimon ben Zoma famously summed up Judaism's view of the role of gratitude in life. "Who is rich?" Rabbi ben Zoma asked. He answered: "He who is happy with his lot" (Pirkei Avot 4.1). This is an immensely powerful idea.

We can be happy too, profoundly, deeply happy — if we can only stop focusing on our next goal, and instead start appreciating what we already have. I once had a teacher in Jerusalem who told me she starts every day by thinking about how shocked her great-great-grandparents would be to see her apartment: how they would marvel at her electric lights, her fully stocked refrigerator, how amazing it would be to them that she lived in modern-day Israel, not the crowded, impoverished European villages they inhabited, where Jerusalem was a distant dream. Needless to say, this woman struck me as an overall very happy, contented person. Thanking God first thing in the morning for our health and our life similarly reminds us of all the blessings we have but often overlook: it forces us to think for a moment about the fact we are alive, that we are free, that we were created by God, and reminds us to thank God for these gifts. It leaves us uplifted and fulfilled.

Years ago, I heard a lecture by a very famous rabbi in Jerusalem, Rabbi Noah Weinberg, may his memory be for a blessing, who founded a well-known yeshivah (rabbinical academy) for previously secular Jews. Rabbi Weinberg told me something I'll never forget. He gazed at the assembled crowd who had come to hear him, and solemnly said, "I am going to tell you the secret to happiness." The secret to happiness is elusive, he explained, and many people claim to know it, but do not really. But he, Rabbi Weinberg, knew it, and was going to impart it to us. I was skeptical and a little amused, unaware that I was about to receive the most useful lesson of my life.

Imagine that you are walking along, Rabbi Weinberg started, and you see a man standing on a high-up window ledge, about to jump. Horrified, you run up to that window and try and persuade him not to jump. When you reach him, he starts to tell you why it is he has decided to jump off a

window ledge. This man starts talking, and you cannot believe how awful his story is. Every tragedy it is possible to experience, God forbid, this man has experienced. He regales you with awful story after awful story, until you can't bear it. He has suffered so much, you don't blame him for wanting to, God forbid, end it all.

But now imagine one more thing. In addition to all these terrible, awful experiences he has had, this poor old man was also born blind. In all his sad, miserable life, he has never been able to see a sunset, never been able to look at a loved one, never was able to know the colors of the world. What an awful story. But imagine this: at the precise moment this poor man is about to jump from his window ledge — a miracle occurs! Suddenly, for the first time in his entire life, he can see!

Would this person still choose this exact moment to jump, to end it all? Of course not. He still has all his problems, but he would nevertheless pause, look around in wonder, and then decide to spend a little time experiencing his new-found sight. He would go inside, off the window ledge, and look at his home, at his friends and neighbors, at flowers and rainbows and the ocean and grass. He would see for the first time in his life. He would probably wander around for a few weeks, eagerly experiencing every new sight and enjoying his new sense of vision.

Then, after a while, the memory of his miserable experiences would once again creep up on this old man. He would remember all the awful things that had befallen him. He would again grow despondent and, eventually, he would once more want to jump off the window ledge.

This is the secret of happiness, Rabbi Weinberg said. "Never get used to being able to see."

"Never get used to being able to see." Are you sitting there, stunned at the wisdom of this, or are you waiting for a better punch line? When I first heard this lecture, I didn't get it immediately; in fact, the large audience listening to this speech tittered a bit. But over the years, the truth of these words has sunk in for me. Who is happy? The person who is happy with their lot. With what they already have. Happiness comes from appreciating our gifts: all our gifts, from the obvious to things we usually take for granted, like sight, or hearing, or taste.

I thought of this story again, many years later, when my brother told me about a friend of his who had become paralyzed (God forbid: it should never happen to anyone else). My brother had gone to visit this friend, and was shaken afterwards. He called me and told me how his friend used a special keyboard activated by his eye movements to communicate, how he amazingly managed to stay active and connected. After describing it all to me, my brother paused and said in an anguished voice, "I wish I had it my power to at least make him able to move his face!" His words haunted me. The next morning, as I said the morning blessings, I recalled them. Everything we take for granted in an "ordinary" life, starting with our very existence and the fact that our bodies work at all, is actually a huge gift from God, and realizing this elevates our entire mood, our entire outlook, our whole lives.

Shabbat breakfast

Friday nights before we go to bed, I change the tablecloth on the dining room table, and put out plates, napkins, juice boxes, fruit, and a tray of muffins. On Shabbat morning, we are not supposed to eat a full meal before saying the Saturday Kiddush over wine or grape juice. Since in Judaism a "meal" includes bread, we eat other things — like muffins, fruits, and cereal — for breakfast on Shabbat instead.

As with everything on Shabbat, most observant Jews try to make breakfast nicer than usual. I know of some people who feed their kids healthy breakfasts all week long, and then on Shabbat allow them to eat all the sugary cereals they want. Other families let their kids have donuts for breakfast on Shabbat, or other sweet treats. Particularly if you think you or your kids might miss the TV or radio during breakfast as you switch to Shabbat observance, it is a good idea to serve something unusual that might tempt and interest you and make your early morning enjoyable. For it is easy to be fired-up about Shabbat at night, when the prospect of a nice dinner party looms; in the morning, however, Shabbat observance might seem less exciting at first. People miss their early-morning routines. It is important to create a Shabbat routine for yourself that satisfies you

and makes you happy. Finding breakfast foods you enjoy that seem "Shabbosdich" (Shabbat-like) is a big part of that.

I find that presentation counts: when foods are arranged beautifully on a plate or serving tray, they seem much more appealing. Here are a few ideas for nice Shabbat breakfasts to get you started:

➤ Slice different fruits; either drizzle fruit with chocolate sauce, or dip the fruit slices into chocolate sauce.

➤ Buy Greek yogurt and serve it with honey; this is so much better than ordinary, flavored, low-fat yogurt.

➤ Set up a yogurt bar, where everyone can choose items to add to their bowls. Include nuts, sprinkles, fruits, and sauces.

➤ Put out various spreads and dips (jam, peanut butter, Nutella, caramel sauce, date spread, etc.). Spread them on fruit slices and crackers.

➤ Serve crudités with salad dressing for dipping.

➤ Wrap cheese slices around bananas. Serve cheese with apples and grapes.

➤ Try the Swiss breakfast dish muesli (recipe included in Chapter 14).

➤ Peanut butter and jelly muffins (recipe included in Chapter 14).

➤ My husband's particular favorite is oatmeal casserole (recipe included in Chapter 14).

Try to find some delicacy that you adore, and save it for yourself and your family on Shabbat. Shabbat is the one day each week we have lots of time to linger over breakfast, and no distractions to take away from our enjoyment of it. I find it is a unique experience, to sit and quietly chat or read a book or the newspaper while lingering over a long breakfast. I wouldn't want to do it every day, but I love doing it on Shabbat.

Dressing for Shabbat

When I was a teenager, I owned a wonderful book about personal style. Like all teenagers, I was beginning to navigate the adult world, and I embraced this book about developing your own style; it addressed every

aspect of the things I was most confused about: how to act appropriately in different situations, what to say to people, how to choose the best clothes and makeup, how to choose a hairstyle. There was one particular piece of advice that the book gave that I found to be intuitively right as a teenager. Years later, as I began to be religiously observant, I was shocked to find that it coincided so perfectly with the religious Jewish way.

The book held up French women as the epitome of style. And, the book pointed out, you will never see a French woman with somebody else's name on her body. French women buy designer clothes, purses, sunglasses — but always with the brand name hidden. Their clothes and accessories are recognizable by their quality and style, instead of by the designer's name emblazoned — like a billboard — on the product. This struck a chord with me at the time. Why would I pay money to have (in the 1980s) Gloria Vanderbilt's name on my jeans? I didn't. When I was in my twenties, and most interested in designer clothes, I remembered this advice again, and noticed that the best, most stylish clothes did not have names or slogans emblazoned on them. After college, I even spent quite a bit of time in the Francophone countries of Europe, and I realized my book had been correct: there was an enormous difference in style between the French (and maybe Italians, too) and other people when it came to dress and personal style. French people almost always looked neat and put together. Their clothes seemed elegant. And, like my book had said, they didn't wear other people's names on their bodies.

If French people look chic, much of it is because they inherently adopt a view that is very Jewish. Your body reflects your inner essence, and it is too important to denigrate it with undignified or ridiculous clothes. In all my time in stylish European countries, I have never seen a native resident wearing anything that made them look anything other than neat, trim and attractive. There must be exceptions somewhere, but in general there is (unfortunately) a huge difference between the style philosophies of the French and the rest of the world, with the rest of the world getting the short end of the stick.

Imagine my surprise, then, when I started hanging around religious Jewish communities, and noticed that religiously observant Jews seemed

a little, well, French in their dress. At first I couldn't figure out what it was. But many Orthodox Jews seemed surprisingly put-together. As I gradually learned what the Torah teaches us about dress, I understood why: Judaism teaches us to value our bodies, and part of that is dressing in a dignified way. It even gives us a few specific guidelines that many people follow in choosing how to present ourselves to the world.

Chapter 3 relates the story about how God continued to know us, the Jewish people, when we were slaves in Egypt. We lost most of our traditions over the long years our people were slaves. But there were three things we never lost, and it was by these qualities that God continued to know us: we kept our own language, we kept our Jewish names, and we continued to dress distinctively. When I first heard this, I was puzzled. Our language — Hebrew — I can understand; Hebrew is an old language, and existed in the time of ancient Egypt. Many traditional Jewish names are likewise old, and date back to biblical days. Yet how can our dress endure? There is no way that any Jew alive today dresses precisely the way our ancestors did thousands of years ago, is there?

Kippah

One of the most obvious ways to dress "Jewish" is for Jewish men to keep their heads covered, either with hats or kippot (the singular is kippah; they are called skullcaps or yarmulkes in English). Surprisingly, this originated as a custom, rather than a commandment in the Torah. Jewish men began to keep their heads covered as a sign of dignity and respect for God. Until very recently, wearing a hat has been a part of dressing in a formal, dignified way the world over. Jewish men, seeking to take themselves seriously and present a decorous face to the world, began to always keep their heads covered. Today, virtually all religiously observant Jewish men wear kippot, sometimes with hats over them. (Orthodox Jewish women would never wear a kippah: it is considered a male garment, and there is a clear ideal in the Torah that men and women do not dress in each other's clothes.)

If you are a man, even if you do not wear a kippah often, Shabbat presents you with the perfect opportunity to experiment with this aspect of Jewish dress. You might want to start by wearing a kippah during important

elements of Shabbat such as meals and Torah study. As you strive to make this day holy, wearing a kippah is another way to connect to God and the Jewish people. Many synagogues provide kippot for use, but I would recommend purchasing your own so you can wear it at home, too. (Plus, you'll probably prefer a dignified version, rather than one in a sherbet color so favored by the nation's bar mitzvah and bat mitzvah kids!) Take a look in a local Judaica store, or shop on websites such as www.kippah.com, www.alljudaica.com, or www.jewishsource.com.

Tzitzit

Most Jewish men know about wearing kippot, but fewer know about an even more important article of clothing God commanded Jewish men to wear: *tzitzit.*

> God spoke to Moses, telling him to speak to the Israelites and have them make tzitit (tassels) on the corners of their garments for all generations. They shall include a twist of sky-blue wool in the corner tzitzit. These shall be your tzitzit, and when you see them, you shall remember all of God's commandments so as to keep them. You will then not stray after your heart and eyes, which (in the past) have led you to immorality. You will thus remember and keep all My commandments, and be holy to your God. I am God your Lord, who brought you out of Egypt to be your God. I am God your Lord. (Num. 15: 37–41)

Tzitzit today are a kind of undershirt with four fringed knots at the hem (two in front and two behind) that Jewish men wear under their shirts to fulfill this mitzvah. The blue dye we used to use came from a species of fish in Israel that is now extinct, so the tzitzit of today are all white. Some men wear their tzitzit with the fringes dangling out below their shirts. The mitzvah to wear tzitzit is incorporated into the central "Shema" prayer we recited twice daily, and some men hold onto the fringes when they recite the "Shema." Others tuck the fringes into their pants, so nobody can tell they are wearing tzitzit.

There are two types of mitzvot in Judaism: those whose purposes we readily understand (called "mishpatim"), and those whose purpose is a

complete mystery to us (called "chukim"). Tzitzit are considered a mishpat: a mitzvah whose purpose we know. The fringes remind us of God and his mitzvot. There is a numerical connection between the fringes and God and His mitzvot too. In Hebrew, letters can also be used as numbers (aleph, the first Hebrew letter, is one, bet, the second Hebrew letter, is two, etc.). The numerical value of the Hebrew word tzitzit is 600. If you then add the five knots tying each fringe, then the eight strings in a fringe, to 600, you come up with 613: the number of commandments in the Torah.

Even men who are not yet ready to wear tzitzit regularly can experience the awesome power of fulfilling this ancient mitzvah on a special day such as Shabbat.

I wish this book could come with a box of ritual items, from kiddish cups to benchers (books containing the "Grace after Meals") to tzitzit. The best I can do, instead, is urge you to take a shopping trip to a Judaica store or website (try www.alljudaica.com or www.artscroll.com). Buy a couple of tzitzit, and experiment with wearing them. Shabbat provides us with an opportunity to try out these ritual items. For men who are beginning to explore different ways to experience Shabbat, wearing a ritual item such as tzitzit can provide a new mitzvah to perform, and a new way to become closer to God. It can also connect us with countless generations of Jewish men and boys that have come before, all the way to the moment at Sinai when God gave us His Torah.

Women's hats

Jewish women who are married, widowed or divorced are required by the Torah to cover their hair. There are a myriad of different interpretations of this rule. Some women cover their hair with attractive wigs, and it is impossible to tell whether they're covering their hair or not. (I remember a friend once telling me that she had met a well-known and very Orthodox Jewish woman — and was shocked to find her seemingly bare-headed! I filled my friend in on the whole wig practice.) Other women wear scarves, snoods (called "tichels" in Yiddish), hats, or even a combination of two of these. Some Jewish authorities hold that the commandment to cover the hair applies to all of one's hair; others say most of the hair should be

covered. Obviously, this is a very personal decision, and one that can be hard to make. Anyone contemplating taking this step should consult with a rabbi, as well as friends and acquaintances who already follow this mitzvah by covering their hair.

What of the person who is just beginning to observe Shabbat? Covering one's hair seems like a radical step to take. Yet for a married, widowed, or divorced woman, wearing a Shabbat hat during important moments, such as lighting the candles, saying the blessings at the table, daavening (praying) and learning Torah can enhance the moment. It is a way to confer further holiness on your actions, and to bring extra spirituality into your Shabbat. It can be easy to do the parts of Shabbat that we have all heard of: lighting the candles, and eating challah, for instance. But Shabbat is a more total experience than that. While covering one's hair if one is or has been married is something that religious Jewish women do every day, incorporating this practice at the very least into our Shabbat can help bring us to a higher spiritual plane on this day.

Throughout our history, it has been Jewish women who have saved the Jewish people, time and again. It was Jewish women who defied Pharaoh's decree to kill all the baby Jewish boys born when we were slaves in Egypt, and it was our women who refused to worship the idol of the golden calf in the desert after we left Egypt. In the days of Purim, when the evil Haman threatened to wipe out all the Jewish people, it was the Jewish woman Esther who ultimately redeemed us and averted the evil decree. Jewish women possess a deep reserve of spirituality, even if we do not always understand God's ways and methods of using it.

In Judaism, human hair is something mystical and important. The Torah says that Jewish men should not shave closely or cut their sideburns, for instance. We don't know God's reasons for this, but it reflects something crucial about our physical form. In biblical times, there were certain people, men and women, called "Nazirim" who attempted to gain an extra measure of holiness. They did this by vowing to abstain from wine, from grapes, from coming into any contact with any dead person or graveyard (for instance, by attending a funeral) for seven years. Most famously, however, Nazirim took a vow to not cut their hair. The most legendary "Nazir" was perhaps

Samson, whose downfall after the wicked Delilah cut his hair is a well-known biblical story. In Judaism, our hair is something intensely personal and holy. This makes no sense at all in the modern, secular world, but it often touches a chord with people. Hair can show our personalities, it can be attractive, it can be seductive. Judaism regards a married (or once-married) woman's hair as powerful, and seeks to protect it; it was mandated that it be hidden from everyone but a husband.

Like most of my religiously observant friends, I have a collection of "Shabbat hats." They are formal and attractive, and I always feel great when I put one on: not just pretty, but somehow impressive, too. I'm wearing the hat because I am commanded to by God, and this feels important and holy. I often treat myself to a new hat before major Jewish holidays, and I always keep an eye out for new and interesting hats, styles, and ways of wearing head-coverings.

If you are just starting out, and want something quickly to wear on Shabbat, try a beret. These are stylish and classic, and extremely popular in religiously observant Jewish circles. You can tuck in a little hair or a lot, you'll always look great, and a classic beret in a neutral color will go with everything. If you want a more modern, edgy head-covering, one look that is very popular currently is a scarf arranged, bandana-style, across the forehead, and tied in back of the head, with the ends hanging down in back. (Use a rough material like cotton; very slippery materials won't hold a knot as well.)

Modesty

The opening chapters of the Torah are majestic in their scope and poetry. They recount God's creation of the world, and then His creation of the first people, Adam and Chava. We read about Adam and Chava's life and trials, and their eventual transformation from innocent beings into the complex, morally complicated people we are today. It is a work loaded with symbolism and multi-layered meanings, and it can teach us a lot about who we are and what God expects of us.

After God created the world, He took some of the red earth of the ground (red

is called "Adam" in Hebrew). He formed a person out of this clay, and breathed into the clay figures' nostrils a living soul. Adam became alive: the first person. God's next act was to plant a beautiful garden in an eastern land called Eden. He placed this man He had formed in it. God told Adam he could eat the fruit of any tree in Eden, except for the fruits of the Tree of the Knowledge of Good and Evil, and the Tree of Life. God warned Adam: the day he ate from those trees would be his last.

God then told Adam it was not good for him to be alone, and He divided Adam into two. God took a part out of Adam's body, and with this part, He created a second person, a woman, to be Adam's wife. The Torah describes her as something that sounds very strange in Hebrew, and is difficult to understand, let alone to translate. This new person, named Chava (which has been changed over the years in Western languages to Eve), is described in the Torah as a "Helper-Opponent" to Adam, reflecting the complex nature of every marriage to this day.

These two people, opposite sides of the same person, existed for many years in the Garden of Eden, eating the fruit of the trees God provided for them, and living in peace. The Torah describes their lives as almost animal-like: they walked through the Garden naked, like the animals, and never worked or built anything. Like the animals, Adam and Chava simply ate fruit that was available to them, growing in plain sight on the abundant trees God had provided. Even childbirth for Chava was to be animal-like: like beasts, it was a routine event, with no pain associated with it. The Torah notes that "they were both naked, the man and his wife, and were not ashamed."

Now, an intelligent, envious animal also lived in the Garden of Eden, however, and this creature wished to see Adam and Chava lose their animal-like innocence. He tricked Chava into eating fruit from the forbidden Tree of the Knowledge of Good and Evil. After she ate this fruit, Chava then fed Adam her husband some. The Torah recounts that, immediately, "the eyes of them both were opened."

How were their eyes opened? What "good" and "evil" did they immediately see? In what way were they now like God? The Torah gives a surprising answer. As soon as their eyes were opened, "they knew that they were naked, and they sewed fig-leaves together, and made themselves loin-cloths." This —

their nakedness — was their first realization and their first activity after eating the Fruit of the Tree of Knowledge was to make clothes.

Adam and Chava hastily sewed themselves some rudimentary garments, and then hid. God of course knows everything, and He could see where they were hiding. God nonetheless called out to Adam and Chava, asking "Where are you?" Adam answered God. Again, his actions are surprising. Adam didn't tell God where he was or what he had done. Instead, Adam called out to God, "I heard Your voice in the garden, and I was afraid, because I was naked, and I hid myself."

God realized that His creations, having eaten off the Tree of the Knowledge of Good and Evil, were forever altered. No more were they the innocent, beast-like creatures He had first made. Adam and Chava had become human beings as we recognize them today, morally complex and different from all other animals. God cast them out of the mystical garden He had created for them, and demanded that they henceforth work for what they gained: through effort and pain they would reap food and bear children. Their leisure in the Garden of Eden was gone forever.

Ever since this incident, clothing has been essential to us, to our identity, to how we present ourselves to others, and to how we relate to God. Men and women have an innate sense of modesty; this is the gift that we gained when we ate the fruit of the forbidden tree. Adam and Chava did not want to appear before God without clothing on; they felt inadequate, exposed, inappropriate. We human beings derive a great sense of ourselves from our clothes. We are able to shape our external identity: to dictate how other people see us. This need and ability separates us from the animals, and it is deep-seated within us. Only human beings are able to decide how we appear to others. Only human beings are able to try to elevate themselves, to act in ways that are dignified and reflect our innate holiness. Only we are able to guard our inner essence through outward modesty.

Traditional Judaism doesn't succumb to the modern notion that "it's what inside that counts." On the contrary! Instead, Judaism teaches us that what is inside will always be reflected on the outside. And because Judaism in general tries to build people up, to see the human being as

dignified and important, it expects our clothing (and our actions) to reflect these elevated qualities.

In a sense, this is obvious. We dress up, for instance, when we go on job interviews. We don't just show up in our most comfortable jeans and broken-in sneakers, and expect our interviewer to somehow divine that, despite our grungy outfit, we are really somehow neat and reliable. On blind dates, we don't wear ugly clothes in the hope that our date will somehow manage to guess that we're actually really attractive, fashionable people on the inside. Clearly, we all realize that how we present ourselves is enormously important, and shapes the impression we make on others.

The Jewish view goes further. There is a crucial idea present throughout Judaism that the external *shapes* the internal. This is a profound thought. When we act in a certain way, we eventually become that way. We grow into the role we set for ourselves. For instance, when we force ourselves to pray, we eventually become spiritual. When we force ourselves to give tzedakah (money to the needy), we eventually become generous. When we force ourselves to invite guests into our homes, we eventually become people who care about others. When we dress in a dignified manner, we grow into that dignity. In the Jewish way, when we dress in a manner that reflects our relationship with God, this aids us in becoming more elevated as people.

I remember this thought hitting home with great force the day I graduated from college. Harvard is an urban campus, and the area around Harvard Yard is crisscrossed with many busy streets. As a student, I was used to dashing across roads all the time, and jaywalking whenever there was a break in traffic. The morning of graduation, I donned my cap and gown along with all the other graduating seniors, and ambled outside. I was all set to dash across the road, when I suddenly became incredibly self-conscious. Here I was, in cap and gown, on one of the most important days of my life. There were tourists on the streets, snapping pictures of the historic buildings, and of us graduates. I somehow didn't feel like jaywalking any more. Instead, I walked sedately to the corner, waited for the crossing light, and crossed the road with dignity, proudly wearing my academic robes. It would have seemed inappropriate to run pell-mell through traffic wearing them.

I had a similar feeling many years later, too, at my wedding. We had an excitable wedding planner, and in the middle of the reception, she interrupted our band mid-song, and made a shrill announcement that the weather was getting worse, and all our guests were going to have a terrible time getting home afterwards! Everyone immediately stopped dancing, whipped out their cell phones, and started making frantic phone calls. Now, to say that I was upset at that moment with our wedding planner's actions is an enormous understatement. (The weather wasn't even that bad.) I was livid. In any other situation I would have walked up to our wedding planner and given her a piece of my mind. But in my wedding dress, with my veil on my hair, there was no way I was going to start shouting at anybody. I was dressed like a lovely princess, and I acted like one (delegating our band leader to go and talk to her instead). I had once seen a funny photo in an art gallery: a bride, dressed in her wedding dress, screaming like a banshee at somebody. I remembered the photo in that instant; its humor derived from its inappropriateness. Nobody expects a beautifully dressed person to act without dignity.

There is one "Jewish" ethos in dress: modesty. Different Jewish communities interpret the demand to be modest in different ways. There is a common Jewish saying: "The glory of the daughter of the king is inside." On a literal level, this reflects the harem culture of the ancient Middle East: a proper princess was kept safe indoors, not paraded outside for everyone to see. But there is a much deeper meaning, which keeps this saying current. We, the entire Jewish people, men and women, are the "daughter," and our father, our King, is God. And if we are to be worthy of being sons and daughters of God, we cannot act like cheap floozies, parading around brazenly. We must preserve ourselves as dignified royalty instead. The Hebrew word for modesty is "tzniut." In English, "modest" also means small or insignificant. In Hebrew, however, this isn't the case at all; the word is instead closely related to "tzinah," or secrecy. It reflects the recognition that not everything needs to be displayed.

Some Jews interpret the commandment to dress modestly to mean that, given the standards of the community they live in, they should dress in a modest way. When everyone around them wears tight jeans, they'll wear

loose ones. When women wear mini-skirts, they'll stick to skirts that go to the knee. When guys go shirtless in the summer, they'll keep their T-shirt on. Most Orthodox Jews, however, go a little further in their dress. While there is not one standard, there are a few guidelines. In general, religiously observant Jews will wear clothes that cover their knees, cover their collarbones, and reach their elbows. Men usually wear long pants instead of shorts, for instance. They don't go shirtless. Orthodox women usually wear skirts (not for reasons of modesty, but for another mitzvah: "beged ish," or the prohibition against wearing clothing meant for the opposite sex) that are knee-length or longer. They'll avoid tops that bare their upper arms or are low-cut. (Or else they'll layer their tops to make sure they're not revealing.) Both men and women avoid clothing with words or numbers on them (unless they are for a specific purpose, for instance when they are playing on a team).

Shabbat offers us a perfect day to begin experimenting with ways to conform to Judaism's expectation of modesty. Certainly, our clothing on Shabbat should be festive. There is an idea in Judaism that Shabbat should be different from the other days of the week. Wear festive clothes on Saturday that you normally reserve for parties or formal functions. And think about empowering yourself on Shabbat by adhering for 25 hours to Jewish standards of modesty. It is possible that this will help you to feel subtly different, better, more dignified, as you take possession of your Shabbat soul.

Makeup and hair on Shabbat

When I was a teenager and drove with my family to synagogue on Saturday mornings, I remember it always used to take me ages to get ready first. Everyone I met at synagogue looked similarly put-together; we all had our hair and makeup just right. Our get-ups reflected hours of effort: we'd all showered, blow-dried our hair, curled it with curling irons (I guess today people use straightening irons instead), and carefully applied eyeliner, mascara, lipstick, etc. Often we didn't want to waste all the effort we made getting ready, and we went on to the mall after services.

I sometimes remember those days with a chuckle as I get ready today on

Shabbat mornings, for nothing could be further from my life as a Shabbat-observant Jew. Not only are my Shabbats much more all-encompassing, but the rules of Shabbat ensure that I'll never again spend half an hour with my cosmetics on a Saturday. (Many of the actions typically associated with putting on makeup violate some of the prohibitions on Shabbat, such as mixing and grinding, anyway, and it is usual in many religiously observant circles to wear very little or even no makeup on Shabbat. Showering, curling irons, and the like are also not used on Shabbat.)

It is all a far cry from the elaborate routine I was once used to, but, strangely, today I find this streamlined routine liberating. It only takes a short time for me to get ready on Shabbat morning, and I find I treasure the simplicity of this day. There is a Shabbat "look" that is (by necessity) very light on makeup and hair styling. In addition to being easy and quick, I find that, ironically, people often look better on Shabbat, when they have spent less time on their appearance and used fewer products. (Perhaps it is a lesson we can heed of during the week, as well, that when it comes to our looks, less is often more.)

The unchanging aspects of Jewish dress and behavior

Here's a final thought about dressing in a distinctive Jewish way on Shabbat. From time to time I teach Sunday school, and when I do, I like to tell the children the following story, based on a lecture I once heard in Jerusalem. It sums up the incredible uniqueness of the Jewish people. Our survival is an amazing aberration in world history; the only way we have remained a separate people, with the same thoughts, dress and traditions as our ancestors, is because God Himself has sustained us.

Scientists invented an amazing time machine! Soon, the world's leaders rushed to form a committee and invited figures from their nations' past to come take a look at the present.

The first dignitary to be invited to the present day was Ramses, Pharaoh of ancient Egypt. In a puff of smoke, he arrived in modern-day Cairo. Excitedly, an Egyptian official took Pharaoh by the hand and led him on a tour.

As he stood on a street corner with traffic whizzing by, Pharaoh was

puzzled. For one thing, he could not understand a thing his guide told him. Thousands of years ago, Egyptians spoke an ancient language that was expressed with hieroglyphics. Today, of course, Arabic is the language of Egypt. As Pharaoh continued to look around, other things baffled him, too. In Pharaoh's day, Egyptians had names like Ramses and Tutankhamun; today, however, Egyptians sport names like Aysha and Mohammed. Also strange for Pharaoh was the dress of modern-day Egyptians. In the ancient past Egyptians wore long white gowns, collars of beaten metal, and elaborate headdresses. Pharaoh could not get over all the new clothes he saw in the modern-day Egypt: blue jeans and T-shirts for men, long black veils and coats for women. Pharaoh's greatest shock, however, came from the casual way he was treated in modern-day Egypt. "Don't you know who I am?" he asked; "I am your living deity!" Pharaoh told his fellow Egyptians to worship him. Surprised, the modern-day Egyptians explained that they are Muslim now, and don't worship kings. Utterly confused, Pharaoh sadly re-entered the time machine and returned to ancient Egypt.

Undaunted, the Time Machine Committee invited a second dignitary to take a tour of the present: the ancient Greek King Antiochus. King Antiochus arrived, and was proudly shown around modern-day Athens by Greek officials. But the ancient king couldn't understand a word they said: modern Greek and ancient Greek are unintelligible to one another. King Antiochus had a hard time pronouncing modern Greek people's names, too. In ancient times Greeks had names like Theseus and Pericles; in modern times, Greeks are more likely to be named Alexandra or Nicholas. As he looked around downtown Athens, King Antiochus was shocked to see the jeans and dresses, the coats, ties, baseball caps and high heels of modern Greek people. "Where are the graceful togas of my Greece?" he cried sadly. Finally, the king exclaimed: "At least my people have surely not forgotten our gods! Show me the temples where you worship Athena and Dionysius." Embarrassed, his modern-day Greek guides explain that in Greece today people have abandoned the old gods, and are Orthodox Christian instead. Utterly bewildered, King Antiochus returned to ancient Greece.

Feeling a little daunted, the Time Machine Committee decided to skip forward a few hundred years, and bring someone a little more modern to visit

the present day. They settled on Julius Caesar, the Roman leader, and Italian officials were appointed to show him around modern Rome. The tour started well, until Caesar spied the Vatican and asked if it housed temples to Hera and Jove. His guides rushed to explain that Italians today no longer believe in these ancient deities. Dazed, the Caesar proceeded around modern-day Italy, but his tour was hampered by a language gap; used to ancient Latin, Caesar had a hard time with modern Italian. Whereas Julius Caesar was used to ancient names such as Flavius and Laelia, he stumbled over modern-day Italian names like Julia and Salvatore. Finally, Caesar was shaken to the core by the clothing he saw all around him. He kept looking for togas, but all he saw were fashionable suits or slacks and jackets on the men, and stylish skirts and blouses on the women. Sadly, the Time Machine Committee sent the Caesar back to ancient Rome.

At a loss for what to do next, the Committee finally listened to their sole Israeli member, a man named Moshe, who suggested trying their machine on an ancient Jewish leader instead. "How about Moses?" the Israeli suggested. After much debate, the Committee reluctantly agreed, and soon the ancient Moses, "Moshe Rabbeinu" ("Moses our Teacher") was being shown around present-day Israel by his modern Israeli guide. Well, this time it was a different experience. For one thing, both men shared the same name: Moses ("Moshe" in Hebrew) remains a very popular Jewish name in Israel and around the world. The ancient Moses was at home with other names, too: he met a modern-day Zipporah (which was Moses' wife's name), a Miriam (Moses' sister's name), an Aaron (Moses' brother's name), and a Gershon (Moses' son's name). These are all still common names in Jewish communities the world over.

Language proved no barrier, either, as both the ancient Moses and his modern guide spoke Hebrew. When Moses visited the synagogues of present-day Israel, again, he felt at home, as his fellow Jews prayed to the one true God with whom Moses himself had spoken. He was pleased to see that each morning Jews even still recite a beautiful, poetic prayer that Moses wrote in ancient times (the "Shir haMayim," or "Song at Sea"). Finally, Moses' noted that much of the clothing of his time and modern-day Jews are the same, too. In ancient times, Jewish men wore tzitzit and garments that covered their

heads; in modern times, Jewish men continue to do the same. In Moses' time Jewish women covered their hair, and continue to do so today. Both men and women have always dressed in a modest fashion, in ancient times and the present.

We modern Jews don't need a time machine to connect with our ancient ancestors; we are part of a people that has never forgotten God's words, in our language, in our names, in our devotion to God, and in our dress. It is amazing that of all the cultures of the ancient world, only the Jewish culture has remained in a constant, recognizable form. While the non-Jewish cultures and civilizations mentioned in the Torah, the Canaanites, the Jebuzites, the ancient Egyptians, Persians, Greeks, and Romans have all either disappeared completely or else evolved beyond all recognition, Jewish culture remains. Our language, our dress, and our names — the three qualities by which God continued to know us when we were slaves in Egypt — continue to define who we are as a people. It is easy to lose sight of the miraculous quality of this unchanging endurance. For alone out of all the ancient peoples, the Jewish nation remains. Shabbat can be a wonderful time to begin to connect with these timeless Jewish qualities, a time to strengthen these eternal characteristics that define us as Jews.

7

Finding a community: Shabbat morning services

By this point in the morning, it is time to go to shul. (Of course, when my kids wake me up early, we have to play a few board games, set up the dolls' house, play doctor, run around outside, and read several books first.) Traditional Jews tend to call synagogue (a word that comes from the Greek) by its Yiddish name, "shul." ("Shul" is related to the Germanic word for school, and indeed, in Orthodox Jewish communities, the shul is used as a place to study Torah as well as to pray.) In Hebrew, it is called "Beit Knesset" (literally, "House of Gathering").

What kind of synagogue should you look for?

This is a question I often hear from friends and acquaintances who are interested in learning more about Shabbat. I know that all Jewish communities celebrate elements of Shabbat, but it is only in Orthodox Judaism that Shabbat is seen as an all-encompassing, transcendent experience. Only Orthodox Judaism views God's mitzvot as imperative, and strives to follow them without exception. Only in an Orthodox shul will you find a community that is fully committed to following every element of Shabbat. This book's wish is to help you find a way to experience a full, meaningful Shabbat in accordance with the mitzvot God gave us for this day, reflecting the way that Jews have celebrated Shabbat for thousands of years. Only in an

Orthodox shul will you find a community that is also seeking to experience a fully authentic, all-encompassing holiday in this way.

Shabbat is so beautiful, and it is so meaningful to incorporate its rituals and traditions into our lives, but attending an Orthodox shul can sometimes seem a step too far. One very good friend of mine once said, only half-jokingly, that she thought of the shul I attend as the "scary Orthodox shul" (even though she has never been there). This reminds me of an old joke.

There was once a Jewish mother whose only son (God forbid) joined a cult. The poor mother was very unhappy, and went to her rabbi to ask if he could help convince her son to leave the cult. The rabbi tried, but was unable to. "Look," he told the mother, "I know another rabbi who is even more religious than me; maybe he will be able to rescue your son from the cult." Well, this second rabbi tried and he, too, failed. The poor mother turned to a third rabbi, then a fourth. Finally, the last rabbi suggested finding a really religious rabbi — an Orthodox rabbi — to help. Reluctantly, the mother agreed.

She visited an Orthodox shul, and met with its rabbi, who had a long beard, long sidelocks and a big black hat. This rabbi assured the mother that he would do his best to convince her son to leave his cult. This rabbi went and met with the son, and had many conversations with him. Eventually, the rabbi was able to persuade the young man to leave the cult.

Three weeks later, the distraught mother called the Orthodox rabbi, more unhappy than ever before. "What is the matter?" asked the rabbi in alarm. "Has your son, God forbid, decided to rejoin the cult?" "No," sputtered, the mother; "it's worse than that. He's left the cult — but now he's an Orthodox Jew!"

Unfortunately, we Jews have learned to be afraid of our own religion, our own traditions.

It wasn't always this way: a couple of generations ago, a majority of Jews were Orthodox, and Orthodoxy was seen as a normal, natural, fulfilling way to live one's life. What happened? There are many theories, but I have always felt we did it to ourselves. Jews assimilated massively once we started settling in the United States, and for a time, being religiously observant was seen as old-fashioned and embarrassing, not modern and

"American." To be sure, there are Orthodox communities that never abandoned their religious traditions, but most American Jews did abandon it. To wear a kippah or daaven (pray) in Hebrew or keep kosher were seen as relics of an unenlightened age, like having bad teeth or wearing homemade clothes. After the first generation that moved to the United States passed away, their children, grandchildren and great-grandchildren rushed to embrace an all-American norm that was far removed from traditional Judaism. It is hard to believe, but the secularism we take for granted today as modern Jews is only a few decades old, coming after thousands of years during which our ancestors kept God's mitzvot.

I think we have created a second stumbling block for ourselves when it comes to following our religion. In the years since we as a community became secular, a few myths have sprung up that have made their way into our communal consciousness. Traditional Orthodox Judaism has been tarred as strange or scary. There are a host of suppositions about Orthodox life that are often repeated but rarely true. Popular culture doesn't help: there are scores of books and movies that depict Orthodox Judaism as bizarre at best and sinister at worst.

This is so unfortunate, because among Orthodox Jews, there is often an extra level of good nature that seems to come from trying very hard to live up to our mitzvot. Most Orthodox shuls are welcoming, rather than frightening. Some of the rituals and traditions of Shabbat might seem a little different to people not used to them, but they are beautiful and enrich our lives. Even if you can't help but feel that the thought of going to an Orthodox shul seems odd, I'd urge you to try it on Shabbat. You'll quickly find a community of like-minded people eager to share with you the beauty of Shabbat. Many Orthodox Jews, in fact, are "baalei teshuva," or returnees to the faith: people who were raised secular and who became religiously observant later on. Orthodox shuls are used to hosting people seeking the beauty of an authentic Shabbat, and will be thrilled to have you attend.

Finally, the spectrum of what is "Orthodox" is very wide. Many of us think of insular communities, where men wear dark suits and black hats, women wear long skirts, and people converse in Yiddish, as the standard of Orthodox. Popular literature and movies often seem to use these identifiable

traits when they wish to include religiously observant Jewish characters. Yet there is no one standard of Jewish dress or behavior. Religiously observant Jews somehow find myriad ways to describe themselves, reflecting the wide variety of Orthodox lifestyles: there is "Modern" (meaning they embrace the modern world), "Yeshiva" (meaning they try to put Jewish concerns ahead of modern, secular ideas and activities), "Chassidic" (meaning they are devoted to a particular rabbi in the mystical, Chassidic tradition), and many other types of Orthodox communities. Given that there are so many flavors of Orthodox Judaism, you can search for one that feels right for you.

What these diverse communities all have in common is an acknowledgement that God's Torah and mitzvot are eternal and unchangeable. Unlike non-Orthodox ways of thinking, Orthodox Jews accept that the Torah is "min Shemayim," from Heaven, in its entirety. It is never altered to suit one's convenience, or to reflect the changing opinions of the secular world. In the context of Shabbat, this expectation is profound. Once you recognize Shabbat as the unchangeable, special day the Torah prescribes, it becomes a day of special holiness. It can't be called off or ignored. Even if you've never considered attending an Orthodox shul in your life before, I would urge you to try it on Shabbat. Shabbat is such a different experience for most modern, secular Jews; we have no other experience of a day that is entirely holy. It is only within an Orthodox shul that you can experience its holiness in the way that God decreed in the Torah, in the way that our ancestors enjoyed Shabbat for thousands of years before us.

If someone were to come to you and try to convince you to enjoy a day of perfect beauty, would you be interested? (Of course you would! It sounds amazing.) If they also told you that during this day of perfect beauty, you would also have the chance to personally speak with God Himself, what would you do? You'd jump at the chance! By observing Shabbat in the traditional way — by praying the full Shabbat services and enjoying the full Shabbat experience found in an Orthodox shul — you are accepting this invitation. There are certain things in life that cannot be described, but only experienced: this is one of them. Even if you've never thought of attending an Orthodox shul, try it. One of the well-known Shabbat morning prayers says: "The people that sanctify the Seventh Day (Shabbat)

shall all be satisfied, and delight in Your goodness." If you are interested in "sanctifying," or making holy, Shabbat for yourself, you will be able to find both company and guidance within an Orthodox shul.

Finding a shul

Because we cannot drive on Shabbat, Shabbat-observant Jews walk to shul. That means that as you embark on traditional Shabbat observance, you will need to find a shul within a couple of miles of where you live. In many areas, this is the most difficult hurdle for people wishing to make the leap to Shabbat observance. A few generations ago, most Jews lived in tightly knit Jewish neighborhoods, close to their shuls and other communal buildings. But it isn't 1910 any more, and today's secular Jews are much more likely to live in outer suburbs, far from the infrastructure of established Jewish communities.

Sure, it is possible to keep the letter of the law on your own, within your own family or your own home, but Judaism is not meant to be a solitary religion. We Jews are meant to practice our religion as part of a community. Men, in particular, have the obligation to pray three times a day — four times on Shabbat — "betzibur": "in a community" of at least nine other adult men. If you are keeping Shabbat yourself, in your home, with no connection to a wider community, you are not yet experiencing it as Jews have traditionally done for thousands of years, and continue to experience it today. Shabbat is meant to be a community experience. You can learn much from books, but to experience a full Shabbat, you must eventually make the leap and celebrate it with other Shabbat-observant Jews.

Luckily, with modern technology, there are many ways to locate nearby shuls. In the United States, the Orthodox Union (OU) maintains a comprehensive database of Orthodox shuls across the country. This "Synagogue Network" can be accessed through the OU's wonderful website, www.ou.org. In Britain, the main Orthodox umbrella organization is the United Synagogue; their website (with shul locator) is www.theus.org.uk.

Even if you don't find any Orthodox shuls near you this way, don't

despair. The Lubavitch Chassidic Jewish movement (a community of Orthodox Jews who follow the late Rabbi Menachem Mendel Schneerson, may his name be for a blessing, and engage in outreach to non-Orthodox Jews) sends rabbis and their wives throughout the world to establish shuls in areas where there is minimal Orthodox Jewish life. Because they are constantly expanding their network, it is possible that there is a new Lubavitch shul near you. (There is an inspiring and fascinating book about the superhuman efforts of these Lubavitch emissaries called *The Rebbe's Army: Inside the World of Chabad-Lubavitch* by Sue Fishkoff, which explains the fire that drives them, and the difficulties they overcome in establishing these shuls.) The Lubavitch movement maintains its own excellent website, which contains a Lubavitch shul locator worldwide, at www.chabad.org.

What if these avenues don't yield an Orthodox shul within walking distance from your home? You still have a few possibilities. Do you live within walking distance of a university or a hospital? If so, call and inquire whether they have a Jewish chaplain; it is possible that he leads an Orthodox service there on Shabbat. If you live near a Jewish nursing or rehabilitation home, call them; you might be able to join them if they hold Orthodox services on Shabbat.

Another possibility is locating an informal Orthodox minyan that meets in people's homes. I have participated in such minyans in several cities, including Washington DC, New York, Oxford, and Chicago; they are popular and have formed in many locations. For help in locating an informal Orthodox minyan in the United States, you might try calling local Jewish community organizations, such as (in the United States) your local Jewish Federation (www.ujc.org), or your local Jewish Community Center (www.jcca.org), and asking if they know of any established Orthodox minyans. Since informal minyanim are by nature spread by word of mouth, the more deeply involved you become in all aspects of traditional Jewish observance, the more likely it is you will hear of and meet like-minded people.

If you are truly not able to find any place to participate in an Orthodox shul or minyan near your home, you still have a number of options. As you learn more about Shabbat, you might eventually want to spend a Shabbat visiting other Jewish families and communities where being "shomer-

Shabbat," or Shabbat-observant, is the norm. Any of the organizations mentioned above can put you in contact with rabbis and other individuals who can arrange for invitations for you and, if applicable, your family. Try asking your friends and relatives, too, if they know of anyone who keeps Shabbat in the traditional manner. It can sometimes be easier to call up a friend of a friend than to phone a rabbi you've never met before. Hosting guests is a crucial part of a traditional Shabbat, and it is the norm in Orthodox circles. While you might at first think that showing up at a new acquaintance's house with your spouse and noisy kids would be an imposition, in the world of Orthodox Judaism it is normal, and is a pleasure for your hosts.

Shabbat morning services

When I was growing up, the order of the Jewish services seemed completely random to me. Whenever I went to synagogue, the service appeared to be one long rambling sequence of prayer after prayer, standing sometimes, sitting others, singing occasionally for brief stretches, then lapsing into silence. . . . I could see no rhyme or reason to the service, and although I enjoyed being in shul, and even found some of the prayers beautiful, I could never discern any reason why the service was structured (if it even was structured) the way it was.

When I became more religiously observant, and learned more about the traditional Jewish prayers, my perspective changed. Eventually, after daavening the three daily services (there are four on Shabbat) for a while, and learning about the order and meanings of the prayers, some themes emerged. The services became less random. There is still quite a bit of filler — prayers which are said as a link between different parts of the service — but now I can see that each service has a clear structure and purpose. (Even the "filler" has a purpose, whether it is to provide beautiful ways to praise God, remind us of His blessings or mitzvot for us, or to tease out a deeper meaning of the surrounding prayers.)

I was reminded of my old confusion about Jewish services some years

ago when a close relative accompanied me to Shabbat morning services in an Orthodox shul. My relative, not being used to Orthodox services, didn't know what prayer we were on. Used to services being one long, confusing, droning experience, chanted by a far-off cantor standing on a far-away stage, my relative expected the Orthodox service to be the same. She looked around, and was annoyed to see, during a lull in the service, that all the women around us were chatting quietly to each other. "Don't they pay attention?" my relative asked, for, confusing as her own synagogue's services always were, at least she and her friends were very careful to stay focused on the activities of the rabbi and cantor on the stage before them.

As soon as my relative spoke, however, the "Shemoneh Esrei," one of the most beautiful and important prayers in Judaism, commenced, and all the women around us, as one, stood up, faced east (towards Jerusalem), snapped to attention, and began daavening (praying) with great concentration. My relative was bemused, but she was also impressed, hearing the impassioned prayers of all the women around us as they said this crucial prayer with great "kavanah," or feeling.

This is another reason to choose an Orthodox shul as you embark on greater Shabbat observance. For when you daaven in an Orthodox shul, where the natural structure of the traditional Jewish service is followed, it is easier to see the order and understand the flow of the service. Each person in the congregation (the "tzibur" in Hebrew) is responsible for their own daavening. There is no stage and no professionals there to pray for you. It is an overwhelmingly powerful, personal, and rewarding, experience. In Orthodox shuls, a lay person almost always leads services. Orthodox rabbis serve their congregations by teaching classes and answering congregants' questions about Jewish law, not by leading services. In my own shul, which is filled with people who grew up secular and became religiously observant as adults, our services are often led by members' kids; these teens have had the benefit of good Jewish educations that their parents never enjoyed, and are able to lead daavening beautifully.

Following is a list of the components of Shabbat Shacharit (morning service). Of course, this is just a guide to what you can expect as you daaven this service. The services are interesting and complex. If you want to really

125

understand them, try daavening with a siddur (prayer book) that explains each component. There are so many wonderful Orthodox explanatory siddurs on the market today, I would encourage you to look for one that explains the services in a way you can easily understand, and buy one — or more — for your own personal use. (See Chapter 3 for a list of some of the most popular ones, and where to find them.)

I know that for many people, buying a siddur full of prayers they are not used to saying seems daunting. However, a clear, well-written siddur with commentaries that will help you to understand the services can be bought for as little as $10. If you are at all interested in learning more about traditional Judaism, investing in your own Orthodox siddur is a crucial first step. The translations, commentaries, and explanations are fascinating; daavening with an explanatory siddur will open up the entire experience of Jewish prayer, making it meaningful and much more understandable.

Finally, a word about Hebrew. I know that for many Jews the thought of praying in Hebrew is off-putting; most of us never learned Hebrew, and sitting through a service that's all in Hebrew sounds about as interesting as watching a Ukrainian film dubbed into Dutch (maybe less interesting). There's no getting around the fact that Orthodox shuls do use Hebrew. But that is no reason for you not to buy a Hebrew–English siddur and daaven from it in English (or whatever your first language may be). Many people in Orthodox shuls — sometimes most of the congregation — say the prayers in translation. You'll soon get used to hearing the communal parts, which are recited in Hebrew, but you don't need to join in if you don't have the Hebrew for it (though you might soon pick up some bits). Much of the service is recited privately, and you will be very much at home using the English side of your siddur for these prayers.

Shacharit ("dawn," or the morning service) on Shabbat
1 "Birkat HaShachar"
These are several brief blessings, thanking God for such fundamental daily miracles as giving us sight, allowing us to wake up and get out of bed in the morning, and having the means and ability to dress ourselves and walk about.

2 *"Pseukei D'Zimrah"*

This means "Lines of Song." This is a short preparatory service that reminds us of God's great kindnesses to us, as we prepare to address Him directly. *Pseukei D'Zimrah* mixes recitations of biblical verses that recall God's nurturing of us, the Jewish people, with psalms praising God and reminding us that when we call out to Him, God is near. My own favorite parts of this introductory service are the first, called "Baruch She'Amar," the prayer Jews used to recite when entering the Beit Hamikdash, the Temple in Jerusalem; and the last, the "Song of the Sea," a prayer written by Moses himself (Exod. 14.30–15.19) after God brought us through the sea and saved us from our Egyptian pursuers. I find it almost overwhelming to say such ancient prayers, steeped with so much holiness.

3 *"Borchu"*

This means "we bless," and this extremely brief blessing marks the beginning of Shacharit. (This is only said when daavening with a minyan; it is omitted by a person praying alone.)

4 *Blessings of the "Shema"*

These come next. Most Jews have heard of the "Shema" prayer, the central declaration of Judaism: *"Shema Yisrael, Adonoi Eloheinu, Adonoi Echad*: Hear, O Israel: God is our Lord, God is One." We Jews are instructed to recite the "Shema" twice a day: in the morning and at night. Before we recite the "Shema" as part of the Morning Service, we recite seven introductory blessings, thanking God for creating the universe and the people in it. In these introductory blessings, we also recall the Seraphim: perfect angels that God created to dwell forever in the Heavens, singing His praises. In recalling the songs of the Seraphim, we hope that our prayers might be as eloquent as theirs.

5 *The "Shema"*

The "Shema" is now said. We recite the famous declaration of our faith, "Hear, O Israel: God is our Lord, God is One." We then recite in an undertone the song of the Seraphim that our ancestor Jacob overheard when he

climbed up to the Heavens in a dream: "Blessed is the Name of His glorious kingdom forever." We then recite the three biblical passages that make up the full "Shema" prayer. The first section, Deut. 6.5–9, is beautiful: it recalls God's instructions to us never to cease thinking, studying, and teaching His Torah. The second section, Deut. 11.13–21, details the bounty that will be the Jewish people's if we cling to God's Torah and mitzvot. The third and final section, from Num. 15.37–41, concerns the mitzvah of tzitzit, which reminds its wearers of God's laws.

6 Blessings between the "Shema" and "Shemoneh Esrei"

The two most central prayers in Judaism are the "Shema" and the "Shemoneh Esrei": both are recited each morning and evening. (The "Shemoneh Esrei" is also said a third time, during afternoon prayers.) Linking these two towering prayers are four brief prayers, which again remind us of all the special blessings God has given us. This is a very holy time in the morning service, and people generally do not interrupt themselves to chat or do anything else extraneous between saying these two prayers.

7 "Shemoneh Esrei"

This means "eighteen" in Hebrew, and during the week this prayer is made up of 18 blessings during which we thank God and ask for a number of things, from our own personal livelihood to a year of prosperity for all Israel, from our physical health to more universal requests like justice and rebuilding Jerusalem. On Shabbat, however, we refrain from making personal requests of God and our prayers are more general in nature.

The Shabbat "Shemoneh Esrei" might better be called the "Seven," rather than "Eighteen," for it includes only seven blessings. The first asks God to recall our ancestors, because we hope the memory of our patriarchs and matriarchs, who did so much to sanctify God's name, will soften God's view of us today. We then utter prayers thanking God for healing people who are sick (two), for being a holy presence in our lives (three), for giving us the holy Shabbat (four), and for having once given us our holy Temple in Jerusalem, and for promising to restore it one day (five). We thank God for giving us miracles and wonders every day (six), and ask that He bless us

and all Israel with peace (seven). Following the "Shemoneh Esrei," we say a beautiful supplication that was written by the fourth-century CE Rabbi Mar ben Rabina, asking for God's help in being humble, and requesting God's protection.

8 Reader's repetition of the "Shemoneh Esrei"

This is only said when daavening with a minyan; it is omitted by a person praying alone.

At this point, the person leading the service repeats the "Shemoneh Esrei" a second time after the congregation has finished saying it quietly for themselves. Everyone says the "Shemoneh Esrei" for themselves the first time; this second recitation is one that the entire congregation participates in and shares. In Judaism there is a concept of "reward" in prayers and mitzvot: not a clear reward for following a simple instruction, but a realization that our words and actions create new realities for ourselves to live in. Praying, for instance, will alter our lives in ways we may not always appreciate, and the intensity of our prayer will affect the intensity with which our life is changed. Thus, by repeating the "Shemoneh Esrei" a second time as a congregation, we all share in the power of the prayers of the congregation with which we pray.

The centerpiece of the Reader's Repetition of the "Shemoneh Esrei" is the "Kedushah," a special prayer we say together as a congregation in which we mimic the holy angels called Seraphim, singing praises to God. We sing words that the prophets heard Seraphim utter, and we even stand like the Seraphim, with our feet together. As we utter the holy words of this brief prayer, we rise onto our tiptoes, as if trying to reach closer to God during this, the most intense and holy moment of the Shabbat morning service.

9 The Torah Service

This service comes next, during which we say blessings over then read the same weekly section of Torah to which Jews all around the world are also listening this morning. (Note: The Torah Service is only done with a minyan. A person praying alone omits it.)

The Torah portions we read are diverse. Some record the early history of the Jewish people and tell exciting stories; others recount the exact method of construction of the ancient Mishkan (tabernacle) in which our ancestors worshipped God, contain descriptions of Jewish holidays, or instructions for ethical behavior. A person can dig deep into the Torah, and never even come close to learning all the lessons it contains. It is an endless, bottomless vessel, full of wisdom and guidance, which replenishes us and sustains us as a people.

When we read the Torah in shul, we do so from a handcrafted Torah scroll, called a Sefer Torah in Hebrew. Professional scribes all over the world still write Torah scrolls painstakingly by hand, using feather quills, on pieces of sheepskin vellum that are hand-stitched together. Each Torah scroll must be perfect: even a minor mistake invalidates a Sefer Torah for use in an Orthodox service.

Here is something I've always found amazing. There are Jewish communities all over the world. Before the advent of high-speed travel and telephones, many Jewish communities had almost no contact with each other. Communities of Jews in Yemen, Afghanistan, India, and other far-flung locales were even cut off entirely from outside Jewish life for centuries or even millennia. Yet when we compare Torah scrolls from these places, even those written after centuries of isolation, they are utterly the same. There are no different, regional versions of the Torah. A Torah scroll written in England in the Middle Ages is identical — word for word — to a Torah scroll written in Morocco 500 years later. The Torah scrolls that were penned in the great yeshivas of Babylonia in the years following the destruction of the ancient Temple in Jerusalem are the same in every respect as those housed in the great yeshivas (rabbinical academies) of Poland, Ukraine, or Lithuania of the nineteenth century. A Spanish Torah scroll from the year 1000 is identical to one written in Texas today. Standing in shul, watching people read from modern-day Torah scrolls, identical in every way to countless other Torah scrolls the world over, we are part of a tradition that goes back thousands of years: a testament to our endurance as a holy people, devoted to God's Word.

We Jews have no king, no supreme religious leader, but we do have the

Torah, and we dress up each Torah scroll in inner and outer robes, and place silver crowns on the scroll handles, just as other nations do their king. In shul, we keep our Torah scrolls in a special cabinet (called an "Aron," or cabinet, in Hebrew), and as we carry them out, we kiss the garments they wear, much as subjects might kiss the hem of a monarch's robe. God is our monarch, and His Torah is His greatest gift to us.

We read the entire Five Books of Moses each year, devoting each Shabbat to reading a section, called a "Parsha," or portion. The cycle takes a year to complete. During the Roman occupation of ancient Israel, publicly reading from the Five Books of Moses was banned. The rabbis got around this law by choosing other sections of the Torah (from the various Prophets) to read each week instead. We retain the custom of reading a selection from the Prophets after each week's Parsha: this is called the "Haftorah."

(This section of the service is in Hebrew. Many people who don't read Hebrew fluently follow along, reading the English translation of the Torah portion and Haftorah during this time.)

The Torah Service commences with some brief prayers recalling God's might and His giving of the Torah. People then go up to the cabinet where the Torah resides, and remove one or, if the shul has more than one, two scrolls. These are then paraded around the shul. Some people go up to the Torah scroll to kiss it, or touch it and then kiss their hands. (This is just a custom; you can decide for yourself what you wish to do.) The Torah scrolls are brought to a table, undressed, unrolled, and then read.

The Parsha is divided into seven sections; we recite a blessing before and after each of the seven sections. This is also a propitious time to say a prayer for a sick person, or to thank God for recovery from an illness, and there are opportunities during the reading to say these prayers. This is also the point at which a new baby girl is named, if this is the Shabbat for her naming.

After all seven sections of the Parsha have been read (we use the Hebrew word to talk about reading it: we "lein" the Torah instead of "read" it), the Torah is held up and everyone present points to it (with their little finger, not their index finger, which is considered more polite) and says loudly:

131

This is the Torah that Moses placed before the Children of Israel, upon the command of God, through Moses' hand.

The Torah is then wrapped up. (It is considered an honor to be asked to hold the Torah, to undress and dress it, and to say the blessings connected with its reading.) The person who is going to read the Haftorah then says a blessing, and reads the Haftorah from an ordinary book, not a scroll. Following the Haftorah, the reader says a final blessing.

10 *"Davar Torah"*

This means "Word of Torah." This is a reflection on the week's Parsha, and is usually delivered (in English) by the rabbi of the shul. When I was growing up in non-Orthodox synagogues, I thought of this part of the service as the "sermon": the rabbi would choose any topic he felt like — often politics — and fulminate for a while. In Orthodox shuls, the custom is very different, and the Davar Torah is very firmly tied into the Torah's portion for that week. While different rabbis have different styles, this is most often a mini-lesson in some new aspect of the week's portion, instead of a wide-ranging talk on other matters.

11 *Returning the Torah*

Returning the Torah to its Aron, or cabinet, is the last act of the Shacharit service. This only takes a few minutes. The bulk of this section is the singing of Psalm 29, a beautiful prayer that describes the voice of God chiming through the wilderness. After the Torah is placed back in the Aron, we recite one more very brief prayer. I have always loved the words that conclude it. Comparing the Torah to a Tree of Life, we sing:

It is a tree of life for those who grasp it, and its supporters are praiseworthy. Its ways are ways of pleasantness and all its paths are peace. Bring us back to You, God, and we shall return. Renew our days as of old.

Mussaf: the additional service

During the week, after the morning Shacharit service, we are finished with formal prayers until afternoon, when Mincha, the brief afternoon service, is said. However, on Shabbat we have an extra service: the Mussaf service, which comes right after Shacharit. ("Mussaf" means "additional" in Hebrew.) Through the Mussaf service, we recall the extra gifts that God has given us for Shabbat, starting with the extra portion of manna He provided us in the wilderness after we left slavery in Egypt, and the extra "gifts," or offerings, we used to offer to Him in the Beit Hamikdash, the ancient Temple in Jerusalem. Each day, the Cohens (the Temple workers) and Levis (their assistants in the Temple) would offer sacrifices of food items to God. On Shabbat and other holidays, they offered an additional sacrifice: the Mussaf offering.

A fascinating way to remind ourselves that this ancient history remains relevant today is to ponder a moment the links that tie us to our ancestors who worshipped in this ancient Temple. The reason so many Jews today are named Cohen, Levi, Levin, and Levy is because they are descendants of the people from the tribes of Cohen and Levi, who worked in the Beit Hamikdash thousands of years ago. In modern times, scientists have even proved this remarkable ancestry: two isolated families of Y chromosomal markers have been identified that indicate approximately half of all present-day Cohens (the priestly cast, not necessarily the last name) share a common patrilineal descent. If you are a Cohen, there is a 50 percent chance that you can literally trace your father's father's father's father, father (etc.) back straight to Aaron himself, with no interruptions.

We cannot bring the extra Mussaf offering to the Beit Hamikdash on Shabbat today, but we can recall it through the Mussaf service. This is a very brief service, which centers on another repetition of the "Shemoneh Esrei." Mussaf begins immediately after Shacharit. Nobody gets up and leaves or takes a break: as soon as the Torah is put away, we begin daavening Mussaf.

1 *"Shemoneh Esrei"*

There is another version of the "Shemoneh Esrei" just for the Mussaf service. This "Shemoneh Esrei" contains just seven sections (instead of the usual 18), and includes a detailed description of the Mussaf offerings (of lamb, flour, olive oil, and wine) that were brought to the Beit Hamikdash on Shabbat. As in the Shacharit morning service, we first daaven the "Shemoneh Esrei" quietly by ourselves.

2 *Reader's repetition of the "Shemoneh Esrei"*

Just as in Shacharit, the person leading services repeats the "Shemoneh Esrei" after everyone's personal recitation of it. This second reading represents and benefits the entire congregation: we all share in its intent and its merit. Here, too, the *Kedusha* prayers are inserted into this second reading of the "Shemoneh Esrei." Everyone rises for them and says them out loud, trying to emulate the perfect Seraphim (celestial beings) who praise God with holy benedictions and song. This only lasts a few moments, but it is one of the most holy and powerful moments of Shabbat. (This is only recited in the presence of a minyan; a person daavening alone does not repeat the "Shemoneh Esrei.")

3 *Studying the Talmud*

Following the reader's repetition of the "Shemoneh Esrei," we launch into some brief Talmud study. First, we introduce this learning with two very brief prayers to God: a short affirmation that we believe in God and rely on Him, and then a short song, *"Ein Keloheinu,"* which ties in with the Mussaf service in recalling how we used to offer sacrifices to God in the Beit Hamikdash.

We then read some sections from the Talmud which discuss the various gifts that used to be offered to God in the Beit Hamikdash. A further section recalls the songs the Levis used to sing in the Beit Hamikdash, Psalm 92. In discussing what Shabbat was like in the Beit Hamikdash, the Talmud repeats the idea that Shabbat is a taste of the afterlife, the World to Come: "A psalm, a song for the Time to Come, to the day that will be entirely Shabbat and contentment for the eternal life."

These days, when I read this line, and gaze around at my friends and neighbors daavening around me, as I think of the guests, meals, and plans I have made for the rest of my Shabbat day, I often think that I can understand this comparison. During the week, many of us run around (certainly I do), worrying about errands, about money, about work. The days slip by. A traditional Shabbat, a Shabbat kept in the manner our ancestors have celebrated this holy day for thousands of years, represents a break from all that. On Shabbat, we pause and remember what we are living for. Whether it is friends, or family, or ourselves (or all three), on Shabbat we finally have the time to know other people, to connect with them, and even to spend time in getting to know our own selves. For one day each week, we can finally tend to the spiritual over the physical. The part of us that will inherit the World to Come — our souls (*"neshamas"* in Hebrew) — is what is nourished on Shabbat. Through conversation, through learning Torah, through song, through the holiness of the day, we do bring a little of the World to Come into our earthly lives.

4 Concluding prayers

The Mussaf service concludes with three prayers. The first of these is "Aleinu," a prayer that recognizes the oneness of God. Following this, we sing a magnificent song, the "Shir HaKavod," or "Song of Glory," an extremely unusual prayer that imagines God in terms of human attributes. The Mussaf service concludes with Psalm 92, the moving prayer that the Levis used to sing on Shabbat in the Beit Hamikdash, and which anticipates God protecting His people from our enemies. In many congregations, young boys who are not yet bar mitzvahs (under the age of 13) lead these prayers. This concluding section of the service has a light-hearted feel.

Following services: Kiddush

Kiddush is the weekly social hour people enjoy after the conclusion of Mussaf services on Shabbat. Some time ago my mother-in-law informed my husband and me that we were "JFK Jews." I thought at first that she

was commenting on our political affiliation, but no, my mother-in-law had a different trait in mind. Often, she noticed, we seem to show up at shul on Shabbat so late, we come "Just For *Kiddush*." My mother-in-law is right. Some mornings, it can be so hard to wake up, get everyone dressed, and manage to make it out the door. I'm sorry to say, but there have been weeks when we've finally strolled into shul embarrassingly late. But, somehow, we never seem to miss Kiddush. (My mother in law, warming to her topic, told me other Jews are FDR Jews: attending shul "For Daavening Reasons.")

The importance of the weekly get-together at Kiddush was brought home to me soon after my third child was born. He was born on a Wednesday, and I came home from the hospital on a Friday, in time for Shabbat. My husband and I were both so sleep-deprived on Saturday morning that I decided there was no way we were going to go to shul. The morning passed in a dazed blur. Our older kids (who were toddlers at the time) began to get bored in the house and, as it was a beautiful day, we eventually decided to put all three kids in their strollers and take a little walk. We enjoyed walking around the block for a while, the kids were peaceful, if felt good to get out of the house, but then I began to get a bit hungry. I also was getting a little tired and wanted to sit down. And a nice cool drink sounded good. . . . And maybe a little chat with some friends. . . . Before I knew it, we had somehow wandered over to shul. Our friends rushed out to meet us and see our new son. Many people said they couldn't believe I had come to shul a mere three days after having a baby. I let them all think I was pious (or crazy). What nobody realized was I just needed Kiddush! The food, the drinks, the break, and the company!

Kiddush literally refers to the Kiddush prayer that we say over wine or grape juice on Shabbat. The Torah tells us to *shamor* and *zachor* the Shabbat: to guard it and to remember it. Traditionally, the Kiddush we make over wine on Shabbat night and the Kiddush we make at Shabbat lunch fulfill these twin injunctions: through one Kiddush we guard Shabbat, and through the other Kiddush we remember it. There is also a tradition that we should make the daytime Kiddush early, before we sit down to lunch, and that we should have a little something to eat in the place where we say it, separate from the Shabbat lunch that is to come later.

Thus, it is the custom in shuls for somebody to make Kiddush over wine or juice in shul following services, and then for the entire congregation to share in a light snack together. Actually, what constitutes a "light snack" varies considerably. Some shuls put out a few cakes, others might offer salads, vegetables, dips, and fruits, and others offer much more substantial Kiddushes. I remember once attending a new shul when I visited New York, and being shocked to see the most lavish Kiddush I'd ever attended: it looked like a wedding, with chocolate fondue and different pâtés carved in the shape of swans. Kiddushes definitely come in all shapes and sizes. If a shul is hosting any sort of *"simcha,"* a happy occasion such as a bar mitzvah or baby naming, then the celebrating family often sponsors an especially festive Kiddush. (My kids love Kiddush so much, they often spend the walk home from shul on such weeks fantasizing about the foods they want to serve when they become bar mitzvahs or bat mitzvahs. My son, in particular, has his bar mitzvah menu planned down to the green onions we'll serve, please God, with the lox and bagels — even though his bar Mitavah is many years away!)

It is said that God sends special angels to sprinkle spices into our Shabbat foods to make it delicious, and shul Kiddushes seem to prove this. The offerings are often pretty ordinary: coffee cakes are ubiquitous, as is soda and instant coffee, but somehow on Shabbat they seem delicious. I remember vividly the Kiddushes from my own childhood. My best friend Allison and I would excitedly make our way to the shul library where the Kiddushes were held, and together we would eat countless chocolate rum balls: our favorites. Today, my own kids run eagerly into our shul's social hall as soon as services conclude, and excitedly jostle for space to help themselves to that week's Kiddush offerings. My kids have a custom, along with their friends, of carefully carrying their plates and cups to a corner of the room, where they all sit on the floor and have a picnic. As I watch them fondly, I'm filled with the gratifying thought that these will be precious memories for them as they grow up: sitting on the carpet with their pickles and slices of cheese (my daughter's favorite choice), chatting with their friends, as their parents mingle nearby.

Like most of my Jewish friends, I want my children to grow up valuing

Judaism. It might look unimportant to see children sitting together each week, chatting over their Kiddush food, but I think this is a crucial part of their Jewish development. Kiddush makes shul each Shabbat into a bit of a party, certainly a festive occasion. I want my children to have memories full of shul being the place where they were happy, where they had friends, where they had adventures like sitting on the floor with their food, where they felt at home.

For adults too, Kiddush can be the highlight of the week. I love chatting with my friends and neighbors, as well as people I don't know so well, and guests who are visiting our shul. Everyone is dressed nicely, everyone is relaxed. Nobody has any place else they need to be. The promise of a long afternoon full of guests, rest, good food, maybe a class on Torah, a good book or a nap beckons. The atmosphere is calm, joyful, and utterly content. Truly a taste of the World to Come.

8

The beauty that is Shabbat lunch

I've always noticed something interesting about children's books: many of the most popular ones star heroes and heroines who live in surprisingly modest circumstances. Whether it is Madeline living in her bare Paris orphanage, Peter Pan with his lost boys, or *Little House on the Prairie* with its background of simple pleasures, many of the most enduring stories feature kids who are poor but happy. For years, I vaguely wondered why that is: why there aren't too many lasting children's stories about kids who are wired up, who rush from tutor to tutor, who play in lots of sports leagues, characters who resemble real kids from the real world. Sure, I've read some books that are a little more modern, more realistic, but the enduring classics seem to be simple. Even Harry Potter eschews telephones and computers and writes his letters by hand. Once I had my own kids, my curiosity only intensified: here were real-life children with lots of toys and adult support, enthralled by tales of boys and girls making do with very little, going on adventures against a background of meager material possessions, little technology, and often no adult involvement. The disconnect is huge.

After a while, however, I think I began to see the appeal. Today, we are all so connected, so fast-paced. Kids and adults alike are linked to our computers and phones; we are scheduled what feels like 24 hours a day, and many of us spend a great part of our leisure hours in front of a screen, whether playing video games, surfing the Internet, or watching movies or television. Adults work longer hours than ever before, and children face long hours of school and scheduled activities. Of course, the idea of spending an afternoon splashing around a country pond or searching for clues to a mystery by exploring a

dusty old house — staples of the "simple" genre of children's stories I mean — seems enticing. The temptation to get out and do something ourselves, unscheduled, real, maybe even a little dirty or dangerous, is appealing. But for most of us, unfortunately, it remains just a thought, an ideal.

Friends often tell me they're burned out and need a vacation. Great, I say, but I wonder how refreshing their vacation will feel when they bring their Blackberries, telephones, and laptops along. I like vacations, too, but I've found over the years that more than time at the beach, it is time spent "unconnected" that refreshes me. Like the characters in all those beloved children's classics, it is moments when I'm taking a walk, when I'm looking for pictures in the clouds, listening to an interesting class or lecture, when I'm talking with friends, chatting with my husband or playing with my kids that satisfy me and leave me renewed.

Years ago, when my husband and I were first married, we watched an obscure Japanese film that had a very interesting conceit: it was about people who had to search out their lives to find their very best, happiest memory. It was a touching film, as it depicted person after person scouring their lives for their most joyous, richest moment. For some of the characters, this was easy, and they had a plethora of memories to choose from; for others, it was painful, as they examined their lives and saw, instead of lots of good moments spent with family and friends, countless hours spent on the phone, or working late, or otherwise solitarily frittering away their time. This film made a big impression on us, and to this day, at particularly nice times, we'll sometimes say, "This could be my 'moment'!" Our "moments" are never while we're at work or watching television. They always come at times when we're relaxed, unscheduled. Many of these best times occur on Shabbat, when we have very few, leisurely plans, and lots of time to sit and chat, to just "be." So how can we make sure to experience the pleasure of unscripted, unwired, "free" time?

On one level, it might seem counterintuitive to see Shabbat as a time for unscripted pleasures, because so many rules govern our behavior on that day. But I've found that the constraints of the day actually do allow — surprisingly — for a great deal of free time and freedom. The many rules on Shabbat against using electronic items, against cooking, against most types

of work, ironically help to free us up. The activities that are permissible on Shabbat include talking with friends, taking walks, reading, playing games, learning new things: the very things that are most likely to refresh us. And the emphasis on Shabbat of spending it with friends (discussed below) means that we are likely to experience it in the company of other people, enjoying the sort of "real," unfiltered interaction that can be so rare during the week. (Of course, there are times when being alone is refreshing and pleasurable, too, and there is also time for being on our own each Shabbat.)

When I contemplate those children's books with their simple pleasures, I recognize that as appealing as they are to modern people, we don't actually want to enter their basic worlds. I love rereading a classic like *Anne of Green Gables*, and wish a little bit that I shared Anne's simple, serene lifestyle, but I don't really want to move into a farmhouse with no electricity or running water; I do love and appreciate my modern conveniences. We all want to experience a less hectic pace of life, but most of us don't really want to give up the modern world. Shabbat provides the perfect solution. For 25 hours each week, one day out of every seven, we eschew our modern, hectic life. We don't go to work, or even call the office. Our kids don't do homework. We don't watch TV or even talk on the phone. For one day each week, we live in the timeless mode of our ancestors, who enjoyed the holy day of Shabbat. For one day each week, we try to tap into what is eternal and real in the world. For one day we aim to aim for, not work or obligations or any of our man-made tasks, but something higher and more timeless. For one day each week, we remember what it is to be human and, as humans, we stretch to catch a glimpse of the Divine.

Shabbat lunch

This "unscripted" time begins after shul. (That is, unless you are like me and get woken up by young kids early on Shabbat; then you too might have hours of "unscripted" time before shul, as well.) After shul, we make our way home — or to friends' homes, if we've been invited — for

Shabbat lunch. Many modern Jews, thank God, are familiar with the joys and beauty of Shabbat dinner. Unfortunately, for many of us, the amazing experience of Shabbat lunch is a little rarer.

I had a fairly typical American Jewish childhood. When I was a kid, growing up in a traditional Jewish but not very observant home, I liked everything to do with our (limited) Shabbat celebrations: Shabbat dinner, and sometimes going to synagogue on Saturday mornings. As far as I was concerned, that was it for Shabbat. In fact, after synagogue, my friends and I often went to a nearby shopping mall for lunch in the food court. If someone had told me that after shul, there were several more hours of Shabbat, I probably would have felt that was onerous: a nice Friday dinner and a few hours at shul represented quite a bit of a time investment for me then. Back then, I was used to spending fairly short periods of time on things that mattered to me. In fact, to be honest, reading books and watching TV were probably the only activities that I engaged in for more than an hour or so at a time. Very few things in my life then required any sort of sustained effort, and I'm sure I would have been surprised at the thought of keeping the special mitzvot of Shabbat for an evening and a night and then the next day until after sunset, too.

This is a huge hurdle in many people's Shabbat observance, for a traditional Shabbat lasts much longer and takes more time than many of us are used to investing. When we celebrate modern, secular holidays, for example, a few hours of attention are all that is needed: four or five hours to cook a Thanksgiving turkey with all the trimmings, then an hour to eat it; a couple hours to watch a Fourth of July parade, maybe a barbecue, then an hour or so to see the fireworks. None of these requires the 25 hours of attention that Shabbat involves. It is no wonder modern Jews risk feeling burnt out at the prospect of a full Shabbat. Yet with great effort comes great reward. I used to love the expression that "you get out of things what you put into them." Once I began to study Torah, I found perfect voice to it: "The reward is in proportion to the exertion" (Pirkei Avot 6.26). Yes, Shabbat requires more effort than many things we modern Jews are used to making, but its rewards, its beauties, also hugely surpass those of other, ordinary days.

This is another reason to make an effort to attend an Orthodox synagogue

on Shabbat, and to immerse yourself in an Orthodox, Shabbat-observant community. It can be hard to make the transition to keeping a full day of Shabbat, and being part of a community where other people are also observing Shabbat helps immeasurably. In fact, I've always felt that inviting guests over for Shabbat lunch — and being invited one's self — is one of the best and most important aspects of Shabbat. Lunches on Shabbat are often long, leisurely affairs, and they frequently lead into afternoons spent together. Friday night dinner is iconic, and many Jews associate it with Shabbat, but a relaxed Shabbat lunch can be even sweeter, coming as it does in the midst of the holy day of Shabbat, when everyone is much more serene, after a morning of socializing and prayer in shul, and is more strongly focused on the holiness of the day.

I myself have particularly fond memories of favorite Shabbat lunches, for it was at a Shabbat lunch table, as mentioned earlier, that I met my husband! I remember there was no pressure, the way there sometimes is at parties or singles events or on blind dates. (The friend who had invited us did want to set us up, but instead of doing it through a date — thank Goodness! — she did it by inviting us both to Shabbat lunch.) Instead, there was just a pleasant, relaxed meal, and a table of interesting people to talk with. The ritual structure of the meal gave us all something to focus on, and broke the ice as well. My husband was a medical resident at the time, and he entertained us with stories about the busy urban hospital where he worked. We enjoyed a great conversation, all of us, and then all the Shabbat guests enjoyed a long, relaxed walk in New York's Central Park together. Because it was Shabbat, none of us had anywhere else we needed to be. Nobody checked their messages, or made phone calls; some guests weren't even wearing watches. Instead, we could all focus on each other. My husband and I were able to get to know each other by talking for hours. I sometimes hear people say — with wonderment — that they had a "marathon" phone conversation and talked with someone for hours and hours. When I hear that I wonder a bit sadly why that should be worthy of comment at all: for on Shabbat, we have the chance each week to connect this way, to spend quality time, communicating deeply with other people, over Shabbat meals and beyond.

The Shabbat lunch table

When we have Shabbat lunch, the table is beautifully set, just as on Friday night. In my own home, we use our good china most weeks, though it is not unheard of for us to have dozens of guests on Shabbat afternoon, and when that is the case, I usually just set out paper plates. After setting the table, as on Friday night, I place two loaves of challah on a dish in the middle, and cover them with an embroidered challah cover. (A plain napkin would also be acceptable, if you don't have a dedicated challah cover.) I place a salt shaker on the table near the challah. I also set out Kiddush cups on a tray, and place a bottle of wine or grape juice (or often both) on the table.

The ritual items required for Shabbat lunch are the same as those required for Shabbat dinner:

➤ wine or grape juice
➤ cup for wine or grape juice (most people put out one cup for each person)
➤ two loaves of challah (or two uncut loaves of another type of bread, if you prefer)
➤ plate or bread-board on which to place challah
➤ napkin or cloth to cover challah
➤ a shaker or dish of salt
➤ cup for ritually washing hands.

Shabbat lunch blessings

The blessings and rituals of Shabbat lunch are very much like those of Shabbat dinner. We don't sing "Shalom Aleichem" or bless our children or sing "Aishet Chayil," though: Shabbat lunch usually begins with the Shabbat Morning Kiddush recited over wine or grape juice. Why "usually"? Because those who attended shul in the morning likely already heard Kiddush recited there. Some people consider the Kiddush they heard in shul in the morning sufficient and skip it at home, beginning their Shabbat lunch with the hand-washing and blessing over the challah instead. Others

begin their Shabbat lunch with Kiddush, even if they already heard it in shul. These people are careful to have it in mind while they hear Kiddush in shul that they will recite their own Kiddush at home, later. (This is a very empowering idea in Judaism: you can hear somebody make a blessing such as Kiddush on your behalf, but you can control whether or not this blessing "counts" for you by mentally thinking to yourself that it does or not.)

The host, or an honored guest, arranges enough Kiddish cups for each person present in front of him or her. (The Kiddush cups can be any sort of cup: some people use ornate decorative Kiddush cups; others use disposable plastic. Both are acceptable.) He or she then fills their own cup with wine or grape juice all the way to the brim. Filling to the brim reminds us that our blessings from God are so numerous as to metaphorically overflow our cups. (Indeed, some people do place their Kiddush cups on a dish, and fill them until they begin to overflow, to take this concept literally.) They then raise their full cups in one hand and recite Kiddush.

The Kiddush of Shabbat day incorporates three moving quotes from the Torah that each present Shabbat in a different light. Kiddush begins with a beautiful and moving passage from the prophet Isaiah (58). In this section, Isaiah delivers God's words to the Jewish people: if we Jews only keep God's Torah and commandments,

> Then shall your light break forth like the morning, and your health will spring forth speedily. And your righteousness shall go before thee; the glory of the Lord will be your rearguard. Then shall you call, and the Lord shall answer; you shall cry, and He shall say, "Here I am."

The passage builds in emotion and urgency, until it reaches a powerful crescendo: after listing all the mitzvot that God has given us, which will hasten this day of perfect union with God (mitzvot such as feeding the hungry, helping the poor), God thunderously concludes with a promise that if we, the Jewish people, only honor His holy Shabbat, then we will ensure our closeness with God forever. It is a phenomenal vision, and one that rivets us as we begin Kiddush:

Kiddush

If you restrain, because of the Shabbat, your feet, refrain from accomplishing your own needs on My holiday day; if you proclaim the Shabbat "a delight," the holy one of God, "honored one," and you honor it by not doing your own ways, from seeking your needs or discussing the forbidden. Then you shall be granted pleasure with God and I shall mount you astride the heights of the world, and provide you the heritage of your forefather Jacob — for the mouth of God has spoken.

We then recite the biblical passage in which God first commanded the Jewish people to keep His holy Shabbat, Exod. 31.12–17:

And the Children of Israel observed the Shabbat, to make the Shabbat for their generations an eternal covenant. Between Me and the Children of Israel it is a sign forever, that in six days did God make the heaven and the earth, and on the seventh day He rested and was refreshed.

We next recite a final biblical passage: the fourth of the Ten Commandments, the commandment to keep Shabbat, which God told Moses on Mount Sinai (Exod. 20.8–11):

Always remember the Shabbat day to hallow it. For six days you may labor and do all your work. But the seventh day is the Shabbat for the Lord your God; you may do no work: you, your son and your daughter, your male servant and your female servant, your animal, and the stranger who is in your gates. For in six days did God make the heaven and the earth, the sea and all that is in them and He rested on the seventh day. Therefore God blessed the Shabbat day and made it holy.

The person making Kiddush then says:

By your leave, my masters and teachers:
Blessed are You, our Lord, our God,

King of the Universe,

Who creates the fruit of the vine.

Everyone present answers "Amen."

The person making Kiddush then pours a little of the wine from their own cup into each of the Kiddush cups grouped together on the table. (Some people add a little extra wine from the bottle to each person's cup, too, so that the cups are full.) Each person present takes a cup, and everybody takes a sip. Because in Judaism we try not to have any interruptions between making a blessing on a mitzvah and performing the mitzvah, there is no talking between the completion of Kiddush and the time when everyone sips their wine or juice.

Washing hands

Following Kiddush, everyone present ritually washes their hands, in preparation for eating the challah. This can be done in any sink: I've seen people wash in their kitchens, bathrooms, or even at wet bars. Because this is a ritual washing, it is important to remove any rings, which would prevent the water from touching all the skin of your hands, and washing them completely. (There are some opinions that if you always wear a ring and it is impossible to remove, you may keep it on to wash; if you have this problem, check with an Orthodox rabbi about what to do.) To wash, fill a cup with water, and first pour water over your right hand three times, wetting your hand up to the wrist. Add more water to the cup, if you need to, and then pour water over your left hand three times. If you are washing in a bathroom, step out of the room to say the bracha (blessing) over this washing. Take a hand-towel and, as you dry your hands, recite the following blessing:

Baruch	=	Blessed
Atah	=	(are) You
Adonoy	=	My Lord

147

Eloheinu	=	Our God
Melech	=	King
Ha	=	(of) the
'Olam	=	World
Asher	=	That
Kidshanu	=	Made us holy
b'mitzva'otav	=	in (through) His commandments
vetzivanu	=	(and) Commanded us
al	=	to
natilat	=	wash
yadaim	=	both hands.

At this point, we've started the sequence of blessing the challah, so we make every effort to avoid extraneous conversation or even interruptions between the acts of washing our hands, blessing, and eating the challah. Some people seek to beautify the moments we wait for everyone to finish washing their hands and reassemble in the dining room by humming appealing tunes; others, however, say that even this humming constitutes an interrupting activity, and has no place here.

Blessing the challah

Once everyone has ritually washed their hands and reassembled in the dining room, the host or an honored guest removes the challah cover. (Please see Chapter 4 for a discussion of the significance of covering the challah loaves.) They hold up the two loaves together, one on top and one below, and say "Birshut," which means "by your leave" in Hebrew. They then hold the loaves and recite the blessing before eating bread:

Baruch	=	Blessed
Atah	=	(are) You
Adonoy	=	My Lord
Eloheinu	=	Our God

Melech	=	King
Ha	=	(of) the
'Olam	=	World
Hamotzei	=	The (one who) brings out
Lechem	=	Bread
Min	=	From
Ha	=	the
Aretz	=	Land

They take the top loaf, and either slice or tear it into at least enough pieces for everyone at the table. They sprinkle the challah pieces with salt, take and eat one piece themselves, then pass around the plate of challah for everyone else.

Ever since the destruction of the Beit Hamikdash, literally the "House of Holiness," known in English as our Temple in Jerusalem, where the very presence of God Himself resided among our people, there has been a terrible absence, a loss within the Jewish people. We no longer have one central place where God's actual presence, actual energy dwelt. (The word used for this essence, for God's presence, in Hebrew is "Shechinah," and it is very hard to translate. For Shechinah means God in an almost tangible form, and the word itself gives some hint as to its incredible complexity. The word is a feminine noun — Hebrew being a language with both masculine and feminine word forms, like French or Spanish — and this hints at the wholeness and complexity of God. God encompasses both male and female attributes; He created mankind, yet is of course completely separate from our physical reality. Shechinah is almost impossible to translate because it is impossible to completely understand. It refers to a concept, a closeness with God, that we utterly lost when we lost our Temple.)

Yet, without our Temple, our religion did not end. When the Beit Hamikdash, the "House of Holiness," was destroyed, God's most tangible and immediate presence was transferred to our homes. Each Jew was given the task to transform his home into a "Mikdash Me'at," which means a "small (the actual meaning is diminished) place of holiness." Our homes became little Temples, and our tables became our altars. Thus, many of

the rituals we perform at our tables on Shabbat and other times mimic the rituals of the Beit Hamikdash itself. Our two loaves of challah represent the double portion of sacrifice that our ancestors offered to God in the Beit Hamikdash on Shabbat (which represented the double portion of manna that God granted us before each Shabbat in the wilderness after we left Egypt), and the salt we sprinkle on our challah is the same as the salt that was used in our Temple in ancient times. By preparing and eating our challah in this way, we become links in a chain that stretches back to 70 CE (the year the second Temple was destroyed) and long before, connecting us directly to our great-great-grandparents and earlier ancestors who brought offerings to God in our Temple in Jerusalem in biblical times.

The Shabbat meal

After we eat the challah, we then enjoy a beautiful Shabbat meal. Although the laws of Shabbat prohibit cooking on Shabbat, it is considered especially festive and therefore desirable to eat hot foods during Shabbat lunch. This is usually accomplished by means of a slow cooker. In fact, the most famous Shabbat lunch dish is a slow-cooking stew called a cholent, probably from the French words that characterize its cooking: hot (chaux) and slow (lent). Though its name might be French in origin, it is popular throughout the Jewish world. This is a rich stew that is made before Shabbat begins and then allowed to simmer slowly overnight. The flavors of the various ingredients meld, and the whole flavor becomes rich and complex. This is a relatively simple and inexpensive way to create a lovely meal for Shabbat lunch. I've included a recipe for cholent in Chapter 14.

Many people serve cholent as only one part of their Shabbat lunch. Shabbat lunches are typically multi-course affairs, beginning with a fish or fruit course, going on to a main course, and finishing with dessert. Because there are many prohibitions against heating food on Shabbat, and because I (and many other Jewish cooks) often serve lunch immediately after returning home from shul, I usually try to serve foods that can be enjoyed at room temperature or even cold, straight from the refrigerator.

Over the years, I've developed some sure-hit menus for Shabbat lunch: here are a few of my favorite meals. All of these recipes are found in Chapter 14. With a little creativity and thought, you can find many other menus suitable for cooking ahead for Shabbat lunch that incorporate your own favorite dishes as well.

Menu one: classic Shabbat lunch

1 Gefilte fish kugel
2 Hot cholent, plus cold cuts and rye bread, onion kugel, and Israeli salad
3 Chocolate cake

Menu two: summer Shabbat lunch

1 Melon slices
2 Fruit soup
3 Fish with egg-lemon sauce, broccoli kugel, and ratatouille
4 Peach crumble

Menu three: all-American Shabbat lunch

1 Cold zucchini soup
2 Oven-fried chicken, served with rice salad and coleslaw
3 Brownies

Menu four: The "I-had-no-time-whatsoever-to-cook" Shabbat lunch

1 Cut-up vegetables served with (purchased) hummus
2 Cold cuts, tomatoes, and lettuce in sandwiches, or wrapped in tortillas or pita. Serve with an assortment of olives, pickles, or fresh vegetables on the side.
3 Fresh fruit and (purchased) cake

Whatever you serve, there are a few shortcuts to making it seem special. One is to serve whatever you are eating from beautiful trays, plates, and bowls. (I have one crystal cake stand that looks like a *fin de siècle* piece of

artwork: it is gorgeous. Sometimes I arrange a mix of red and green grapes on it and elicit oohs and ahs from everyone — it makes me wonder why I ever bother to bake.) It is also a nice touch to serve coffee and tea at the end of a meal, after dessert. Clear off the table, and bring out a box of candy or chocolates to eat with drinks. It looks elegant and makes the whole meal seem more festive.

I learned the importance of presentation from my friend Gila. Her Shabbat meals are lovely, but what sets them apart is their impression of sheer opulence. After each meal, my husband and I find ourselves talking about how amazing Gila's food is on our walk home. Yet, when we think about the actual menus, they don't seem so unusual. Eventually, it always hits us: what sets her meals apart is the lavish way they're arranged. Gila will spread rice on a platter, arrange chicken pieces on top, and sprinkle the whole thing with herbs. She serves salads out of a gorgeous serving bowl, and onto interesting, arty plates. She bakes cupcakes, and then makes them extra special by icing them beautifully, adorning each one with a perfect strawberry, and arranging them like jewels on gorgeous trays. I've learned from Gila that you can take a nice, ordinary meal, and by means of arranging it and serving it beautifully, make it extraordinary. It is a valuable lesson to have.

"Hachnosas Orchim": welcoming guests

A crucial component of Shabbat meals is the presence of guests. We all like inviting guests, but in traditional Judaism, doing so is a mitzvah: a commandment from God. The mitzvah is called "Hachnosas Orchim," or the giving of hospitality. The Hebrew word for hospitality is linked to the word for travelers, and this mitzvah implies more than simply inviting over friends because you enjoy their company (although this can certainly be a part of having guests): it implies giving shelter and sustenance to people who need it. The difference is huge. In the secular way of thinking, we invite someone over, perhaps because we are already friends, or maybe to repay a social obligation. Yet Judaism charges us to do even more than this;

it challenges us to strive for an even higher level of hospitality. Traditional Judaism spurs us to empathize with our guests, to put ourselves in their shoes so we can figure out what they want; Hachnosas Orchim demands that we entertain not only because it is fun to do so, but also because giving to others is a way of connecting with them and, ultimately, of connecting with God, as well.

There is a puzzling statement in the Torah: Hachnosas Orchim is even more important than speaking with God. This sentiment has fascinated many Jewish thinkers over the years, for why should extending hospitality be even more important than communicating directly with God? What is the connection?

One beautiful and well-known answer was provided by a famous sixteenth-century Czech rabbi, Rabbi Yehudah Loew. Rabbi Loew is perhaps best known today for the popular legend that he constructed a Golem, a monster made out of clay, to protect the Jewish denizens of Prague, who suffered greatly from anti-Semitism. In real life, however, Rabbi Loew wrote many philosophical and mystical works, and discoursed with great beauty on the concept of Hachnosas Orchim. The reason that extending hospitality to guests, Rabbi Loew famously wrote, is greater even than conversing with God, is because God dwells in each and every person. We are all created "betzel Elokim," in God's image, and when we extend hospitality to each other, we are extending this mitzvah and kindness to a spark of God. There are very few ways in which a human being can give something back to God; our relationship with God is so much about our receiving gifts from Him, not offering gifts in return. Yet in hosting our fellow men and women, we are extending kindnesses not only to other people, but also to the sparks of God that dwell within them.

One way in which you can begin to enrich your Shabbats is to gradually change your attitude towards guests, from one of modern hospitality to the traditional concept of Hachnosas Orchim. The Torah goes into great detail about what is required to fulfill the mitzvah of Hachnosas Orchim. Specifically, there are four requirements. When we invite guests into our homes, we must offer them shelter, food, and drink. When it is time for our guests to leave, we are required to walk them to our door, and even

accompany them for a few steps as they leave our homes. These rules are simple, but they imply a great deal. My favorite has always been the obligation that we are to see our guests out the door. To me, this implies that the connection we are to create, through food, through drink, through conversation and companionship, is to be so strong that we are even reluctant to part ways at the end of the visit. It is a beautiful ideal to strive for.

The most dramatic example of Hachnosas Orchim in the Torah (and the source for many of the contemporary rules surrounding this mitzvah) concerns our ancestors Abraham and Sarah. Abraham and Sarah had responded to God's call to leave their homes, and even their old names behind. They followed God to a new land, the Land of Israel, where they changed their names and worshipped God, pitching their tent by a busy crossroads so that they could greet large numbers of travelers, and teach everyone they met about God's existence, too.

When Abraham was 99 years old, he entered into the covenant of "brit milah," or circumcision (which every Jewish boy is meant to share) with God. As Abraham recovered, God sent three angels disguised as people to visit Abraham and Sarah.

> God appeared to (Abraham) in the Plains of Mamre while he was sitting at the entrance of the tent in the hottest part of the day. (Abraham) lifted his eyes and he saw three strangers standing a short distance from him. When he saw (them) from the entrance of his tent, he ran to greet them, bowing down to the ground. He said, "Sir, if you would, do not go on without stopping by me. Let some water be brought, and wash your feet. Rest under the tree. I will get a morsel of bread for you to refresh yourselves. Then you can continue on your way. After all, you are passing by my house." "All right," they replied. "Do as you say." Abraham rushed to Sarah's tent and said "Hurry! Three measures of the finest flour! Knead it and make rolls." Abraham ran to the cattle, and chose a tender, choice calf. He gave it to a young man who rushed to prepare it. (Abraham) fetched some cottage cheese and milk, and (then) the calf that he prepared, and he placed it before (his guests). He stood over them as they ate under the tree. (Gen. 18.1–8).

The Torah goes on to recount that after receiving this amazing hospitality, the "travelers" (really angels) then went to go speak with Sarah, who had never been able to have children, and promised her that she would have a child (Isaac) within the year.

What does this story mean for us? Clearly, the Torah is setting us an example of extremely generous hospitality, but what does this mean for us, practically, as we go about our Shabbat?

On one level, we can learn how to treat all of our guests. Even though Abraham was much weakened at the time of this story, when he was recovering from his brit milah, he didn't focus on himself, but directed all his energies towards his guests. Moreover, he *ran* to meet them: he was eager to make them comfortable, and didn't show any reluctance. He offered them rest, as well as several types of food and drink: the hospitality that Abraham and Sarah extended was not partial or half-hearted; it was complete and total. In fact, our sages recount that not only did Abraham serve his guests meat, he prepared mustard for them to eat with it, too: it is not enough to provide food, even rich food to our guests: the example of Abraham shows us we have to go the extra mile, and offer garnishes and extra comforts, as well. We have a unique example of hospitality to live up to, and it exceeds much of the secular world's concepts of holding little get-togethers and inviting guests in those contexts. In Judaism, we can (and should) invite over our friends for a nice chat. But we are also charged to extend an even deeper hospitality: an invitation to those who perhaps need our hospitality a little more, a recognition that we host guests not only for our own benefit and amusement but also because perhaps our guests need something we can offer them, as well.

This deeper meaning of hospitality has been brought home to me so many times over the years, as I've been extended the most amazing hospitality at all times, but particularly on Shabbat. One of the most beautiful examples of Hachnosas Orchim I ever experienced occurred many years ago, in Paris. One summer, while I was a graduate student, I received the single best job offer of my entire life: how would I like to teach a course on the Single European Market to a group of students, and travel with them all through Europe as they visited the sites and institutions I'd be teaching

about? I think I knocked over my chair in my haste to say yes. The vacation (I mean job) was amazing, but arranging my Shabbat plans on the trip posed a challenge. I'd arranged most of my Shabbats with local communities, but I had no plans for my first Shabbat on the trip, in Paris. That Friday morning, I took the Metro to the Marais district, an elegant, Jewish area in central Paris, and walked into a kosher restaurant. I thought perhaps I could buy some Shabbat meals to eat in my hotel room alone, but to my surprise, the proprietress told me to come back to the restaurant later on, on Shabbat, to eat there. My French wasn't great, and I was confused; I wondered if she was saying the restaurant would be open on Shabbat, perhaps for people who paid ahead of time? No, she was insistent, she didn't want my money, but repeated that I should return to the restaurant on Shabbat.

Puzzled, I returned to my hotel, and the next day walked across Paris on Saturday morning, arriving at the kosher restaurant around noon. It was empty but unlocked, and the tables inside were set with crisp linens, china, and the Kiddush cups and challah of Shabbat. I sat down and waited. Presently, the owners of the restaurant, their children, and a huge assortment of guests arrived from a nearby shul, entered the restaurant, and sat down for Shabbat lunch. I couldn't believe it. There were at least 50 of us. Some were tourists, some seemed to be old friends of the proprietors, some were young college kids, and at least a couple appeared to be sick or eccentric, and possibly in need of a meal. There were a few American visitors, and I sat with them, conversing in English.

Our host made Kiddush, and we all ritually washed our hands, then listened as our host made the blessing over the challah. The restaurateurs then served us all a magnificent, multi-course lunch. I still remember that meal: it was a typical Alsatian meal (many Orthodox French Jews have roots in the Alsatian region of eastern France) of veal stew, egg noodles, and other beautiful side dishes. Our hosts didn't skimp or cut corners because they were feeding so many people; on the contrary, they served us all a meal fit for a king. I'm sure our host family didn't need to eat in the restaurant; their apartment probably had adequate space for some close friends to dine with them. But it was clearly their custom to invite huge numbers of guests back for Shabbat meals. Located as they were in central Paris, there were

certainly lots of people who were passing through, or otherwise in need of a home and a meal on Shabbat. I was blown away by the hospitality I was witnessing; here was a religious Jewish family, living according to the ideals of our ancestors Abraham and Sarah.

As the wonderful meal concluded, we all sang "Birkat HaMazon," the blessing after the meal. The party started to break up, and my hosts walked me to the door. With my basic French and their basic English, we could barely communicate, but they didn't treat me like the charity case I clearly was as I thanked them for their family's hospitality and wished them a Good Shabbat. Far from appearing condescending or perfunctory, my hostess shook my hand warmly, her husband looked me in the eye, and both thanked me for coming. We spoke for a few moments, as if we were old friends. They asked me to make sure I visited again whenever I was in Paris, and with a few more warm "mercis," I left, with the tender feeling of having been included in an amazing gathering, not as a poor stranger who was helped out of pity, but as a warmly valued guest.

The mitzvah of Hachnosas Orchim directs us to invite not only those we wish to see for our own enjoyment but also those people who might *need* our hospitality. Sometimes "need" can be a tricky quality to pin down, and it is not always clear which party gains more: hosts or their guests. The beauty of Hachnosas Orchim is that it charges us to give of ourselves to other people. Once that connection is forged between us and our guests, however, we both benefit.

I learned about the value that Hachnosas Orchim can give to a host, as well as a guest, at around the same time I experienced this example of warm hospitality in Paris. At the time, I lived in central London, where (as in central Paris) there were many transient people: tourists, students, young people who had recently moved to London for work. I used to attend a lovely Orthodox synagogue there that had a very mixed congregation: there were many families living nearby, but also many of these younger, more transient members. One afternoon, I was invited to lunch at the home of a woman I knew slightly who lived nearby. She was one of the more "stable" members of the shul: she was married, with several grown children who had long ago moved away to start their own families. As I enjoyed a

delicious Shabbat lunch with this woman and her husband, we chatted, and it became apparent that my hostess had only one topic she was burning to talk about: a few months previously, her youngest son had died, tragically, in an accident. (May nobody else ever know such sorrow.)

As you can imagine, this poor woman was raw with grief. We talked for hours, about many things, though the conversation always came back to her son. This woman and I felt such a connection that afternoon, and she invited me many more times to her apartment for more Shabbat meals. Over the months, I noticed, this woman began to invite more and more people to her Shabbat meals. For each Shabbat meal, she hosted at least several guests. She once told me that she looked forward to Shabbat so much each week, and the companionship and festive feeling it gave her, that it was the focus of all of her days; every day that was not Shabbat she spent planning and thinking about the next Shabbat, when she would again entertain widely.

Now, of course, this was a short-term coping strategy, and reflects a way to deal with shocking, overwhelming grief. This was not a "normal" approach to inviting guests for Shabbat. But the several meals I spent with this lovely woman, her husband, and other guests taught me a great deal about hosting guests. Everyone knew why this woman was channeling all her energy into her Shabbat meals: she needed companionship, love, and the chance to talk about the terrible tragedy in her life. But I'll always remember the lesson that the benefit of hosting guests goes both ways. We often think of having guests as an opportunity to give. But when we invite a person into our home, and share some of our life with them for a time, we can be enriched by the resulting companionship and human connection, as well.

As you transition to a more fully observant Shabbat, one way you might think about enriching this day is to include guests at your meals. On a practical note, having guests around sometimes induces people to be on their "best" behavior, which can be useful if you're trying to encourage your family to stay focused on Shabbat. Entertaining is also an important way to become integrated into a wider community of Shabbat-observant friends. If you begin to invite other Shabbat-observant people to your

home, you will soon find yourself with plenty of invitations to go "out" for Shabbat meals, as well. Spending Shabbat with friends is an integral part of the day; nothing enriches our lives more than spending quality time connecting with other people. Finally, as you become more secure in your own Shabbat observance, you can try reaching out to other people whom you can benefit through your hospitality. Whether it is a family who is going through a difficult time, a person who is new to your area, or an elderly person who lives alone, including new people in your Shabbat meals is a wonderful way to practice Hachnosas Orchim and, often, to make lasting new friendships with people outside your immediate social circle, as well.

As I said earlier, only four simple concrete steps are required to fulfill the mitzvah of Hachnosas Orchim: we must offer our guests food, offer them drink, offer them shelter, and accompany them to the door when they depart. This seems straightforward enough, but there are a few extra tricks to helping us uncover the beauty inside each of our different guests.

➤ We might think we know our guests well, but often we do not. I was once shocked to discover that the husband of a friend of mine had been out of work for several months, and her whole family was extremely anxious and depressed! I'd spoken to this friend many times, but I'd never really enquired how her life was going. (I was always satisfied with "how are you doing/fine" and never went beyond that.) Instead of only talking about minor topics, ask how your guests are, and be sure to really listen to the results. Often, we don't know people half as well as we think we do.

➤ The Torah says: "The ways of a simpleton seem proper to him, but he who accepts counsel is wise" (Prov. 12.15). Ask your guests' advice. You might be shocked at the wisdom you receive, even from people you would never have thought to ask.

➤ Judge favorably. There is a powerful injunction in Judaism to judge other people favorably. In fact, even if it seems that someone is guilty of doing something wrong, we have an obligation to imagine that we don't know all the facts of the case — and to assume that our perceptions are mistaken! When you start to feel judgmental,

try to force yourself to see an issue from the other person's point of view. (As an added incentive, Judaism also teaches that God will be judgmental with us if we judge other people harshly, and God will be lenient with us if we judge other people favorably. So start giving other people the benefit of the doubt today!)

➤ I have always been amazed at my mother's ability to speak to every person, no matter what their situation, with immense interest and dignity. She loves talking to people, and often strikes up conversations with people of all walks of life. I have seen my mother chat easily with the very young, the very old, with people who are developmentally delayed, with people who are homeless, even with people who act eccentrically and whom other people might avoid. I remember in particular once walking with my mother, when we were asked for money by a family who was begging. Instead of passing by, as most people were doing, or even handing over a dollar, my mother, in her typical fashion, stopped, chatted with the parents, then went into a nearby café to get a glass of milk for their child. When she returned, my mother chatted more, asked the family lots of questions, and shared heartfelt advice. Afterwards, I asked my mother the secret to her easygoing rapport with people. She thought for a minute. "I find people interesting," my mother explained, pure and simple. (How many of us can say the same?) She sees in every person a worthy individual, a story, and a person she can relate to on some level. My mother is able to look inside, past a person's externals, to view the spirit within. I've tried over the years to emulate my mother's way of looking at others (with mixed success). Try to regard every person as interesting: it is simple advice, not always easy to follow, but when we succeed it can make us extraordinary hosts.

➤ Speak to each of your guests. This might sound obvious, but it isn't at all; I've noticed that many people seem to assume their guests are happy when the general conversation flows, and guests are talking to one another. Yet each person craves attention; each person wants to be seen, to be recognized and valued. You invited these people into your home, so talk to them. Even if your exchanges are brief, each

person invited into your home should feel that you have valued them personally.

➤ Try to see what each person needs. Again, it might sound obvious, but is someone thirsty? Does a guest want second helpings? Don't assume everyone is forceful enough to demand what they require. Try to see the visit from your guests' point of view.

➤ Don't forget children. I've noticed that kids often get ignored in social settings. They might be immature, but they of course have needs and feelings, too. If you've invited kids into your house, spend some time speaking with them and including them in the general conversation. They'll appreciate it, their parents will appreciate it, and taking the time to interact with even your littlest guests will remind you that we all, young and old, wise and simple, are blessed with a Divine spark within us; we were all made "betzelem Elokim," in God's own image.

➤ One of the best lessons I ever learned came from my own rabbi, Hershel Berger. I have been privileged to be a guest at his table on many occasions, and I have always been impressed with the ease with which he converses with every person. I have seen him go around the table throughout a meal or a conversation, and ask each person at the table interesting questions that only they are likely to be able to answer. He will ask businesspeople their thoughts on recent business news, political junkies their thoughts on current events, high school kids questions about American history or chemistry. Nothing affects his sangfroid: when he's speaking with really young kids, who don't have too much to say, he'll ask them the names of their teachers, and then listen intently, with great interest, to the answers. At Rabbi Berger's table, each person seems immensely interesting. I've never been able to quite master the ease with which Rabbi Berger lobs questions at his guests, but I do attempt it. Everyone likes to be questioned about something at which they are expert: it is a way to put them at ease, and often to spark a good general conversation, as well.

Should we invite only Jewish friends to share in our Shabbats?

There is one difficult issue regarding guests on Shabbat that many people have asked me about over the years. How much should we include (if we include them at all) non-Jewish family and friends? Many modern Jews find that their greatest friends and favorite relatives are not Jewish at all. Sometimes, people find that their friends who are most interested in spirituality come from other faiths. I've seen Jews embark on quests to incorporate Jewish ritual in their lives, and bring along their good non-Jewish friends (or boyfriends or girlfriends), who also become interested in Judaism. Many Jews today are in interfaith marriages, and I've seen both Jewish and non-Jewish partners become interested in incorporating Jewish rituals into their lives. So how much should we strive to include non-Jews in our Shabbat plans?

Jewish tradition teaches us that our patriarch Abraham was unsure whether or not he was Jewish. Abraham was the first monotheist, and he and his wife Sarah founded the Jewish people through their son Isaac, but they also founded another people, too (the Arab nation), through their son Eisav. Abraham was gifted with great foresight, and he saw that the Jewish people would develop and that someday God would give them the Torah with its 613 mitzvot (commandments). Abraham rushed to embrace the mitzvot, and followed them faithfully, all except one. Abraham was unsure how to behave on Shabbat.

The Torah tells us that Shabbat is a gift from God to the Jewish people. God has given each nation of the world various gifts and commandments, but Shabbat is a gift intended for the Jewish people only. Abraham had a dilemma: if he was Jewish, he should follow Shabbat. But if he was not Jewish, he would be violating God's plan by keeping Shabbat faithfully. (In fact, to this day, people who are desirous of converting to Judaism take it on themselves to live an Orthodox Jewish lifestyle for some months before their conversion. They keep all the mitzvot of the Torah, except for one: Shabbat. Before their conversions, they are required to violate one Shabbat-related mitzvah each week, so as not to faithfully follow Shabbat before they are Jewish.)

Abraham eventually came up with an ingenious solution. He knew that if he were not Jewish, he was not required to wear tzitzit, fringes on the corners of his clothes. Thus, he wore tzitzit on Shabbat. The solution was neat: if Abraham was Jewish, he was required to wear tzitzit, and his tzitzit counted as a garment he was wearing on Shabbat. If Abraham was not Jewish, however, he was not required to wear tzitzit. They wouldn't be considered a garment, in this case, but an item he was carrying. Carrying things out of doors is prohibited on Shabbat, so if it was the case that Abraham was not Jewish, he would be violating this mitzvah on Shabbat. It was a brilliant resolution to a difficult problem.

Judaism discourages us from sharing Shabbats with friends who are not Jewish. In cases where one is Jewish but one's spouse or children are not, I would recommend having a heart-to-heart talk with an Orthodox rabbi you like and with whom you feel comfortable; they can help you to come up with strategies and solutions that are right for your family. When it comes to friends, though, traditional Judaism urges us to maintain Shabbat as an event for Jewish friends only. In fact, the Shabbat morning liturgy actually says this. As we bless Shabbat during the morning "Shemoneh Esrei" prayer, we say, "You did not give it (Shabbat), Lord, our God, to the nations of the lands . . ." Among other things, we thank God for making Shabbat a special gift for the people of Israel.

But what if you don't have many Jewish friends who are interested in exploring Shabbat? This is a very common situation. One possibility is joining a shul or a Jewish organization that can help you connect with other Jews who are also interested in Shabbat. Even if you live in a very isolated place without a large Jewish community, computers and telephone connections can help you to at least "virtually" meet other Jews who are interested in their heritage, too. One good example of this is Partners in Torah (www. partnersintorah.org), which pairs up people to learn Jewish texts weekly over the phone. In Britain, the United Synagogue also pairs people for learning Torah over the telephone (www.theus.org.uk). These are amazing resources for people who felt that they were alone in their desire to learn more about traditional Judaism. There are many other Jewish clubs and

organizations that can provide a community. I'd urge you to reach out to a local (or at least the nearest) Orthodox rabbi or shul to learn more about social options that exist in your area.

I know that the idea that Judaism sees Shabbat as something that is to be experienced by Jewish people only seems to modern ears to be exclusionary, prejudiced, and worse. There is an idealism in contemporary society, and almost everybody today rejects the discrimination and racism that was the norm just a few years ago. (I always get irritated when people complain that things are too "politically correct"; I want to ask them: "Why — would you prefer to go back to a time when most people were horribly discriminated against?") In this context, the idea that Judaism regards the Jewish people as a separate "nation" with its own religious obligations is unfashionable, even troubling. We Jews, particularly, have been on the vanguard of anti-racism movements from South Africa to the American South, and are for most part vigilant about not falling into the traps of prejudice or exclusion. To many of us, to be asked to regard Shabbat as a Jewish activity reminds us of segregation and discrimination. So how does regarding the Jewish people as separate, with our own rituals and obligations, differ from racism?

The view of traditional Judaism is that to have our own rituals and religion is not unfair to people who do not share them. In fact, the very word for "Hebrew" (in Hebrew) comes from the word "other," and was first used to describe Abraham, who crossed over the Jordan River, and dwelt separately there, worshipping God. Abraham didn't seek to coerce or harm other people, but simply to live with his own beliefs and rituals, beside them. This remains our model today. Judaism recognizes that everyone has their own way to connect with God. Jews, however, are expected to follow the Jewish way of life, to perform specific mitzvot (God's commandments) that are meant for the Jewish people exclusively. As much as it seems old-fashioned or even unfashionable, Judaism is not meant to be a universal religion, but a special covenant between the nation of Israel and God.

When people ask me about including friends who are not Jewish in our Shabbat activities, the only personal story that I can ever think of that seems relevant is my life-long friendship with one of my very best girlfriends, who

is not Jewish. We met in high school, and when we were in our twenties, we each took our own paths to become observant in our respective religions (me in Judaism, and my friend in her own monotheistic religion, which is based in India). Instead of driving a wedge between us, though, our religiosity instead brought us closer. We never discuss theology, recognizing that our own religions are very separate and personal. But of course there is so much that we do have to talk about: our lives and our families and our thoughts on everything from politics to books, even the intense joy we each have found in our own religious rituals. Our friendship is not hampered by the fact we cannot share all the religious aspects of our lives with each other. On the contrary: we each understand that the other is grounded in her own religion and her own community, and we are happy for each other. I have seen first-hand that it is possible to be very, very good friends with someone from a different faith, yet never to seek to share that faith: simply being compatible is more than enough to bind us together, instead.

Judaism is a very open religion in some ways. It recognizes that all people have their own path to God. Yet Judaism is also an insular religion, too: it recognizes a unique identity, and a unique path to holiness for the Jewish people. Shabbat is one of our greatest gifts from God. It was given to the Jewish people, not to share, but to enjoy intensely, within our community. All peoples can enjoy a day of "rest," but only the Jewish people are charged with Shabbat: with this day of holiness, of reaching towards God, not in a universal way, but within a particularly Jewish context.

Striving to live on a higher level

More than simply feeding and nourishing ourselves physically, on Shabbat our meals can nourish us spiritually, as well. There is a great word in Hebrew: "madrega." It means stair, but the image it conveys can be profound. Religiously observant Jews often speak of striving to reach a higher "madrega": a higher step, a higher level of existence.

I don't mean this in the sense of some non-Jewish religions, where the goal seems to be to somehow ignore the physical realities of life. (A life of

165

solitude, celibacy, long fasts, etc. has no place in Judaism.) Judaism urges us not to try to escape from the world, but to refine it. We don't try to ignore the physical world. On the contrary, traditional Judaism revels in the physical world that God created for us, and seeks to bring sparks of holiness into even the most mundane acts. Every human activity — talking, getting dressed, bathing, giving charity, eating, drinking, doing business — is celebrated in Judaism. Judaism teaches us not to be ashamed of these activities, nor to try to avoid them, but to elevate them, and use each aspect of human behavior as a way to get closer to God. No matter how seemingly base an activity, there is always a "Torah" way to approach it, a way to act that is governed and regulated by mitzvot, by God's commandments. Each activity we do in life gives us an opportunity to reach a higher "madrega": a higher level of existence.

Now, to some extent, exactly what constitutes a higher "madrega," or level, of life is subjective. Many Orthodox Jews stress Torah learning as their ideal. Some observant Jews feel that they have reached a high "madrega" by helping others through charitable activities. I once heard a musician say that by playing religious songs on the guitar, he was inspiring his fellow Jews to feel a love of God, and that playing his guitar thus brought him (as well as his listeners) to a higher madrega. I know some women who see raising their families as their highest life's goal: the way they can most closely connect with God. Everyone identifies for themselves what high level they want to aim for, but traditional Judaism does give us some clues about how to move upward along the steps, the various "madregas," of holiness.

Living our lives according to God's mitzvot brings us closer to Him. Judaism teaches us that God is completely good: He created humankind with the ultimate goal of making us completely and utterly happy. To aid us along the path of happiness, God gave us His Torah, with its holy rules for living. In order to make our embrace of His Torah even more satisfying, God gave us free will, to accept or reject His gift: because the decisions that we make for ourselves are ultimately the most rewarding ones.

You, Reader, are poised in an amazing, holy, position right now. As you learn about Shabbat and begin to keep it a Torah-based, all-encompassing, traditional manner, you are moving up many, many levels, many

"madregas," towards God. This is a unique opportunity to transform your life. I once heard of a fascinating discussion between two eminent Orthodox rabbis about the way to bring the most holiness into our lives, to move up the most "madregas" ("madregot" in Hebrew). One rabbi said that "people who have learned Torah from birth, who have been steeped in mitzvot their entire lives, can reach levels of learning and knowledge that other people simply cannot match." "Fair enough," said the other rabbi, "but even the most devout Jew who was raised keeping the mitzvot can never know the incredible passion, the overwhelming excitement, of someone who was raised secular and found the beauty of God, of Shabbat, of Torah as an adult. This passion brings the person who became religiously observant later in life to a much higher madrega!" I agree. As a woman who found traditional Judaism later in life, I will never know as much Torah as some. But I'll always remember the giddy feeling of falling in love: the joy and passion I felt as I began to make Shabbat (and other aspects of Judaism) a part of my life.

Just sitting down to Shabbat lunch lifts us to a high "madrega." By not rushing home and microwaving a pizza while we watch the news, but instead having a beautiful, traditional Shabbat lunch, we are achieving a high level of holiness. By focusing on those people around us, and resisting the temptation to check our phone and IM messages, we are celebrating Shabbat the way God intended, and are elevating our souls.

But many people take the opportunity of Shabbat lunch to elevate themselves still further. In Chapter 5 we learned that God Himself dwells in our homes when we study Torah: "if two sit together and words of Torah are between them, the Shechina (Divine Presence) rests between them" (Pirkei Avot 3.3). In order to elevate the holiness of their Shabbat table, many people make an effort to discuss Torah — usually the weekly Torah portion that was read in shul — during Shabbat lunch. This doesn't have to be a big discussion. Many traditionally observant Jewish families have a custom on Shabbat to ask their children questions about that week's Torah portion. This is a nice way to introduce a little Torah into the conversation. But I've found over time that these weekly sheets (my kids' school sends them home each Friday) can stimulate discussion among adults, as well.

(I've learned a lot from them.) Particularly in families where everyone is new to Torah study, having a few basic questions to answer each week about the Torah portion can be a nice way to structure a brief, low-stress discussion. I've included some questions for each week's Torah portion in Chapter 11. These can be handy guides to help stimulate discussion.

Other ways to use your Shabbat to reach a higher "madrega," or level, might include reading books on Jewish subjects, attending (if you are able) lectures on Jewish topics, or making an effort to follow new mitzvot. You might want to be very careful on Shabbat not to gossip, for example, or to make an effort to judge each person favorably. You might try to relate to your family and friends in a refined way, discussing more elevated topics than you are used to. Many people refrain from talking about money and business on Shabbat. Others try to make every conversation they have relate to Torah. It is very common to resist talking about plans one wants to make for after Shabbat; many people who are Shabbat-observant feel that is disrespectful to Shabbat, and prefer to act and think on Shabbat as if Shabbat might last forever. It might be that simply by maintaining the rules and commandments related to Shabbat is enough of a challenge. People's mood and temperament also vary week to week: on some Shabbats it is easier to reach for higher "madregot," or levels, than others. It is rewarding, however, to think of Shabbat as a chance each week to nudge yourself higher: to go further in prayer, in Shabbat observance, in study, etc., than you normally do otherwise.

"Zemirot"

As on Friday night, after lunch on Saturday, it is customary to sing zemirot, or Shabbat songs. There are a number of traditional songs that people sing following Shabbat lunch, and these are included in Chapter 12. It might sound odd to modern, secular Jews to think of having a sing-along at their dining room table after lunch, but it is a lot of fun. There are no rules about what songs you can or can't sing. Though there are some zemirot that are traditionally associated with Shabbat lunch, you can also sing other songs,

both Jewish and secular. (Though it is helpful to keep in mind the sanctity of the day, and select songs that enhance Shabbat's holiness.) Some other popular songs are included in Chapter 12, as well.

I've found that our modern, secular culture really devalues singing. Other people often recognize the power of song much more than we do. Some of the most beautiful prayers ever composed, for instance, are the Psalms of King David. These prayers speak beautifully of man's longing for God, of our hopes, our fears, and our trust in our Creator. Yet they were written as songs. I can only assume that King David recognized that the power and beauty of singing his prayers would greatly enhance their beauty, and would help people to make their prayers to God even more heart-felt.

For centuries people realized that singing offers us a profound way to transcend ordinary life. It is only recently that the many beautiful folk and traditional songs that used to be common knowledge for all people have fallen by the wayside and been forgotten. Most of us simply don't sing any more, though even in our recent past, song used to be much more common. Coincidentally, in Israel today, song is making a bit of a comeback. Over the past several years, big public sing-alongs have become popular in Israel, even (mostly) among secular Jews there. Perhaps we in the modern West would be embarrassed to attend a sing-along, would think it quaint, but many Israelis who have embraced this new fad recognize the strong feelings of fellowship and joy that publicly singing together can engender.

If you are at all like I was before I started keeping Shabbat in a traditional manner, you are probably thinking to yourself, "Right, I'll just skip this singing bit, then; it's not really my scene." But I would urge you to embrace the singing of zemirot and other songs after Shabbat lunch, anyway. Trust me: it is one of those things that can't be explained, that has to just be tried. Singing is a big part of Shabbat lunch in traditional Jewish circles. It enhances the meal, and creates a wonderful feeling of closeness and joy among those present.

"Birkat HaMazon"

Shabbat lunch, like Shabbat dinner, closes with "Birkat HaMazon," the blessing after the meal (Chapter 15). It is a chance for us to pause once again, to reflect on the many blessings that God has given us. Psychologists have noted in recent years that the process of thinking positive thoughts makes us happy: smiling and being grateful — counting our blessings — actually releases endorphins in our brains that relax us and give us a feeling of contentment. The Torah expresses this beautifully: "All the days of the poor (the person who regards themselves as lacking) are evil: but he that is of a merry heart has a continual feast" (Prov. 15.15).

"Birkat HaMazon" is a way of ensuring that we have a continual feast in our hearts. It is a way of departing from our lunch table as happy and sated in our souls as we are in our stomachs. "Birkat HaMazon" reminds us to thank God for giving us food and the land to grow it on (specifically, our own Land of Israel), for our families, for being invited out to lunch if we are guests, and for the gift of Shabbat.

9

The holiness of Shabbat afternoon

Many people translate Shabbat as a "day of rest." I think this is a mistranslation. "Shabbat" in Hebrew means a cessation more than a rest. Just as God ceased creating the world on the Seventh Day, so we try to copy God by ceasing our own physical work on Shabbat. This doesn't mean, though, that we do nothing on Shabbat. Shabbat is more than a day to catch up on our sleep or recharge our batteries for the week ahead. If these were the primary functions of Shabbat, it would put Shabbat on a lower level than the rest of the days of the week. On the contrary, however, Shabbat is meant to be the pinnacle of our week: all the other six days of the week lead up to Shabbat. The function of Shabbat is not simply to "rest." It is to cease some functions — to pause in much of the physical that we do each week — and instead to concentrate on something else. On Shabbat, we shift our focus away from the material, and concentrate on the spiritual. On Shabbat, we do rest in some ways. We take a rest from the clock, from errands, from our jobs, from shopping, from the mundane. But other parts of us don't take a rest at all. Our senses, our minds, our emotions and thoughts: all these are stimulated on Shabbat.

Years ago, I lived in downtown Washington DC. It is a beautiful city, and often on Shabbat afternoons, I used to take long walks along the National Mall and the banks of the Potomac River, reveling in the views of national monuments and nature that make the District of Columbia so majestic. One weekend, an old friend from graduate school visited. We had a great time together, and on Shabbat afternoon, I took her on one of my habitual long walks around the monuments. We had a fantastic day; my friend had never

visited Washington before, and we talked for hours about the meaning behind the monuments, about the city, and generally catching up.

My friend was not Shabbat-observant, and even though she knew I would never do so, she stopped frequently on our walk to buy coffee, to buy T-shirts, to buy snacks, and souvenirs. By the end of the afternoon, as we returned to my apartment, my friend sighed that she had had a wonderful time, but regretted that she'd spent so much money. I smiled and commented that I hadn't spent a penny. Even though my friend was aware I hadn't bought anything, nor even carried a purse, during our walk, she was still startled. "Not a penny?" she cried; "I should start keeping Shabbat, too," she joked.

I occasionally remember that exchange on Shabbats today, as my family enjoys Shabbat afternoon. During the week, it often seems as if every little thing involves a commercial transaction. My kids take art classes and ballet, I take exercise classes, we go to pools, museums, water parks, stores. Everything is structured; everything comes with a calculated price tag. Sure, we all enjoy hanging out, taking walks, and reading at home, but sometime these unstructured activities wind up taking a back seat to the relentless demand of pre-arranged ways to spend our time. Increasingly, I find, the times that we really do take the time to be creative, to entertain ourselves, are on Shabbat, when many other activities are prohibited. I also have found that when my family and I look back on the most happy, memorable occasions of our weeks, they are almost always found (surprisingly, perhaps) among those open, free hours during which we shape our own agendas and invent our own amusements to share.

More importantly, perhaps, Shabbat also gives us the chance to strain to reach a higher "madrega": to live for a few hours each week on a higher level. Shabbat is my main time each week not only to enjoy the company of my family and friends, but also to read books on Jewish topics, to study Torah, and to contemplate deeper thoughts than laundry and what to make for dinner. Many of my friends and I enjoy going to lectures on Jewish subjects given on Shabbat afternoons. If you live in an area where this is an option, you might want to try attending a lecture (called a "shiur" in Hebrew): studying the Torah and Jewish traditions inspires us on Shabbat

and helps to enrich the day. If you live in an area without a strongly established Orthodox Jewish community, you might want to try finding a study partner with whom to read and discuss books on Jewish subjects on Shabbat. Many people also set aside time each Shabbat to read books on Jewish subjects by themselves. I often read Jewish books to my children on Shabbat; by studying Torah and pondering ethical and philosophical questions on Shabbat, we can elevate ourselves, and make our Shabbats even more holy, meaningful, and transformative to our Jewish souls.

Like all other areas of Shabbat, enjoying a successful Shabbat afternoon takes planning ahead of time. I'll always remember speaking once with a Jewish man who reminisced to me that when he was a child, his parents demanded that he and his siblings be Shabbat-observant, but they lived in a town with no other Shabbat-observant families, and he was incredibly bored and resentful each week with "nothing to do." Needless to say, when he was an adult, this individual was no longer Shabbat-observant in the slightest. (Although his siblings were: you can never tell how even a limited experience of Shabbat will affect impressionable children.) When I heard this man's story, I made a promise to myself that I would do everything in my power to make sure my own family experienced Shabbat as a day of promise and fun, instead of a day of limitations and monotony.

This isn't always easy, especially at first, as people begin to transition towards observing Shabbat in a traditional way. Many of us are used to being very busy outside our homes much of the day, and plugged in when we are at home, communicating, watching, and playing with electronic items. The thought of turning all that off can be daunting. The thought of turning it all off so we can sit around and talk about Torah can be beyond daunting: it can be downright off-putting. It is all very well to hear little homilies about Judaism occasionally, or even to attend a class or some services, but the thought of devoting 25 hours to a traditional Jewish Shabbat can seem overwhelming, even if you are attracted to the idea of trying it. If you are trying to drag along a reluctant or skeptical family, it can seem nearly impossible.

Singles

For singles, Shabbat observance poses some special challenges, but it also promises great rewards. As a single person, particularly if you live alone, you have a special challenge to find other people with whom to enjoy Shabbat. I've had plenty of solitary Shabbat meals over the years, and while at times a little solitude can be refreshing and relaxing, too many weeks of being on your own can begin to feel lonely and cheerless. (At its worst, I remember thinking once that keeping Shabbat alone was akin to sitting at a red light at a deserted intersection late at night: what was the point of following these rules when I was all alone in keeping them?) Shabbat is a time for creativity and growth, not for inertia and loneliness. It is crucial — for your mental health, and your spiritual health — to share Shabbat with other people. Yet it can be hard to approach others when you want to be included in their Shabbat plans or invited over for Shabbat meals: nobody wants to feel like a charity case, looking for a host.

The most attractive solution is to seek out shuls and communities that have large, active single populations. If you are lucky enough to live in an area with several Orthodox shuls, try visiting each of them to scope out the social life there. Ideally, you'll find a fun community of like-minded people who share Shabbat with each other, trading meal invitations, plans for Torah study, walks, and other activities. Many religiously observant singles are lucky enough to live in shared apartments with other Shabbat-observant roommates. Even if you find only one or two like-minded others, it can still be invaluable. For a while, one good friend and I called each other our "Shabbat partners." We ate meals with each other, introduced each other to our friends, and in general ensured that our Shabbats were meaningful and fun. Even though my "Shabbat partner" and I have lived many thousands of miles apart for many years now, I still have such a warm feeling of fondness whenever I think of her: we shared so many wonderful hours of Shabbat together; some of our most intense hours each week were spent in each other's company. Together, we learned Torah on long Shabbat afternoons, had heart to heart conversations, or sometimes just sat reading the newspaper together. We were in a similar place in our

lives then, and each was able to share what the other was going through and be supportive.

Another way that single people can ensure they enjoy meaningful company on Shabbat is to be the one who does the inviting. Invitations for meals are common currency in Shabbat-observant communities, and once you begin inviting people to your home for Shabbat lunch or dinner, you will likely soon find yourself receiving invitations in return. If your shul offers Shabbat afternoon classes or lectures, that's another way to connect with people on Shabbat. Attending a weekly lecture on the weekly Torah portion, for instance, is a common Shabbat activity in many communities, and a great way to help make your Shabbat afternoon meaningful.

As a single person, you also have the unique ability to spend significant time with old or sick people who often long for visitors. For years, while I lived in London for graduate school, I spent every Shabbat afternoon with my Great-aunt Cissie (may her memory be for a blessing). Aunt Cissie had very few visitors, and I know the many hours I spent sitting with her in her tiny kitchen on Shabbat were one of the highlights of her week. But (something I didn't anticipate) they were also the highlight of mine. I had the liberty in those days to spend my time doing what I wanted, with whom I wanted; there was no place else I had to be those Shabbat afternoons, and nobody else I had to be available for. I was able to develop a deep relationship with my great-aunt that has enriched and comforted me my entire life, even in the many years since her death. If you are a single person, looking for a community on Shabbat, and wishing to develop deep bonds with people that enrich your life and your Shabbats, spending time getting to know older people in a Shabbat setting is yet another option to consider.

Finally, aside from the issue of company, Shabbat is a valuable time for people to pursue holiness. Being a single person places you in an optimal role to do this. I remember the years I lived alone as the most intense, personal time of my life. Never before nor since have I been able to develop my thoughts as precisely, to explore avenues of knowledge that interested me, to work on my own character traits and religious observance, trying to reach higher "madregas," or "levels," of being. It was only when I was an adult and single that I was able to easily become religiously observant in

the first place: I was beholden to no one, and could follow my passions and my interests in Judaism wherever I desired. I was able to attend lectures, travel to Shabbatons (conventions where people spend a Shabbat together as a group, often sponsored by clubs or big Jewish organizations such as the Orthodox Union, www.ou.org), and befriend new and different people.

For a while, while I was single, my Shabbats were on a much higher "madrega," or level, than I've ever been able to enjoy since. On Shabbats when I was single, I had my own personal custom never to read secular books or magazines; everything I read on Shabbat had a Jewish component. (I wasn't being original: many Shabbat-observant Jews make efforts to occupy themselves with Jewish thoughts instead of secular reading and conversation on Shabbat.) I studied Torah each Shabbat with a study partner, and made a wide range of friends and acquaintances from whom I learned a great deal. If you are single, treasure these Shabbats. Reading books on Jewish subjects, taking long walks, even just napping and relaxing, can all create a beautiful Shabbat afternoon, even during those times you are not sharing it with anyone else. Resist the urge to not make an effort; even when you are alone, Shabbat is still a special time. It can be a time to pause, to recognize those things in life you are grateful for, to reorient yourself towards God and Judaism, and can, if we let it, be a time of great personal growth.

Couples

Ideally, if you are married, your growing interest in traditional Shabbat observance will be mirrored precisely by your supportive, loving spouse, whose every thought and inclination corresponds perfectly, at all times, with your own. Sigh. Of course, in the real world, even though our spouses might be very loving and supportive in general, it will often be the case that one partner will be more interested in pursuing more traditional Shabbats than the other. This was certainly the case when my husband and I were first married. I was much more used to traditional, Orthodox Shabbats than my husband was: he loved many of the rituals and ideas surrounding

Shabbat but had rarely kept all the mitzvas of Shabbat for a full day (and was not exactly raring to try).

Many of my friends over the years have described similar scenarios to me. In fact, some of my friends tell me I was incredibly lucky that my husband had a positive attitude towards Shabbat at all; unfortunately, many modern Jews harbor deep-seated antipathies to Jewish practice, and can be hostile to their spouses' experiments with traditional Judaism.

If your spouse is downright hostile to Judaism, I think there is little point in trying to win them over with conversation. The more you try to explain why you are interested in keeping Shabbat, the more you might find yourself at odds, eventually even arguing. Instead, you might try to remember that actions speak louder than words. As you explore keeping Shabbat in a traditional manner, it is possible that your spouse will come to enjoy some aspects of it with you: Shabbat dinner, for instance, or taking a Shabbat walk on Saturday afternoon. There are so many aspects of Shabbat that are fun and non-threatening; you might find yourself winning over your spouse with the pleasantness of these rituals. (I often think of some of my relatives in this regard. An Orthodox Shabbat dinner is not what many are used to, yet over the years I've noticed our relations have accepted a remarkable number of invitations for Friday night dinner, returning again and again to share this meal with us. While in the beginning we listened to the occasional — or not-so-occassional — protest about all the ritual involved, over the years the protests have died down, yet our relatives have kept coming. It seems that a traditional observance of Shabbat has grown on them, winning them over through its sheer beauty.)

More importantly, whether you are facing indifference or actual hostility from your spouse, if you show that you value your Shabbat observance and are serious about doing it, you will eventually earn respect, and then acceptance. People value authenticity. And they sense authenticity, too: if you waver in your beliefs, other people will too, but if you are strong in them, you'll earn others' respect. Think for a moment of any vegetarians you know. Many people know someone who is strongly, ideologically, committed to vegetarianism. Do the people around them ridicule them? Demean them? Try to get them to change? That's not the case for the

vegetarians I know; on the contrary, people respect their decisions not to eat meat, and cater to their dietary needs. People value authenticity. Once a person adopts a deep-seated belief or practice, it is very often the case that those around them grow to respect it. Not everyone might share your Shabbat practices, but if you demonstrate your commitment to them and remain true to them, those around you will eventually come to accept, even admire, your decisions.

On a practical level, there is a great deal you can do to make Shabbat palatable to a reluctant spouse. First, you can make Shabbat pleasurable for them. This is what I tried to do when I was first married. I made nice Shabbat meals, of course, and made sure that our apartment felt "Shabbosdich" (Shabbat-like): I'd tidy up, and shower and change into nice clothes before candle lighting. (Notice: I did it all myself. I knew that this was my interest more than my husband's, so I made the effort; I didn't want my husband to associate Shabbat with being nagged to do something he wasn't even that excited about.)

My husband loves reading about current affairs, so I used to stop by a newsstand on my way home from work on Friday afternoons and buy him the latest issue of every news magazine I could find. I made plans for Friday night and Saturday afternoon. I tried to be pleasant on Shabbat. When my husband wasn't ready for a particular piece of Shabbat observance, I tried very hard to bite my tongue and not complain. Above all, I wanted Shabbat to feel like an enjoyable, special time for him. I never wanted it to become a source of tension and irritation for us. (I'm not saying that I always succeeded, but my goal was for everything connected with our Shabbats to be peaceful and pleasant.) To some extent, I did succeed: our Shabbats became special times, better than the rest of the week. After a while, my husband began to find the Shabbat-related activities he enjoyed more satisfying than other activities like talking on the phone and watching TV.

Another major part of working out a way in which you and your spouse wish to keep Shabbat is the presence of guests. Inviting guests to our homes on Shabbat is important for many reasons, but it has one central, very practical benefit: having guests around keeps us on our best behavior. When you are aspiring to create a nice Shabbat atmosphere in your home, the presence

of a guest can go a long way to helping everyone stay civil and focused on Shabbat. I once shared an apartment with a very funny friend who used to joke that when we wanted to end a party, she and I should just start screaming at each other about the cleaning-up, and everyone would leave. In real life, this is precisely what most of us avoid. Guests keep us civil. If you worry that your spouse might lose interest in Shabbat dinner mid-way through, inviting Shabbat guests can help keep the evening focused. It is a sad truth that we are often nicer and kinder to acquaintances than we are to our own families; we can turn this to our advantage, however, by giving our Shabbat meals the formality that entertaining bestows.

Closely related to this is another important benefit of guests. The relationships we have influence us, and the "couple" friends that spouses have together often help shape their marriage. As you embark upon a Shabbat-observant lifestyle, you will be aided immeasurably by friendships with other couples and families who are Shabbat-observant. We can learn a lot from friends whose religious observance is something we want to emulate. Most importantly, perhaps, we can simply enjoy ourselves as we share our Shabbats with other people. Judaism is meant to be practiced in a community; we are not meant to experience it alone, nor even only with our spouse. Reaching out to other people and sharing our Shabbats with them enriches not only our Shabbat experiences, but also our lives, as we share this important time in our weeks with others.

Families with children

Shabbat with kids is wonderful and rewarding. It can also be exhausting. There are few things more pleasurable than asking our children questions about the week's Torah portion on Shabbat, than taking a walk with them, than finally having the time to read them a long story or to share a snuggle. Shabbat can be a magical time to connect with our kids. Unfortunately, though, there is a converse side we have to work hard to keep at bay. I find there are few things more stressful than the cry "Mommy, I'm bored!" over and over again on Shabbat, knowing that my usual arsenal of distractions

(CDs, art projects, calling up friends) is unusable. How do we ensure that our Shabbats are times of pleasure and bonding, and not times of tedium and frustration for children?

I vividly remember one particular Shabbat that was a turning point for me, when my kids were very young. The entire Shabbat I felt sluggish; I thought I was coming down with something. My kids were bored and restless, and I felt bad for all of us that I was too under the weather to play with them more. I remember thinking to myself that once Shabbat was over, I would go to bed early. Well, to my great surprise, Shabbat ended, the kids started playing a CD and got out their art supplies, and I suddenly felt wide awake and fine. I couldn't believe it, and wondered why I hadn't felt so good all of Shabbat. The answer hit me: I'd had no plans during the day. Instead of focusing on all the wonderful things I could do with my children on Shabbat, I think I was concentrating in the back of my mind on all the restrictions instead. Shabbat is obviously meant to be relished rather than endured, and that Saturday night I made a resolution for myself: to plan activities, guests, fun, wonderful things for my family on Shabbat. I realized that, just as I need to cook and clean before Shabbat if I want my Shabbat to go smoothly, so, too, I need to spend a little time planning activities. There is a lot of preparation that goes into a fun Shabbat; especially with children, they don't just happen. But with some work and effort, the return can be huge.

One of the first things I did in my new Shabbat mindset was scour the house for fun toys that my kids didn't usually play with. I emptied out an enormous cardboard diaper box, covered it with wrapping paper, and labeled it "Shabbat Toys." Into this box I put some of my kids' best toys. I felt a little mean taking them away from my kids, but I comforted myself with two thoughts. One was that like many modern kids, my children have so many toys they don't always have the time to focus on them all. By reserving some toys for Shabbat only, they might play more often with them than if those toys were available every day. (And, indeed, I've found that's been the case: they play with their Shabbat toys each week as if they were really special.) Also, I was confident that by reserving some exclusive toys for Shabbat, I was going to enhance my kids' Shabbats, and thereby

give them a more valuable gift than any toy. The toys in the box have changed a bit over the years, but some have remained classics: a beautiful bingo set; some old-fashioned dolls I picked up in a sale; books; and a set of dominoes. Other great Shabbat-friendly toys you might want to consider setting aside for fun Shabbat play include dolls houses, dress-up costumes, a puppet theatre, and board games.

When Shabbat rolls around, I find that these special toys my children don't see the rest of the week can see them through at least a few hours. Some weeks we luck out, and they remain in great moods throughout Shabbat. My husband and I also try to make Shabbat magical for our kids in many other ways. On Shabbat (unlike the rest of the week), they can eat lots of dessert, we let them camp out in each other's bedrooms or sleep in the guest room, and I try to set out especially appetizing foods for breakfast, like muffins or cut-up fruit they can dip in sugar. We try to invite their (also Shabbat-observant) friends over for lots of play dates, and we're often lucky enough to be invited out to friends' homes as well on Shabbat.

But all of this only goes so far. There comes a time each Shabbat when, as parents, we must make a big effort to keep the atmosphere "Shabbosdich" and nice. The moment might come late in day on Saturday, after the kids have exhausted all their play and want to hear a story. (On very bad weeks, it comes at 6 a.m. on Shabbat morning, as they start fighting with each other.) I want my children to love Shabbat, so at these moments, I paste a (fake) smile on my face, and make a big effort to take them for a walk, or set up a board game, or read them a book. At times, I feel like dumping them all in the basement and lying down for a nap myself, but I don't. In Hebrew, I would say this is my "avodah," or vocation: I want to raise my children well, and I want to instill a love of Shabbat in them. So, just as I would somehow muster my strength for the task at hand if I were at work, I also shake myself awake, and focus at home when my children need me to help maintain a Shabbat atmosphere.

One major activity my husband and I do with our kids on Shabbat is read them books. My older kids can read on their own, but Shabbat is our time to plow through long classics and read them aloud. My husband calls it being the "reading slave," and indeed there have been Shabbat afternoons

when he and I took turns reading to our kids for hours. One year at parent–teacher conferences, I was shocked (and heartened) to find that by doing so we are helping our kids create beautiful memories. I went in to meet with my son's teacher, and she told me that each of the children in her class kept a journal. Every Monday morning, the students opened to a new page and recorded an event from their weekend. The teacher handed me my son's journal, and I got a lump in my throat as I flipped through it. On nearly every page was a picture of my son sitting on a couch with my husband or me, and a caption describing the book we had read to him on Shabbat. He could have drawn and written about anything, his teacher told me, but week after week, my son, thinking about the highlights of his entire weekend, thought of those Shabbat hours that we spent reading to him.

Another wonderful Shabbat activity for families is board games. I always felt a little guilty about playing all these frivolous games with my kids on Shabbat; I felt we should somehow be doing something more spiritually elevated instead. Then one day a very good, extremely Orthodox, friend of mine called me, mortified. She and her kids had gone somewhere and been introduced to a great, eminent, famous Orthodox rabbi. The rabbi chatted with her children, and asked them, in teacher mode, what it is we do on Shabbat. My friend fully expected her young children to say "make Kiddush" or "go to shul," but instead, they answered the rabbi loudly: "We play Monopoly!" I had to laugh. It might not be as spiritual as studying Torah or praying, but playing family board games can be lots of fun, and can lead to some great conversations and wonderful moments of togetherness. My own kids love the game "Sorry"; it takes a long time, and we don't seem to get to it much during the week, but on Shabbat, we often find the time to set it up and play together. Even if the thought of playing a board game with your kids is unappealing, remember that your children will love it. We might not always feel like playing on their level, but if we want them to love Shabbat, we as parents have to make an effort to ensure it is a special time for our kids.

Learning Torah

Traditional Judaism places a high value on learning Torah at all times, and particularly on Shabbat. It is natural on this day when we seek extra holiness to look for it through this, one of the most important of Jewish activities. (In fact, Judaism teaches that the world rests on three "pillars": prayer, good deeds, and learning Torah.) Unfortunately, in English, many people talk about "studying" Torah. This makes it sound hard, boring, and unpleasant. I used to study algebra in high school; there is no way I want to study it again, and the phrase "studying Torah" makes me think of it, and all the homework I used to do as a kid.

In traditional Jewish circles, people say they "learn" Torah. This comes from the Yiddish word for studying, "lern," but it has a very different connotation today. "Learning" Torah is gaining new insights into the Torah: it is hearing and thinking about different ways to regard God and the world that He created for us. Hearing a five-minute devar Torah ("word of Torah") in shul thus counts as "learning" Torah. Having a spirited discussion with a friend about what the Torah is trying to teach us in a particular story or passage is also "learning" Torah. Reading a book about Shabbat or the Jewish holidays to our kids is "learning" Torah, too. There is of course a place for more rigorous Torah learning in traditional Judaism: people often set aside time each week (or each day) to study Jewish texts with a study partner, and many Jews attend weekly classes on Jewish topics, as well. But any contemplation of the Torah and its many commentaries counts as "learning," too. Particularly if you are just beginning to observe Shabbat in a traditional manner, you might find it more manageable to take small steps at first to learn Torah, and to add spirituality to your Shabbats in this way.

One of the main stumbling blocks for many modern Jews in their quest to learn Torah seems to be, ironically, the "Torah" they already learned as a kid in Hebrew or Sunday school. I think the entire system of Hebrew and Sunday schools through which most secular Jewish communities transmit Jewish knowledge is broken — and I'm speaking as a former Sunday school teacher! We teach our kids "Bible stories," unconnected to

anything practical in their lives, for a few years. Then our kids turn 13 and graduate, rarely to hear anything about these Bible stories again. We might not actually say to our kids, "Look, the Bible is confusing and strange, but don't worry, because it's not too important anyway," but our kids get that message loud and clear.

I sometimes think that many Hebrew and Sunday schools are like the ice skating lessons I arrange for my children. I don't really care whether my kids can ice skate or not, but lots of other children seem to enjoy it, so I signed up my kids for lessons, too. But I'm not too invested in it. I never ice skate along with them, and I don't really expect them to pursue ice skating for many years, anyway. Is it possible that one of my children will (shockingly) turn out to have a passion and a talent for ice skating, and become a serious skater for their entire life? Doubtful. So it is with much Jewish education today. It is entirely possible, of course, for children to be touched by a few years of Hebrew School and seek to integrate Jewish values into their lives, but it doesn't happen often. We drum the message into our kids that Jewish learning is something just for children, that it will take place once or twice a week for a few years, that it will consist of pleasant homilies and sweet stories, not that it is a deep and crucial part of all of our lives. By the time we are adults, many of us have an aversion to learning those childish "Bible stories" we recall from our pre-bar mitzvah and bat mitzvah days. It is like being asked to take the story of Goldilocks and the Three Bears seriously, and to try to somehow find life lessons in it: pointless and a little silly.

However, when adults (and children, too) do begin to learn about the Torah in a traditional way, they are often amazed at the real, grown-up wisdom and profundity it contains. The traditional Jewish approach to learning Torah is extremely different from that taught to many Jewish children. We are not meant to read an (often inaccurate) translation of a Bible story into English, ponder it for a moment, and then shrug our shoulders in confusion and move on. The many narratives the Torah contains are perplexing at first glance, and the traditional Jewish way of reading them is with the use of a cornucopia of rich Jewish commentaries that clarify their meanings, and often elucidate new concepts for us to ponder. The

stories of the Jewish Bible are often used as jumping-off places for writers to tease out their deeper meanings, and to put forward different ideas and worldviews. Just as in everyday life there is more than one way to view a situation, in Jewish commentaries on the Torah, there are myriad ways of reading one text.

There are two paths that I'd advocate for the beginner who is interested in learning Torah in a more traditional Jewish context. They might seem contradictory, but I've done both, and have gained great insights in different ways. One is to study Jewish texts from adult books and classes, especially those aimed at beginners. There are many excellent texts aimed at adults with limited backgrounds, and the number keeps growing; I cite a few recommendations to get you started at the end of this book. My other piece of advice, which I sometimes share with friends who are looking for a way to start acquiring familiarity with Jewish texts, came about when my children started school. I attended public school when I was a kid, but my husband and I decided to enroll our children in Orthodox Jewish day school. To my great surprise, the books and tapes my children started learning from weren't childish and obvious. They bore no resemblance to the Jewish books I'd studied as a kid, nor even to the texts I had been given to teach Sunday school. They were detailed and sophisticated, and conveyed real, concrete knowledge in ways that were clear, basic, and easy to understand. My kids' textbooks have taught them so much, and they have also taught me a great deal, more than I would ever have thought possible.

I'm not alone in thinking this. One of the funniest conversations I've ever had was with a good friend of mine, who also became religiously observant as an adult. She is very clever, has an Ivy League MBA, and has one of the best jobs of anyone I know, managing a multi million-dollar project for a huge multinational company. She flew into town one day to address an industry dinner at a conference, and before her speaking engagement, made the time to stop by my house for a chat. There she sat, poised, well-dressed, well-spoken, competent and bright, having just been flown a thousand miles to address a crowd of professionals about her sector. We talked mostly about our children. My friend told me excitedly that

she has learned so much about Judaism from her kids, and mentioned her young son's ArtScroll beginner's siddur (prayer book) and how informative it was. "My son has an ArtScroll siddur too!" I exclaimed, and I asked him to go get it. He did so, and carefully showed my friend all the prayers he'd learned and what he recites each day. My friend listened, then looked at me, cracked up, and said, "I meant the siddur for even younger kids — the one with pictures"! We couldn't stop laughing. Here we were, two women with advanced degrees, my friend with her amazing job, and we were learning so much from Jewish books aimed at preschoolers and young elementary-aged kids! It is funny, and maybe a little sad, but also informative. If you have children, I'd urge you to get some Jewish books aimed at the (Orthodox) youth market. You can read them together, and I guarantee you will learn a great deal, along with your child.

At the end of this book, I've included a very partial list of books and topics you might want to use to kick-start your own Shabbat Torah learning. Everybody has their own interests of course; the books and topics I recommend have been good for me as I have learned about Jewish topics, and will help introduce you to the world of Torah learning. In thinking about what Torah topics and sources to study, I have been inspired by the words of Rabbi Abraham J. Twerski, MD, when he commented on the opening lines of the book of Deuteronomy: "These are the words that Moses spoke to all of Israel." Rabbi Twerski expounds, drawing on the words of two famous Chassidic rabbis who also addressed this passage:

> The Rabbi of Lelov said that, "Every person felt that Moses' words were intended only for him, and for no one else." The Rabbi of Kosov said, "Whenever I speak to a group of people, I have no intention for anyone in particular. But if anyone feels my words were directed toward him, then it was really him for whom they were intended."

We no longer have the privilege of prophets who convey to us messages from God. Today, God speaks to us through various people. When we hear a person speak about character defects and the need for spiritual development and growth, and we feel that his words were intended for us, we

may be sure that they were indeed so. Somewhere deep down we have an awareness of what it is that we are lacking spiritually. When someone strikes a chord that calls our attention to our spiritual needs, that message was indeed intended for us.

We each find our own interests, our own ways of learning Torah. I hope the recommendations at the end of this book introduce you to some classic Jewish works. As you make your way through the world of Torah, there will be many beautiful books and articles that speak to you and draw you in. This is such an awesome journey to begin; Torah learning can lead us to greater wisdom, to more ethical behavior, to a feeling of closeness with God, and to a greater connection with our fellow Jews. Spending Shabbat learning Torah can transform our day, and can beautifully alter our entire week as well.

Other Shabbat activities

Traditionally, people who keep Shabbat in an Orthodox manner use Shabbat afternoon for learning Torah, for taking relaxing Shabbat naps, for visiting friends, reading and playing games, and for taking Shabbat walks. If you live in an area where other people are observing Shabbat, too, seeking them out can enhance your Shabbat; there is nothing like a friendly visit or shared activity to enrich a Shabbat and make it more satisfying. If, however, you live in an area with few or no other Jews who are keeping the laws of Shabbat, planning fulfilling Shabbat afternoons can be a challenge, particularly in the summer, when the sun sets late into the day and Shabbat lasts until well in the evening.

I have been in this situation many times, and have found that the best way for me to maintain a "Shabbosdich," or Shabbat-like atmosphere for myself was to avoid places and activities that were far removed from Shabbat. There is an idea in traditional Judaism that on Shabbat we refrain from doing "ordinary" things: that we avoid activities and actions that we are used to doing during the week, even if those actions do not technically violate any of the prohibitions of Shabbat. Thus, for instance, Jews

traditionally do not exercise on Shabbat. Doing so might not technically violate any laws of Shabbat, but exercising is seen as something that belongs to the work week, and thus not to the special day of Shabbat. (Shabbat-observant Jews can and do take long walks on Shabbat, so we can get a bit of physical activity that way.) I once walked to my local library on Shabbat, and was shocked at how "un-Shabbosdich" (not Shabbat-like) it felt to be there, surrounded by people oblivious of the holiday.

It can be a slippery slope on Shabbat to engage in activities we are used to performing when it is not Shabbat. Shabbat is our day to be special, to be holy, and in order to do so we have to make a break with the rest of the week. Our quest to live on a higher plane on Shabbat is helped by acting, dressing, and praying differently on this day. Our externals greatly influence the way we think and feel internally: when we behave differently on Shabbat, we come to regard it as a day apart. Only in this way can we hope to achieve the promise of Shabbat to raise ourselves to a higher, more holy level.

Finally, when I speak with friends about beginning to observe the traditional rules of Shabbat, I often, and surprisingly, find myself talking about taking Shabbat walks. Perhaps it is because in our modern, fast-paced lives there is little room for nature, but I have found that for some people, taking walks outside is one of the most profound, enjoyable activities they engage in on Shabbat. I have had so many conversations with people who at first dismissed the idea of Shabbat walks because they live in uninteresting locations: there doesn't seem to be much to see on a walk. I have found, though, that once I at least start walking, there are often an astonishing number of interesting things to observe. Maybe because so few of us are used to taking walks, seeing birds, trees, the occasional spring or pond is wonderful, unexpected, and intensely refreshing. Also, because during the week we so often drive places, there are a surprising number of unexplored locales near many of our homes. A healthy walker can cover three miles in an hour: that's a great distance. I have found some picturesque places to walk within that distance from my home. (And believe me, I live in pretty boring suburbia; it is not exactly Yosemite in my Midwestern American town.) And yet there are new places to explore, and pleasant routes to walk;

I always return from taking Shabbat walks feeling renewed and grateful to God for creating the nature that I usually only take the time to appreciate each Shabbat.

10

Saturday evening

Shalosh Seudos, the third meal

There was once a holy rabbi who wanted, more than anything else, to know the identity of one of the "Lamed Vavniks" — the 36 righteous men and women in each generation, without whom, Judaism teaches, the world cannot stand. This rabbi yearned to know the identity of them. He wanted to know what a perfectly righteous person looked like. "Please," he pleaded with God, "I desire more than anything to know a Lamed Vavnik. Meeting just one of these holy people would suffice!"

After years of pleading with God to show him a righteous person, God finally relented. God spoke to the rabbi in a dream, and disclosed to him the identity of one of His precious Lamed Vavniks. "There is a righteous man in a town on the other side of the mountains," God told him, "a Lamed Vavnik, by the name of Mordechai Goldstein." "This is all I will reveal." The rabbi awoke from this momentous dream feverish with excitement. As soon as the sun rose, he saddled his horse and set off to find Reb ("Sir") Goldstein.

The rabbi rode for days over the mountains until, at last, he arrived at the village of the precious Lamed Vavnik. It was Friday morning, and the rabbi knew he would have to get ready for Shabbat soon, but in the meantime he searched. "Where can I find Reb Mordechai Goldstein?" the Rabbi asked over and over. The people of the town merely shrugged: nobody seemed to know who this man could be. At last, as the sun hung low in the sky, a passer-by directed the rabbi to a crude wooden hut. He said, "Motti the town beggar lives here. Motti is a nickname for Mordechai; perhaps he is the Reb Mordechai you seek." The

passer-by shrugged hopefully, and walked on. Trembling, the rabbi knocked on the door of Motti the Beggar, wondering if this was the man he sought.

There was no answer. The rabbi knocked again, a little louder. Suddenly, the door was yanked open, and there stood a thin old man. He looked at the rabbi for a moment, then gave a kind smile. "How may I help you?" he asked. His voice was coarse and uneducated. "I am searching for Reb Mordechai Goldstein," the rabbi whispered. "Then you have come to the right house, the old man replied: I am Mordechai Goldstein, or, as I am usually known here, Motti the Beggar! Come in!"

The rabbi stepped over the threshold and looked around Motti's modest home. He couldn't help being a little disappointed. He had expected to find volumes and volumes of Talmud and other Jewish law, but instead saw just one or two books, occupying one small shelf. He expected to see hordes of people, come to benefit from the Lamed Vavnik's great wisdom and charity. But besides the rabbi, Motti had no visitors. Motti's wife stepped into the room. Motti informed her they had a guest for Shabbat, and she, smilingly, laid an extra plate at their small table. After a few last-minute preparations, Motti and the rabbi set off for shul to usher in the Shabbat.

All the way on their way to shul, the rabbi waited to see something special. He wondered what insight, what goodness, what extra holiness the Lamed Vavnik he accompanied possessed. Surely, the rabbi thought, something amazing will happen in shul.

But to the rabbi's surprise, all was ordinary as they daavened the Kabbalat Shabbat service, welcoming the Shabbat bride. His host daavened in an ordinary fashion, with no particularly special "kavana" or concentration. "Perhaps," thought the puzzled rabbi, the Lamed Vavnik will reveal his extraordinary holiness tonight, during dinner, maybe with a special devar Torah: the speech on a topic of Torah that one often delivers during Shabbat meals.

In due course, the rabbi and Motti returned home, but to the rabbi's shock, they enjoyed a small, ordinary Shabbat meal. Motti didn't even give a devar Torah, or mini-speech about the week's Torah portion. They enjoyed their meager food in companionable silence. Nothing seemed unusual, nothing seemed out of the ordinary, and the rabbi began to be bewildered. "Maybe something will happen tonight," he mused, as he went to sleep.

However, nothing strange occurred during the night, and the next morning when the rabbi accompanied Motti to shul to say the morning prayers, once again nothing remarkable occurred. Following services, the rabbi, Motti, and Motti's wife enjoyed another sparse Shabbat meal, and then Motti lay down for a long Shabbat nap. As Motti snored loudly in the next room, the rabbi grew frustrated. "I wanted so much to meet one of the righteous of the world," he lamented, "a Lamed Vavnik, and instead God has led me to this simple beggar!" Just then Motti gave a particularly loud snore, and the rabbi wept with disappointment.

Late in the afternoon, Motti roused himself and began to prepare for Shalosh Seudos, the third meal of Shabbat. Listlessly, the rabbi also rose and went to the table. He no longer expected to see anything unusual. But what he saw at the table shocked him.

Shabbat dinner and Shabbat lunch had been small, modest meals. Yet here on the table ready for Shalosh Seudos was spread a feast: a banquet fit for a king. With wide eyes, the rabbi sat down and took in the pheasants, the wine, the great loaves of golden challah bread, the salads, the soups, the steaks, stews, kugels, potatoes, the whole chickens, and the dazzling trays of iced cakes. He couldn't believe his eyes. Especially not when his host sat down and served himself heaping portions of each dish, as his wife sat proudly at the head of the table. Motti ate and drank with an appetite the rabbi had never seen. Each time the rabbi was sure Shalosh Seudos was over, Motti would reach across for another helping from one of the heaped serving dishes.

For an hour or more, the rabbi stared in amazement. Eventually, it dawned on him that here was the secret to Motti's extraordinary holiness. For how many people engage with gusto in this most forgotten of mitzvot, Shalosh Seudos? How many of us endow the third Shabbat meal with all the holiness and majesty which Motti afforded it? At last, the rabbi understood the secret of Motti the Beggar's greatness.

Shabbat's third meal is a peculiar meal. The Talmud instructs us to partake of three meals on Shabbat. Shabbat dinner on Friday night is the first of these meals. We might enjoy a bite to eat on Saturday morning, and another snack after shul at Kiddush, but these don't count as full meals in

the traditional Jewish sense. Traditional Judaism defines a full meal as one at which bread is served. According to this definition, the second Shabbat meal is Shabbat lunch, eaten after shul on Saturday afternoon. What of the third meal? After eating a large holiday lunch on Saturday, many of us don't feel like eating again a few hours later, near the conclusion of Shabbat. Yet this is precisely what the Torah directs us to do.

The third meal we eat on Shabbat, a late afternoon supper just before sundown on Saturday, is also puzzling because it is imbued with many mystical attributes. The Torah teaches us that being scrupulous in regard to eating the third meal on Shabbat saves us from the suffering that is foretold at the end of days, before the Messiah appears and ushers in an era of perfect happiness. It is also meant to help protect our souls after death. These are weighty matters, and it has always struck me as odd to contemplate a connection between them and the act of sitting down to a meal.

Many commentators through the years have discussed this surprising link. The most common explanation of this association is that this is a meal we eat entirely because God has commanded it. While we eat Shabbat dinner and Shabbat lunch in order to honor God, we also enjoy these repasts because we are hungry, as well. However, when Shalosh Seudos comes around, we are usually no longer hungry. Yet we force ourselves to sit anyway and rejoice a third time over a festive meal. This third meal is not for us; we partake of it purely to honor God. For this reason, Shalosh Seudos commands towering respect. In fact, there are two ways to refer to the third meal in Hebrew. We can say "seudah shlishit," which means "third meal"; many people do refer to the meal this way. A more common term to refer to it, however, is "Shalosh Seudos": "Three Meals": such is the importance of Shalosh Suedos that all three meals of Shabbat are present in this one.

It is still an odd thought that the best, most important way we can honor God is to eat an extra meal for Him. Certainly, there are many more difficult mitzvot. There are other mitzvot whose purpose we can clearly perceive, and which seem very important, for instance helping the poor or saving a life. Yet, the Torah singles out this mitzvah, Shalosh Seudos, as the one that will stave off disaster long after our present lives are over. Why? The connection between Shalosh Seudos and the events of the after-world and

Messiah are murky at best. All we can do is trust that God Himself sees this link more clearly than we do. Yet perhaps, as we contemplate this puzzling association, and wonder why the third meal on Shabbat is so important, we might gain extra insight into what God wants from us.

The fact that the most crucial mitvah we can perform to safeguard our souls from some bewildering metaphysical trials after our death is to enjoy a festive meal now hints at a profound truth. God wants us to be happy. He might not always want us to be happy in the ways we think we'll best find happiness. (I'd love to win the lottery, but obviously God has other plans for me.) But perhaps in being forced to enjoy many festive meals, to sit down to beautifully set tables with friends and family again and again, week after week, we are best conforming to the vision that God has for us. Perhaps the seeds of our highest joy are contained in the formula of sitting down, with our fellows, to an agreeable meal. When we think of the conversation, the hospitality, the song, and the words of Torah that are typical in Shabbat meals, perhaps we have found the key to achieving perfect human happiness.

When I plan Shalosh Seudos, I sometimes think of the dilemma posed in Pearl Buck's 1931 novel *The Good Earth*. The main character, a poor Chinese peasant, eats simple meals of pancakes with a little garlic for seasoning almost his whole life. At the end of the book, however, the peasant becomes rich, is able to eat his fill, and he suddenly finds that he requires special gourmet foods in order to feel hungry again. The book goes into great detail describing the exquisite delicacies he orders to stimulate his appetite, the rare vegetables, the tofu, the fine jasmine rice; when I read these passages, my mouth waters. This is what we have to do for Shalosh Seudos. It is not enough to serve some cholent and a kugel again, not after lunch, when we are usually no longer extremely hungry. In order for us to enjoy Shalosh Seudos, we often need something extraordinary to tempt us to the table.

Many Jewish sages have discussed what it is necessary to eat to satisfy the requirements of Shalosh Seudos, and there are various opinions. Many rabbis have said we only need to eat a tiny snack, such as a piece of fruit, to fulfill the mitzvah of Shalosh Seudos. Most authorities agree, however, that it is strongly desirable to eat bread at this meal. Shalosh Seudos

must commence before sunset (the time we lit Shabbat candles on Friday night). In the summer, this timing works out well; Shabbat lasts very late, and Shalosh Seudos can be eaten at a normal dinner time. In the winter, however, sunset can come mid-afternoon; at these times, I often think of Shalosh Seudos as more of a mid-afternoon tea.

Over the years, I've developed some Shalosh Seudos menus that my family and guests seem to enjoy. The meal can be more fun if you prepare unusual or entertaining food. My favorites are sushi, antipasti, and other spicy, Asian or Mediterranean dishes. Several piquant Shalosh Seudos recipes are found in Chapter 14. When all else fails, I've even served banana splits with all the trimmings; this has probably been my most successful Shalosh Seudos meal yet!

Shalosh Seudos "entertainments"

Shalosh Seudos often has a bittersweet quality to it. It is fun, and gives us another chance to sit together with guests or family, but it also means that Shabbat is drawing to a close. Because I find that my mood and my kids' moods are somewhat subdued then, we have started a number of family traditions for this meal. (These are not required in any way by Jewish law, but they simply have served my family well as a way to lend even greater meaning and enjoyment to our Shalosh Seudos.) My kids always want me to tell them a story. (I suspect that some older children might enjoy a good story during a quiet family meal like Shalosh Seudos, too.) Over the years, we've developed two long, ongoing stories together. One is a whimsical tale about a family of birds. When we sit down at the Shalosh Seudos table together, we often start thinking immediately about what new adventure the birds can have that week: it is a fun, bonding experience that brings us all closer together.

The other "series" is about a group of children, much like my own, who travel the world together, experiencing new things. Shabbat afternoons are so leisurely, I have the time to spin tall tales with my kids, and my kids have the time (and, in the absence of distractions from the non-Shabbat world,

the patience) to listen. This is my time to teach my kids things, in guise of our weekly stories. Some weeks I tell them about travelling to different countries, so we can talk about different cultures and Jewish communities around the world. Some weeks we imagine they are visiting far-flung relatives, so they can feel closer to their cousins, aunts, and uncles. (My kids have one cousin who lives in Jerusalem whom they've never met, yet they feel they know her intimately because of these weekly Shalosh Seudos stories, in which they "visit" her often.) I don't always feel like making the effort late on a Shabbat afternoon, but afterwards I'm always glad I forced myself. With a little planning and a lot of effort, we're able to make Shalosh Seudos feel like a special, magical time each week.

Even if you don't go in for stories during this meal, it is easy to create a beautiful aura around Shalosh Seudos in a traditional way: by singing the beautiful "zemirot" or songs that are customary for this third meal. These are moving songs, with bittersweet melodies. The most traditional songs to sing at Shalosh Seudos, which usually cap off the singing during this meal, are Psalm 23, which famously declares "though I walk in the valley overshadowed by death, I will fear no evil, for You are with me," and the beautiful sixteenth-century song "Yedid Nefesh," or "Beloved of my Soul," which talks about the yearning our souls have for God. I find there are so few occasions during the ordinary work week to express or even think about sentiments such as these. Shalosh Seudos is a perfect platform for us to pause and take one last lingering look at Shabbat, and to recognize the enormity of this gift that God has given us. The words to these and other songs you can sing at Shalosh Seudos are found in Chapter 12.

Blessings over food

Before Shabbat lunch and dinner, we make the blessing over bread, and that covers our entire meals. In Judaism, however, there are six blessings to make over various foods. "Hamotzi," or the bread blessing, is the best known. But what if we are not eating bread? Then we choose the appropriate blessing to match our meal.

Baruch Atah Adonoi, Eloheinu Melech Ha'Olam . . .
Blessed Are You My God, King of the World . . .

(over bread)
. . . *Hamotzi Lechem min Ha'Aretz.*
. . . Who Brings forth bread from the Land.

(over pastries)
. . . *Borei Minei Mizanot.*
. . . Who Creates types of grain.

(over wine or grape juice)
. . . *Borei Pri Ha-Gafen.*
. . . Who Creates Fruit of the Vine.

(over fruits:)
. . . *Borei Pri Ha-Etz.*
. . . Who Creates Fruit of the Tree.

(over vegetables:)
. . . *Borei Pri Ha-Adama.*
. . . Who Creates Fruit of the Ground.

(over all else:)
. . . *She-hakol Ni-hi-yeh Bi-Devaro.*
. . . Who Brings everything into being through His word.

Prayer following a meal

Following Shalosh Seudos, we say the concluding prayers after a meal. If we've eaten bread, we recite "Birkat HaMazon," the blessing after a meal with bread (Chapter 15). For meals that contain no bread, Jewish tradition provides us with two other, much shorter, blessings:

For most meals and snacks, we say the short, beautiful blessing thanking God for providing food that maintains all living things:

Blessed are You, God, our Lord, King of the Universe, Who made many souls, and their needs; for everything that You Created to be there for them, to maintain their lives. Blessed is the life of the world.

If our meal consisted of any of the seven foods that our ancestors used to bring as offerings to God in the Beit Hamikdash, our ancient Temple in Jerusalem, then we recite a slightly longer blessing after our meal. The seven foods are wheat, barley, grapes (including wine or grape juice), figs, pomegranates, olives, and dates. This blessing recalls the beauty of our Temple in Jerusalem, where in ancient times we would bring these foods for feasts and offerings before God, and looks forward to the rebuilding of our Temple in Messianic times.

Blessed are You, Our Lord, King of the World,

(for grain say)
for the livelihood and for being provided for

(for wine say)
for the vine and the fruit of the vine

(for fruit say)
for the tree and the fruit of the tree

The blessing of Israel
And for the crops of the field, and for the good, spacious, desirable Land (of Israel) that You designated for and that you bequeathed to our ancestors, for its fruits and for the goodness of its weeks.

The blessing of the Temple
Have mercy, God, Our Lord, on Your people Israel, and on Jerusalem Your city, and on Zion, the place of Your Honor, and on Your Altar and on Your Temple.

The blessing of Jerusalem
And rebuild Jerusalem, Your holy city soon, in our days, and raise us up to it, and make us happy in its buildings, and allow us to eat of its fruits, and be

satisfied from its goodness, and allow us to bless You greatly in its holiness and in its purity.

(Note: these blessings are meant to be recited after all meals, not just Shalosh Seudos, and not only on Shabbat. Even if you do not habitually recite them, however, doing so on Shabbat is yet another way you can enhance your experience on this holy day.)

Mincha: the afternoon service

There is no one particular time we have to daaven Mincha, the afternoon service, on Shabbat (nor any other day). It should simply be recited sometime between the middle of daylight hours and sunset. In some shuls, people daaven Mincha together after eating Kiddush, before they go home for Shabbat lunch. (This is particularly common in winter, when the days are short.) Some shuls hold the mincha service right before sunset, and then offer Shalosh Seudos to the congregants. (This is common in summer.) For those who cannot make it to shul or do not have access to an Orhthodox shul on Shabbat, you can daaven Mincha yourself at any point during Shabbat afternoon.

Mincha on Shabbat begins with the prayer "Ashrei," which enumerates all the wonderful qualities of God. This is followed by a mystical prayer, which incorporates words known to be uttered by the Seraphim, the angels that God created in the Heavens who sing praises to God all day long. Following this enchanting, moving prayer, if we are daavening with a minyan, we remove the Torah from its Aron, or cabinet, with blessings and psalms, read the first three sections of that week's Parsha, or Torah portion, and then, with more songs, blessings and psalms, return the Torah to its Aron. (Note: each Jews who is at least 12 if a girl and 13 if a boy is considered a "bat mitzvah" or "bar mitzvah"; it does not matter at all if they ever had a ceremony, party, certificate, or other event to mark the occasion.)

Following the Shabbat Mincha Torah service, we daaven yet another version of the "Shemoneh Esrei" prayer. If we are daavening with a minyan,

the person leading the service makes a second recitation of the "Shemoneh Esrei," during which we recite the holy "Kedusha" prayer. We conclude the service with the prayer "Aleinu," in which we thank God for making Israel a distinct nation, and a recitation of the traditional Jewish mourners' prayer.

Havdalah: marking the end of Shabbat

Shabbat is 25 hours long: it begins at sundown on Friday (though you can light your candles and bring it into your home a little earlier, if you prefer), and it expires 25 hours later, an hour after sunset.

On clear evenings, it is very easy to know when Shabbat is over: we step outside and look into the evening sky. When three small stars are clearly visible in the sky, Shabbat is over. Sadly, for many of us, star-gazing is a lost art. Yet this weekly hunt for stars to mark the ending of Shabbat ensures that we spend time each week looking into and appreciating the magnificent night sky. Even if it only takes a few minutes, it is refreshing to peer at God's handiwork this way. Spending this time, searching for stars in the darkening sky, provides an appreciation of the natural world that is lacking in many of our modern lives.

For me, standing outside with my family in the late Saturday evening, waiting for stars to appear in the sky, is a beautiful ritual. The sky is a stunning sapphire color at that hour, we hear the last frenzied cheeps of the birds as they end their days, in warmer weather we appreciate a cool evening breeze, and in winter the air is so cold and still and the snow sparkles like jewels. We often remain outside for a while, just appreciating the evening and enjoying this unusual encounter with the outdoors.

When my oldest son was very young, he reminded me of how divorced we are from the natural world most days outside of Shabbat, and how beautiful it can be on Shabbat to live our lives according to the rhythms of nature. Once, on an ordinary weekday, we walked to visit some neighbors after dark. As I pushed my son in his stroller, I told him, "Look up in the sky! The stars are so pretty." My tiny son looked up and was shocked.

"Mommy," he cried, "I thought there were only stars on Shabbat!" For this little boy, steeped in the magic and ritual of Shabbat, the appearance of twinkling diamonds in an indigo sky each week at the conclusion of Shabbat seemed a natural part of this dazzling, special, and holy day: yet one more wonder with which God has blessed us. When it is not Shabbat, we somehow always seem to be too busy to take the time to gaze at the night sky and appreciate the stars. The magic of the stars, for us and for many Jews, belongs to the slower tempo of Shabbat.

When we step outside each Saturday evening at the conclusion of Shabbat to examine the night sky, we are claiming some of the beauty and enchantment of the natural world for ourselves: we are embracing the beautiful world that God has made for us. As with many other aspects of Shabbat, this weekly holiday forces us to experience the beauty of the world around us, forces us to enjoy nature, to experience the best of everything we can muster, regularly, each week. When we spend a full 25 hours enjoying the fruits of all our labors, the abundance of God's gifts to us, the experience is overwhelming, opulent, and exquisitely satisfying. Capping it all off by gazing at the beautiful stars in the night sky seems appropriate.

What if it is cloudy? What if we cannot see three stars in the night sky? How do we know when Shabbat is over then? There's an interesting answer.

In Judaism, each "day" begins, counterintuitively, not in the morning or at 12 midnight, as in the secular calendar, but at sunset ("shkia" in Hebrew). The evening portion of the Jewish day is called "erev," or "evening." Thus, for instance, Friday night is known as "Erev Shabbat." (My grandmother of blessed memory even used to celebrate everyone's birthday the night before: she called it "erev birthday.")

For most purposes, a day ends at shkia, or sunset, too. But there are big exceptions: important days, such as Shabbat and holidays, end one hour *after* shkia. This prevents anyone from accidentally violating the sanctity of the day by making a slight mistake about the exact time of sunset. It also accrues precious extra moments for holy days, and allows us to imbue even more time with the power of Shabbat and holidays. If for some reason you are unable to see three stars in the sky on Saturday evening, wait one hour

after sunset. (You'll know what time sunset is, because that's the time you lit your Shabbat candles on Friday night.) Some authorities add a further 20 minutes, to make sure there are absolutely no mistakes and to prevent anyone from accidentally violating Shabbat, but these extra minutes are not universally accepted.

Once Shabbat is over, we say a brief prayer to acknowledge the passing of the day. This allows us to engage in all the activities that were prohibited on Shabbat, such as using electricity, travelling, bathing, writing, etc. We say:

Barukh atah Adonai, hamav'dil bein kodesh l'chol.
Blessed are You, Who Divides what is Holy from the Rest.

This ends Shabbat for us, but not fully. There is a longer ceremony to more completely mark the end of Shabbat, and to note the contrast between the holiness of Shabbat and the "ordinary" nature of the rest of the week. "Havdalah" in Hebrew means "division," and a ceremony known as "Havdalah" marks the final close to each Shabbat.

Before Havdalah, some women have the custom of reciting a beautiful prayer that was first composed by the great Chassidic (Jewish mystical) Rabbi Levi Yitzchok of Berditchev in Ukraine in the late eighteenth century. This touching prayer is written in Yiddish, the everyday language of many religious Jews then and now. Even though I'm not Chassidic, I like saying it: it focuses my thoughts on what is truly important in the coming week, as I ask God to bring me close to Him, to ensure that I have good friends, that I have a week of health and blessing. Because I cannot easily read Yiddish, I say this prayer in English.

"Gott fun Avrohom" ("God of Abraham")

God of Abraham, and of Isaac, and of Jacob, protect your beloved people Israel from all danger, in Your Goodness. As the beloved holy Shabbat slips away, bless us that this week and this month and this year should see us have perfect faith. Bless us with faith in the Torah scholars. Bless us also with love and closeness to good friends, with closeness to the Blessed Creator, with belief in the 13 principles of faith, in the coming of the Messiah, may it be soon, in

the Resurrection of the dead, and in the prophecy of Moses, our teacher, may peace be upon him.

Our Master of the World, You are the one who gives strength to the weary. Give your beloved Jewish people health and strength so we can love you and do your bidding, yours and no other, God forbid.

May this week, and this month, and this year, come to us with mercy, and health, and promise, and blessings, and success, and riches and honor, and children, and life, and bread, and Divine Providence, for us and for all of Israel, Amen.

Timing of Havdalah

There are some differing customs concerning the timing of Havdalah. Almost all Jews perform Havdalah as soon as possible after Shabbat ends. In fact, most Jews traditionally refrain from eating until after Havdalah. (This is incentive indeed!) However, this is custom, not law. In fact, we are technically permitted to perform Havdalah until Tuesday evening. This is because in mystical Jewish thought, the week is divided in two, with Shabbat as its hinge. Sunday, Monday and Tuesday are all meant to be bathed in the afterglow of Shabbat. Wednesday, Thursday, and Friday are part of the preparation for the next Shabbat. Thus, since a little of the Shabbat glow lingers until sundown on Tuesday night, it is permissible to make Havdalah until then.

In general, there are two types of people who seem to wait until Tuesday to make Havdalah: some adherents to the more mystically minded "Chassidic" Jewish groups, and lazy people. (I've made Havdalah on a Tuesday exactly once in my life, having neglected to purchase the necessary items before then, and found it a dispiriting occasion, lacking the grandeur and beauty of Havdalah performed on Saturday night. But some other people feel that delaying Havdalah until Tuesday gives the first half of their week extra holiness. To each his own.)

Havdalah is a short, beautiful ceremony that engages all our senses. It requires a few special supplies, which are easy to arrange. For Havdalah, you will need:

1   A candle with a least two wicks. The Torah stipulates that the flame

we use for Havdalah must be very bright, like a torch: it must have at least two wicks, so that its flame blazes brilliantly. There are many candles that are specially made for Havdalah; these can be purchased from almost any Judaica store or website. (Most Havdalah candles are very distinctive: a common style is a long, braided candle made up of six smaller candles.) If you do not have a special Havdalah candle with at least two wicks, that doesn't matter at all. Simply tie and hold two candles together so that their flames merge.

2 A cup of wine or grape juice. (The Torah says that when no wine or grape juice is available, we can use as a substitute something that people in our community drink instead of wine — but not water. Some people have the custom of only using other alcoholic drinks such as beer or whiskey when no wine is available; other people use milk or apple or orange juice when they have no wine or grape juice.)

3 At least two fragrant spices mixed together, to symbolize the sweetness we hope for in the week ahead.

4 Most Shabbat-observant Jews acquire special boxes in which to keep their Havdalah spices. We were given a very typical, ornate Havdalah set, which includes a spice box, for a wedding gift; it is beautiful, and sets can be purchased in many Judaica stores or websites (such as www.alljudaica.com or www.jewishsource.com). Later on, my children made all sorts of handmade spice boxes as projects in school. These are obviously more fun to use, even if they do somehow leak trails of dusty spices everywhere they're carried. You can try making your own out of matchboxes or any small box that can open, allowing you to smell the spices inside.

5 Here are some ideas for popular spices to use for Havdala; don't forget to use at least two: cinnamon, cloves, cardamom, nutmeg, allspice, ginger. In a pinch, I've even used herbal tea bags that contained a blend of spices.

It is customary at the start of Havdalah to turn off the lights. This allows us a clearer view of the light of the Havdalah "torch," which reminds us of the dazzling light of Shabbat. It also starkly illustrates the difference between

the holy, shining nature of Shabbat, and the darker, murky quality of the rest of the week. We light the Havdalah candle and give it to someone to hold. (There is a superstition that when an unmarried woman holds the Havdalah candle, the height at which she holds it signifies the height of her future husband; lots of single women consequently hold their Havdalah candles up very high!)

We next fill a cup with wine so that it is overflowing, and the person who is to lead Havdalah holds it in their hand, usually over a plate to catch the inevitable spills.

Havdalah opens with various quotes from the Torah, primarily from Psalms, which remind us that God will always help and protect us. At this moment of transition, when we leave the extra holiness of Shabbat behind, it is comforting to remind ourselves that God is always with us, every moment and every day.

We recite:

Behold God is my salvation, I shall trust and not fear — for God is my might and my praise — Lord — and He was a salvation for me. You can draw water with joy, from the springs of salvation. Redemption is God's, upon Your people is Your blessing, Selah. Lord, Master of armies, is with us, a stronghold for us is the God of Jacob, Selah. Lord, Master of armies, praised is the man who trusts in You. God save! May the King answer us on the day we call.

The above section is spoken only by the person performing Havdalah. (There is a tradition that Havdalah should be recited by a man, if one is present, since men have the stronger obligation to hear all of Havdalah; as in many Jewish rituals, men are presumed to need the discipline of rules and regulations much more so than women. Only if there are no men present do women lead Havdalah.)

The next line is recited by everyone present, young and old, male and female. This is the famous line from Megillat Esther, the Book of Esther, which tells the story of the Jewish holiday of Purim. After Mordechai and Esther thwarted the evil plan to destroy all the kingdom's Jews, the Torah

recounts that God heaped blessings upon our (the Jewish people's) heads. We recall this miracle, and God's many other, continuing miracles that He has performed for us, all reciting out loud together:

For the Jews there was light, gladness, joy and honor (Esther 8.16).

The person leading Havdalah then continues alone:

So may it be for us. I will raise the cup of salvations, and I shall invoke the name of God.
By your leave, my masters and teachers:
Blessed are You, Lord our God, Kind of the universe, Who creates the fruit of the vine.

All present say "Amen." (This is the blessing over wine or grape juice. We will drink the wine or juice, but only after Havdalah is completed.)

Blessed are You, Lord our God, King of the universe, Who creates types of fragrance.

All present say "Amen."

At this point, everyone present passes around the fragrant spices and smells them, hoping that the coming week will be (symbolically) scented as sweetly as these spices's perfumes.

Blessed are You, Lord our God, King of the universe, Who creates the illuminations of the fire.

All present say "Amen."

This blessing is over the Havdalah light. After we respond "Amen," we gaze at the reflected glow of the Havdalah flame in our fingernails. There are many mystical explanations for this curious ritual. My favorite of these is that one's fingernails always grow, and thus represent the continual nature of our of blessings.

I have always found this to be an intimate moment, as we internalize the Havdalah flame. Instead of simply responding "amen" to this blessing and gazing at the naked light, we enjoy its reflected glow on a part of our own bodies. This creates a beautiful, sensory experience, and I often find that the memory of these moments, gazing silently at my hands by the light of a candle, smelling sharply spicy scents, declaring my faith in God by the light of a flickering torch, stay with me strongly the rest of the week. They are so much more beautiful, real and visceral than anything that occurs in my ordinary day.

The leader continues:

Blessed are You, Lord our God, King of the universe, Who separates between holy and secular, between light and darkness, between Israel and the nations, between the seventh day and the six days of labor. Blessed are You, Lord, Who separates between holy and the rest.

The person leading Havdalah then drinks some of the wine or grape juice in his or her cup. (If he or she does not want to, it is acceptable to have someone else present drink it instead.) They then extinguish the candle by dipping it into the remaining wine, or into the wine that has sloshed out of the Havdalah cup into the dish below.

Some people at this point have the custom of dipping their fingers into the remaining Havdalah wine or grape juice. The thinking is that some last vestiges of Shabbat remain in it, making it holy, and some people dab their wet fingers on their eyelids (to give them perception) and in their pockets (to give them wealth).

Post-Havdalah songs

There are many traditional songs to sing immediately after Havdalah, before we turn on the lights and rejoin the ordinary, weekday world. In my own family, we sing two. Some people link arms and sway when they sing at this point. Jewish conceptions of modesty would prevent this in mixed company, but if you are with friends of the same gender, or with your close family, it can be very nice to link arms and sway. I always use

these moments to embrace my children while we sing together. The whole ceremony of Havdalah is so unusual, so beautiful, that this is always a moment of great tenderness and fellowship.

We first sing the opening verse of "Eliyahu HaNavi," or "Elijah the Prophet." Jewish tradition teaches that Eliyahu HaNavi will herald the coming of the Messiah, and at this moment of great importance we look forward to Messianic times by recalling Eliyahu HaNavi.

Eliyahu HaNavi	Elijah the Prophet
Eliyahu HaTishbi	Elijah the person from Tishav (where he was born)
Eliyahu HaGiladi	Elijah the person from Gilad (where he also lived)
Bimheira Bimheira	Quickly, Quickly
Yavo Eleinu	He will come to us
Im Moshiach Ben David	with Messiah, son of David (the Torah teaches that the Messiah will be a descendant of King David.)
Im Moshiach Ben David.	with Messiah, son of David.

Some people sing the much, much longer version of this iconic song (it can be found in Orthodox prayer books), and many other songs, as well, but my own family then segues into an easy, simple song (that is perfect for us, with our limited Hebrew backgrounds). Using the same tune, we sing the words "Shavua Tov," or "Good week," the traditional post-Shabbat blessing:

Shavua Tov	Good week
Shavua Tov	Good week
Shavua Tov	Good week
Shavua Tov	Good week
Shavua Tov	Good week

We then turn on the lights and look at each other, blinking. The majesty of Shabbat is over. We perform our Havdalah ceremony in our kitchen,

and I'm always amazed at how lurid the room looks after Havdalah. True, things are often a mess, and I often have little to look forward to the rest of the evening except cleaning up and doing a load of laundry, but I think it goes deeper than that. Following Havdalah, I always find that the lights seem too bright, the surfaces too harsh, people's voices too loud. As I come out of the holiness of Shabbat with a sharp bump, I'm always shocked at how ordinary everything seems: how flat. I soon get used to it, but it always makes me realize why the Torah calls Shabbat a taste of the World to Come: a foreshadow of Heaven.

Once you begin observing Shabbat in the traditional way, you too will see the amazing holiness that rushes at you throughout the day: the million opportunities for pleasure, for company, for thinking more creatively than ever one does amid all the distractions of the week, for the deep, profound satisfaction that Shabbat offers. In the moments after we switch on the lights following Havdalah, in that minute of adjustment between the "Holy" and "The Rest," the gap is easy to see. As I wrote at the beginning of this book, the feelings that one has on Shabbat are difficult to describe in words. If nothing else, I hope that this book can be a siren, a loud alarm, clanking, and calling insistently to you to "try it!" Of course the thought of following a traditional Shabbat with all of its rituals and constraints seems strange at first. But for the thousands upon thousands of Jews who do observe Shabbat in an Orthodox manner, and for the millions of our ancestors who did so before us, Shabbat was not strange at all. It was (and is) wonderful and perfectly natural: the focus of their week.

There is nothing so foreign, really, about reaching out and taking Shabbat for ourselves: it is there for us, a dazzling gift from God. If you are curious about Shabbat but don't feel you could ever take the leap to celebrating it, I will tell you to ignore the messages of the modern, secular world. Discard your prejudices and claim the gift that God has given us. This is what you were born for. This is the life you were meant to lead. It might feel odd to claim this gift, to pick up the tradition that you or your parents or your grandparents discarded, but it is there for you. It is waiting for you to take it. Shabbat is an enormous present. It is the sweetest day imaginable. Its traditions and its rituals, its prayers and its meals and even its strictures and

its requirements offer so much. Taste it. Allow yourself to live the life you were meant to have. Experience the deeper joys that Shabbat can give you, as you lead your life for one 25-hour period each week on a higher plane: as you spend a day each week sampling a taste of the World to Come.

Melava Malka

Although Shabbat ends an hour after sundown on Saturday night, many people try to extend the holy mood of the day with some sort of party or festivities. "Melava Malka" literally means "Escorting the Queen," and it is a way of escorting the Shabbat Queen on her way, as she departs from us for another week.

There are few rules for what constitutes a Melava Malka. In fact, the only qualities I've noticed over years of attending various Melava Malkas is that they all begin with Havdalah, and they all involve some sort of meal or snack. I've been to fancy dinners, casual get-togethers, school concerts, and even an art auction that were all billed as Melava Malkas. Some Saturday evenings, I pop a big bowl of popcorn and play fun CDs with my kids, and we call that our Melava Malka. Many enjoyable events can become Melava Malkas if you begin to think about them in a new way: as a way to usher out the Shabbat Queen.

I've noticed this myself first-hand, when I've planned events for Saturday nights. I'll always remember the first evening that my husband and I organized a Melava Malka. We were planning to have over some friends' on a Saturday night to play a game. (It was one of those complex board games with lots of players that last for hours; our husbands were enthusiasts.) We'd gotten together with these friends before, and though we were all Jewish, there had seldom been a particularly "Jewish" or spiritual feeling to the times we entertained with them. But this Saturday night my husband and I decided to subtly shift the tone of our "Motzei Shabbat" ("Post-Shabbat") into a Melava Malka mode. It started with us thinking that it would be nice to include our guests in our Havdalah ceremony, so they could fulfill this mitzvah with us.

Once all our friends were assembled at our house Saturday night, my husband performed Havdalah. Afterwards, we turned on the lights and we all wished each other a "Shavua Tov," a good week. I could feel a subtle difference in our interaction already. Although our friends were not traditionally observant, we all began thinking and feeling in terms of the Jewish weekly cycle, and using Hebrew greetings with each other. One friend suggested singing the song "Hine Ma Tov," the perennial Jewish camp favorite, which talks about how wonderful it is to be together with friends. (The words to this and other songs are found in Chapter 12.) We all joined in, enjoying the way it made us feel even closer than ever before. We soon exhausted our repertoire of Jewish songs, however, and slowly made our way to the living room to set up our game.

The ritual portion of our evening was over, but I noticed an unusual new quality to our interactions throughout the entire evening. We talked about Jewish topics more than ever before. At one point, somebody had a question about a story in the Hebrew Bible, and I went to look it up, thinking to myself as I did so how surprised I was that these secular friends were so interested in Jewish topics that evening. When we decided to play a CD, I chose a compilation of Jewish music; it seemed to fit the tone of the entire night. Never had this group of friends and us enjoyed such a spiritual, meaningful occasion, infused with Jewish thoughts, songs, greetings, and questions. We played our game, and talked about other topics as well, but I remember feeling at the time that we really were accompanying the Shabbat bride: that starting off our evening with Havdalah had elevated us all, and bathed us in a little of the holiness of the departing Shabbat.

If you are planning an evening with some Jewish friends on a Saturday night, you also might like to infuse the evening with a little extra holiness by rethinking your occasion as a Melava Malka, too. Here are a few ideas to get you started in planning your Melava Malka:

➤ **Havdalah:** Try beginning your Saturday night event with a group Havdalah ceremony. Even Jews who are unfamiliar with the words and the ritual cannot but be moved at the beauty of this ceremony. The darkness, the flame, the wine, and the spices are all so evocative.

211

This is a very moving event. Plus, it is very brief, so even people unfamiliar with it won't have a chance to grow bored.

➤ **Food:** Melava Malkas include some sort of a meal, whether fancy or casual. Don't forget to make the appropriate blessings before and after your Melava Malka meal, and to ritually wash your hands if you are going to eat bread; this will set apart your meal as a specifically Jewish, spiritual event.

➤ **Music:** Music is another common component of Melava Malkas. Whether you are playing a CD or hiring a band, consider choosing some Jewish music to play, too, to help set the tone of your evening as a Jewish occasion.

➤ **Song:** Sing-alongs are fun on Shabbat, and they are fun (and common) at Melava Malkas, too. Search for Jewish-themed music and lyrics you like. This is a time to sing all the old songs you learned at camp or Sunday school. I guarantee, once you see the words of "David Melech Yisrael" written down on paper before you, it will all come rushing back. (The words to this and other fun songs are included in Chapter 12.)

➤ **Events:** You can also organize something a little more ambitious. Some wonderful Melava Malkas are really fancy dinner parties, or larger parties, where guests mingle. In the past, I've arranged some really fun events for groups of friends by inviting people to speak to us about their work or hobbies. Some of the more successful get-togethers I've organized included: inviting an amateur photographer who had visted Jewish sites in Eastern Europe to come show guests her pictures of them; inviting a fundraiser for a local Jewish museum to talk to a group about the museum's collection; and inviting a local outreach rabbi to explain to a group of friends exactly what "Kabbala" is. These sorts of occasions are entertaining and interesting, and of course meaningful, too. If you ever feel like arranging a more serious, ambitious evening, you might try thinking along the lines of arranging a dinner, lecture, or a class to entertain people at a larger-scale Melava Malka.

➤ **Have fun:** Above all, have fun. Even if your Melava Malka is

nothing more than munching on snacks while you chat with some friends, the very act of starting your evening with Havdalah, and the consciousness that you give yourself by labeling your evening a Melava Malka, will make you feel more spiritual. This is a very easy way to introduce some extra Jewish feeling into your week, and to start the following six days on a wonderful note.

11

Torah questions for your Shabbat table

One traditional element of Shabbat mealtimes is some discussion of the weekly Parsha, or the Torah portion for that week. That sounds nice in principle, but, for many of us, studying Torah sounds daunting. Where to begin? What exactly is the weekly Parsha, and why study it?

The term "Torah" can refer to many things. At its broadest, "Torah" refers to the entirety of Divine knowledge that God transferred to Moses atop Mount Sinai. This includes the "Written Torah" (which we call the Bible in English) and the "Oral Torah" (which is variously, and confusingly, also called Mishna, Gemara, or Talmud). The Oral Torah was intended to be transmitted verbally from teacher to student, but after many years people began to worry about forgetting its details, and committed it to paper. The name "Talmud" is derived from the Hebrew word for "Studying."

However, when we go to synagogue, we see a "Torah" there too: this is the Torah scroll (called "Sefer Torah" in Hebrew, which means "Written-Down Torah"). The Sefer Torah is a handwritten scroll that contains the first part of the Bible, the books of:

1 Genesis ("Bereshit" in Hebrew)
2 Exodus ("Shemot" in Hebrew)
3 Leviticus ("Vayikra" in Hebrew)
4 Numbers ("Bemidbar" in Hebrew)
5 Deuteronomy ("Devarim" in Hebrew).

These five books are sometimes referred to as the "Five Books of Moses." (To be even more confusing, sometimes people refer to them by their ancient Greek name, the "Pentateuch.") In Hebrew, they are called the "Chumash" (from the Hebrew word for five). These five books make up the first section of the Hebrew Bible. They are so important that the Torah itself instructs us to read them publicly each year.

In biblical times, we accomplished this by having someone read a section out loud every week in the market places. This worked well while we were an agrarian people living in the Land of Israel, but today, of course, it is impractical. Instead, for the past two thousand years, ever since the Roman Empire crushed the ancient kingdom of Israel and scattered many of its Jewish inhabitants far and wide into exile, we Jews have read the Torah out loud each week in our synagogues. (Interestingly, in addition to Shabbat, we still read the Torah in synagogue on the old market days, as in ancient times: Monday and Thursday. If you've ever wondered why many stores today stay open late on Thursday nights, it is because the ancient schedule of market days was copied and continued in other lands, through countless generations, until today, when Thursday still retains some slight remnant of its original origins as a day of commerce, in the form of longer trading hours.)

The books of the Torah are divided into weekly portions so that it takes a year to complete each cycle of Torah-reading. We begin and end each cycle on the Jewish holiday "Simchat Torah," when we celebrate God's giving us His Torah. On Simchat Torah, a reader completes the last Parsha, and then immediately begins reading the first Parsha of the Torah, without a break, symbolizing the eternal nature of our commitment to the Torah: our reading it never ends.

This Jewish love of the Torah permeates everything we do. The Jewish people were the only people in ancient time to accept God's Torah. In doing so, we became defined by our relationship to God through His Torah. There is a very famous Jewish story that sums up the central role the Torah plays in the relationship between the Jewish people and God.

Many, many years ago, after God created the world, He looked for a nation that would accept His holy Torah. This was the greatest gift that people could receive from God, and God offered it to the various nations on His Earth. However, nobody wanted it. One nation looked at the Torah and complained that it prohibited stealing. "We enjoy stealing," they explained, "and we don't want to give it up," so they rejected the Torah. Another nation complained that they didn't like the Torah's laws of keeping kosher, and rejected it. Other nations explained that they did not want to give up human sacrifice, incest, idol worship, and many other practices that the Torah outlawed. One by one, each nation rejected the Torah.

Finally, God asked the Jewish people if they would accept His Torah, and the Jews, alone out of all the nations, agreed. "We will observe Your laws," they told God, "and we will study them." The Jewish nation thus accepted God's Torah: its beauty and its blessings, and also its rules and its obligations. In doing so, the Jews accepted a special position in God's world: the only people bound to God through His holy gift to us, His Torah.

As a people, we have embraced the mitzvot (commandments) of God's Torah. Whether or not we study the meanings behind them, whether or not we understand them fully or at all, Judaism stresses we are still obligated to keep the holidays, the celebrations, and the rules of the Torah. This is what we promised to God first: "We will observe Your laws." Before we even understand them, we will perform them.

However, the second part of the contract we made with God is to study His holy Torah. We will observe God's laws, and we will study them, too. This is central to the mission of living a Jewish life. Other people have called the Jews the people of the book. Throughout Jewish history, we have been known as a people apart, a people defined by our intense joy and love of trying to understand God's meanings in the world. Throughout our history, we have studied the Torah, have grappled with its intricacies, and have sought clarification of its hidden depths. As mentioned in Chapter 5, the great third-century Rabbi Ben Bag Bag expressed this Jewish love affair with God's Torah and the wisdom it contains when he said "Delve into it (the Torah) and continue to delve into it, for everything is in it; look deeply

into it; grow old and gray over it, and do not stir from it, for you can have no better portion than it" (Pirkei Avot 5.26).

The writings of the Torah touch on so many subjects. Studying the Torah brings us into contact with poetry and science, history and philosophy, literature, and deep insights into human nature and motivations. The Torah can be studied at any level of intellectual and spiritual engagement, from the most basic to the most advanced. Virtually every passage in the Torah has been interpreted in fascinating ways over the years, creating a rich tapestry of commentaries, stories, and differing perspectives that is enticing to explore. More personally, there is a saying in Hebrew: *"Ma'aseh avot"* ("What happened to our patriarchs") *"siman l'banim"* ("portends what will happen to their descendants"). Not only is the Torah full of interesting, absorbing stories and profound moral lessons, the experiences of our ancestors that it describes have a direct bearing on our own lives today. We inherit our patriarchs' and matriarchs' character traits, their faith, even their relationships with God. When we study the Torah today, we are also studying ourselves.

Yet it can all seem so overwhelming. With so many commentaries on the Torah, with so many translations, where do we begin?

One way to do this is through the delightful traditional Jewish ritual of asking Parsha Questions at the Shabbat table. Each week, in Shabbat-observant households, people study the Parsha for that week. Adults read it, usually with their favorite commentary, and kids learn it in school. Then, on Shabbat, there is a tradition of parents asking their kids a few questions about the Parsha so the children can show off their knowledge.

This is fun, but I have found the value of the Parsha questions we ask to be even greater than giving my kids a chance to shine. In our home, we are all beginners when it comes to Torah study, and we all enjoy talking about each question and trying to answer them. Whether we're alone for our meal, or joined by guests, we find it is fun to discuss a few questions about the Parsha at our Shabbat table. At times, our Parsha questions lead to bigger discussions about Torah and other topics. Usually, though, we have enough to contend with coming up with the answers. Often we run to get a copy of the "Chumash" (Hebrew for the Five Books of Moses) and look

up our answers. This ritual helps us to understand the weekly Parsha, and also introduces the elevated discussion about Torah that we crave to help make our Shabbat even more holy.

One of the greatest surprises my husband and I received when our children started attending Jewish day school was the list of Parsha questions they brought home with them each Friday. We had never even heard about asking Parsha questions before this, and having our kids' lists of questions has enriched our Shabbats enormously. For those of you who do not have the benefit of a Jewish day school sending you questions to your home every Friday, here is a year's worth of questions to ask at your own Shabbat table.

These questions are simple, and can be answered with a quick reading of the weekly Parsha. They remind me of a cartoon strip I once read. Two high school boys are talking to one another. One boy asks his friend, "What are you learning about in Honors History?" His friend replies, "We're learning about the social, political, and cultural roots of the Peloponnesian Wars. What are you learning about in Regular History?" The first boy replies: "The *dates* of the Peloponnesian wars."

Some areas of my life are on the level of that Honors History kid. But most are on the level of the Regular History kid: I'm happy if I understand some concepts at all. When it comes to learning about the weekly Torah portion, I always try to aim for the "Honors" understanding, but I'm pleased if I just get the "Regular" familiarity with them, too. (Luckily, I've found that even a basic reading of the weekly Parsha really elevates my week and makes me feel closer to God by understanding His Torah and the wisdom He wants to teach us with it.)

These Parsha questions are "Regular" level. If you crave more advanced, complex questions, there are so many sources to turn to. Some ideas to get you started are contained at the end of this book. As you become more adept at Torah study and read more books about the weekly Parsha, you can find your own favorite sources for commentary and questions, too. I hope that the following questions start you off. If you aren't sure what the Parsha is for a given week, you can refer to a Jewish calendar or newspaper, or else to websites such as the Orthodox Union (www.ou.org), United

Synagogue (www.theus.org.uk), or the Jewish educational center Aish Hatorah (www.aish.com).

Below, I've provided the Chumash (Bible) verses that make up each Parsha. The Hebrew text is constant, but there are many different English translations and commentaries available. I'd recommend buying at least one good, hardcover copy of the Chumash, with an English translation. (There are also excellent editions that translate the Chumash into other languages such as Russian, French, and Spanish, if you prefer.) Here are three excellent versions you might like to consider.

➤ *The Chumash: The Stone Edition* by Rabbi Nosson Scherman (1993).

➤ *The Living Torah: The Five Books of Moses and the Haftarot — a New Translation Based on Traditional Jewish Sources, with Notes, Introduction, Maps, Tables, Bibliography and Index* by Rabbi Aryeh Kaplan (1981).

➤ *The Pentateuch and Haftorahs: Hebrew Text, English Translation and Commentary* edited by Rabbi Dr. J. H. Hertz (1981).

The Book of Bereshit (Genesis)

Bereshit

This famous first Parsha encompasses so many profound concepts and famous stories. It also contains a dark vision of human depravity. God creates the world and everything in it. Adam and Eve, the first people, dwell in the Garden of Eden, break God's laws, and are expelled. They have children, but one of their sons kills the other. At the end of the Parsha, God decides to blot out mankind, with the exception of Noah and his family.

Read Gen. 1.1–7.8.

1 There are four versions of the creation of Eve, the first woman. How do they differ?

2 There is a famous discrepancy between what God told Eve about the Tree of the Knowledge of Good and Evil and what Eve repeated to the serpent. Can you spot it?

3 What was the difference between the sacrifices that Cain and Abel offered to God?

Noah

Because of man's sins, God warns he will destroy the world. Only Noah and his family heed God's warning, and save themselves, as well as samples of all the animals of the world. This Parsha details the subsequent resettling of the earth and God's promise that He will never destroy the world again. It also contains the evocative story of the Tower of Babel.

Read Gen. 6.9–11.32.

1 Who, exactly, did God want to destroy? Why?

2 What does the rainbow signify in this Parsha?

3 What did Noah's son Ham do to earn Noah's curse on his descendants, and what did Noah's sons Shem and Jafet do to earn Noah's blessing?

Lech Lecha

God tells Abraham and Sarah to leave their idolatrous city and travel to the Land of Israel. ("Lech Lecha" is a poetic way of saying in Hebrew "You shall go.") Afterwards, God creates an eternal covenant with Abraham and Sarah, and their descendants.

Read Gen. 12.1–17.27.

1 What spoils of war was Abraham willing to take after he rescued his nephew Lot?

2 How long did God tell Abraham his descendants would live as strangers and slaves in a land not their own?

3 In this Parsha, God tells Abraham of two sons he will have, and promises different blessings for the descendants of each son. (Jewish commentators have generally regarded the descendants of Abraham's son Ishmael to be the Arab nation, and the descendants of Abraham's son Isaac to be the Jewish nation.) What different blessings does God promise for these two nations?

Vayera

Abraham bargains with God over the fates of the cities Sodom and Gemorrah. Later, God instructs Abraham to sacrifice his son Isaac to God. Additionally, a powerful underlying theme in this Parsha is the challenge of infertility in the lives of our matriarchs.

Read Gen. 18.1–22.24.

1 This Parsha opens with God sending three angels disguised as men to Abraham and Sarah. In what condition was Abraham when they arrived? How did he greet the angels?

2 This Parsha contains an amazing passage in which Abraham argues and bargains with God. Over what did they negotiate?

3 How many times was the angel sent to stop Abraham from sacrificing Isaac have to call out to Abraham before he got Abraham's attention? Why do you think the angel had to repeat itself?

Chaye Sarah

Although this Parsha is called "Chaye Sarah," or the "Life of Sarah," it deals almost exclusively with the events after her death. Abraham buys the Cave of Machpelah as a burial place for her, forming the Jewish people's oldest connection with the Land of Israel. Perhaps most famous is the moving story of Eliezer's selection of Rebecca to be Isaac's wife, and join the monotheistic clan that Abraham and Sarah had founded.

Read Gen. 23.1–25.18

1 After a lifetime living and fighting alongside him, the children of Heth were willing to give Abraham land in which to bury his wife Sarah. What was Abraham's response?

2 Where is the Cave of Machpelah located?

3 What sign did the servant Eliezer look for when he went to choose a wife for Isaac?

Toledot

Isaac's and Rebecca's twins, Jacob and Esau, fight each other inside their mother's womb. When they are adults, they struggle over their birthright and the blessings they are each to receive from their father. The outcome of these two brothers' struggles will shape the history of the Jewish people.

Read Gen. 15.19–28.9.

1 In what unusual manner did Jacob and Esau emerge from their mother's womb?

2 How did Jacob and Esau differ once they grew up?

3   How did Rebecca and Jacob trick his father into believing that Jacob was Esau when it was time for Jacob to confer his blessing?

Vayetze

Jacob works for his uncle Lavan and marries Lavan's two daughters, Leah and Rachel. After 20 years of acrimonious coexistence, Jacob and Lavan divide their possessions and part company.

Read Gen. 28.10–32.3.

1   This Parsha opens with a stirring blessing given by God to Jacob. What five promises did God make to Jacob and his descendants?
2   How did Lavan trick Jacob?
3   What did Rachel remove from Lavan's house before she left?

Veyishlach

Returning to Israel, Jacob wrestles with, and is blessed by, an angel. Later, he confronts his brother Esau. This Parsha also relates the assault on Jacob's daughter Dina by the native inhabitants of the city of Shechem (Nablus), and Jacob's sons' revenge.

Read Gen. 32.4–36.43.

1   Jacob was afraid that his brother Esau still wanted to kill him. How did Jacob first approach Esau on his return, and try to win him over?
2   In this Parsha Jacob wrestles with an angel sent by God. How does this angel bless Jacob?
3   Why was Jacob angry with his sons Shimon and Levi?

Veyeshev

Jacob's sons turn on their brother Joseph and sell him into slavery. Joseph works for a high-ranking Egyptian minister for many years, until he is falsely accused of attacking his master's wife, and thrown into prison. In prison, Joseph interprets the dreams of his fellow prisoners.

Read Gen. 37.1–40.23.

1   What happened to the Egyptian Potiphar when he bought Joseph to be his slave?

2 What two reasons does Joseph give for not wanting to be with Potiphar's wife?

3 What do the dreams of the butler and the baker signify?

Miketz

Joseph is released from prison, and rises to become a great leader of Egypt, second only to Pharaoh himself. In the midst of a drought, Joseph's brothers travel to Egypt to buy food. Joseph recognizes his long-lost brothers, but they do not recognize him.

Read Gen. 41.1–44.17.

1 What did Joseph interpret Pharaoh's dreams to mean? What did Joseph recommend that Pharaoh do?

2 Most of Joseph's brothers travelled to Egypt to buy food. Why did Benjamin, the youngest, remain at home?

3 What does Joseph require his brothers to do?

Vayigash

Joseph's brothers return to Egypt a second time, this time bringing Benjamin with them. This reunion proves to be a decisive one for the Jewish people, as this Parsha marks the beginning of the Jews' long, tragic sojourn in Egypt.

Read Gen. 44.18–47.27.

1 How does Judah explain why he cannot leave his brother Benjamin in Egypt? How does Joseph respond to Judah's plea?

2 Is Joseph angry with his brothers? Why or why not?

3 There is a splendid passage in this Parsha, in which God speaks to Jacob. What three promises does God make to Jacob?

Vayechi

At the end of his life, Jacob blesses his 12 sons, each of whom will go on to found one of the 12 tribes of Israel. After his death, Jacob's sons carry his body back to Israel, and bury him with his father Isaac and grandparents Abraham and Sarah.

Read Gen. 47.28–50.26.

1   What did Joseph's brothers fear after they buried their father Jacob?
2   How did Joseph react to his brothers' fear?
3   What was Joseph's final wish?

The Book of Shemot (Exodus)

Shemot

A new Pharaoh becomes ruler of Egypt, and enslaves the Jews. Moses is born to a Jewish midwife, who hides him in a basket of reeds placed in the River Nile. Moses is discovered by the Pharoah's daughter Batya, and raised in the palace of the Pharaoh. After killing an Egyptian taskmaster, Moses flees Egypt, and has his first, dramatic contacts with God.

Read Exod. 1.1–6.1.

1   Jewish tradition tells that Moses' mother and sister were midwives. In what way did they and other Jewish midwives defy Pharaoh's orders?
2   Who served as Moses' baby nurse? What effect do you think this had on Moses' personality and development?
3   What was Moses' initial request to Pharaoh? What was Pharaoh's response?

Va-ayera

When Pharaoh refuses to let the Jewish people go, God sends plagues to torment Egypt. This story is famous from books and film. Reading the original, however, is an even more exciting experience: there are so many details of these famous stories that are unique to the Torah, that are challenging, even troubling.

Read Exod. 6.2–9.35.

1   It is one of the Thirteen Principles of Faith in Judaism that Moses was our greatest prophet. God Himself implies this in this Parsha. Where?
2   How did the Jews first receive Moses when he came to rescue them?
3   Pharaoh offered the Jews the right to sacrifice to God. Why did this offer not please God?

Bo

Plagues continue to rain down on Egypt, until Pharaoh finally consents to let the Jewish people go. We are then instructed to commemorate the events that are about to take place — God's redemption of the Jewish people from slavery in Egypt — through the holiday of Passover.

Read Exod. 10.1–13.16.

1 God instructed each Jewish household to slaughter a lamb the night before they left Egypt. What two things did God tell the Jews to do with this lamb?

2 How many years had the Jews lived in Egypt?

3 How many Jews left Egypt?

Beshalach

As the Jewish people leave Egypt, Pharaoh has a change of heart and pursues them, eventually trapping them against the raging foam of the Red Sea. God splits the sea, allowing the Jews to escape. Once in the desert, God protects the Jews, providing a delicious food called manna each day. Yet there is a dark side to this Parsha, too: the anger of the Jews against Moses, and the brutal assault on the Jewish travelers by a nomadic desert tribe called Amalek.

Read Exodus 13.17–17.16.

1 When the fleeing Jews saw that Pharaoh was chasing them with all his soldiers and with 600 chariots, what did the Jews say to Moses? Did they trust his leadership?

2 In this Parsha, we see the Jews turn on Moses again and again, doubting his authority and God's mercy. What are some of the things the Jews complained about to Moses? How did God respond to these complaints?

3 During their sojourn in the wilderness, God admonished Moses and the Jewish people to be scrupulous in keeping which holiday?

Yitro

If there is a climax in the narrative of the Jewish Bible, this is it. The Jews prepare themselves before Moses climbs the mountain to receive a precious

gift from God. God's voice rings like a shofar (ram's horn), echoing over the people below, and God begins to give us His holy Torah.

Read Exod. 18.1–20.23.

1 Who was Yitro? How did he advise Moses to manage disputes?
2 What did God promise the Jews if they keep their covenant with Him?
3 Before the giving of the Torah, Moses called together all the elders of Israel. What did Moses ask them, and what did they reply?

Mishpatim

God relates a long list of crucial commandments to Moses. Moses then ascends into the thick cloud blanketing the top of Mount Sinai, and remains there 40 days, continuing to receive the Torah.

Read Exod. 21.1–24.18.

1 What is the Torah's penalty for murder? For accidental homicide? How do they differ?
2 How does this Parsha instruct us to treat an item of clothing that was given to us to secure a loan?
3 In this Parsha, it is written that the elders of Israel "saw" God. What did they see?

Terumah

In the midst of the riveting narrative of God appearing to Moses atop Mount Sinai to give him the Torah, there is an interlude of two Parshas to describe the way God wants us to house the tablets on which He wrote this Torah. They were to be kept in an Aron (a cabinet), housed in a portable structure composed of curtains and jeweled decorations, called a Mishkan.

Read Exod. 25.1–27.19.

1 How was the Aron (the "Ark") to be decorated?
2 From whence did God tell Moses he would speak to the people of Israel?
3 What decorations did God instruct the Jewish people to place inside the Mishkan?

Tetzaveh

God describes the services that will take place inside the Mishkan, our portable synagogue in the desert. The services will be beautiful and ornate, featuring offerings given to God.

Read Exod. 27.10–30.10.

1 Who were the original Cohens (people who conducted services)?
2 What was fastened to the hem of Aaron's robes? What was to be written on the golden plate worn around Aaron's forehead while he conducted services?
3 What foods were sacrificed to God to sanctify the Mishkan?

Ki Tisa

While Moses receives the Torah, the Jew at the base of Mount Sinai grow restless, and decide to fashion an idol to worship. Moses returns from the mountain, beholds the bacchanal below, and breaks the tablets on which God had written the Torah. Moses then pleads with God not to forsake the Jewish people. God relents, and allows Moses to ascend Mount Sinai one more time.

Read Exod. 30.11–34.35.

1 How did Moses finance the Mishkan and all the ornate decorations inside it?
2 What holidays did God tell Moses the Jewish people must keep?
3 What reasons does Moses give to God not to turn His back on the Jews?

Vayakhel

Moses tells the people of Israel the importance of keeping Shabbat. The Parsha then relates the efforts of Israel to come together and create a beautiful Mishkan ("synagogue") in which to worship in the desert. Men and women, young and old, all come forward to offer their services building and decorating, and donating materials. (You might have heard of the famous Bezalel Academy of Art and Design in Jerusalem; it is named after the talented artist in this Parsha.)

Read Exod. 35.1–38.7.

1 Did the people of Israel donate enough materials to adequately build the Mishkan?

2 What materials were used to build the Aron ("Ark"), containing the tablets God gave to Moses atop Mount Sinai?

3 What materials did the serving women who worked in the Mishkan donate for decoration?

Pekuday

This Parsha describes the conduct of the Cohens (service leaders) when they worship God in the Mishkan (synagogue). This Parsha concludes with the stirring image of God sending alternately a cloud (during the day) and a pillar of fire (at night) to stay with the Jewish people, and to lead them through the wilderness.

Read Exod. 38.21–40.38.

1 Who built the ornaments used in the services in the Mishkan? Who designed them?

2 After each person donated a half shekel to the building of the Mishkan, the number was tallied. How many Jewish men over 20 years old were there during the time of the building of the Mishkan?

3 There is a custom in Judaism never to count people. (The idea of assigning a mere number to a human being is anathema to Judaism.) Yet, there are times when it is helpful to know how many people are present. This Parsha hints at a commonly employed Jewish solution; what is it?

The Book of Vayikra (Leviticus)

Vayikra

"Vayikra" is one of the more technical Parshas, concerning the details of sacrifices offered in the Mishkan (tabernacle). Yet, in Orthodox Jewish communities, when little children begin to learn the Torah, they traditionally begin by studying this Parsha. Why? Because although the details in this Parsha might be dry, although they might strike some as gory (concerning, as they do, animal sacrifices), studying them is a little bit like bringing the sacrifices to God ourselves: we gain some of the merit of these ancient sacrifices today. By reading this Parsha, we are actually participating, in

a small way, in the worship of God that Aaron and the ancient people of Israel performed.

Read Lev. 1.1–5.26.

1   Who brought sacrifices to the Mishkan for God? When?

2   What did Aaron and his sons do when an animal sacrifice was brought to the Mishkan? What did they do when an offering of flour and oil was brought?

3   Could the Jews offer breads and cakes to God in the Mishkan?

Tzav

Five groups of sacrifices are offered to God each day in the Mishkan. All day, from morning until nightfall, Aaron and his sons, dressed in magnificent attire, burn sacrifices to God on the Jewish people's behalf, infusing the Jewish people with holiness.

Read Lev. 6.1–8.36.

1   How often did Aaron and his sons have to kindle the fire for sacrifices in the Mishkan?

2   When were Aaron and his sons *not* allowed to eat the meat from the sacrifices?

3   How long did Aaron and his sons remain inside the Mishkan during the consecrating ceremony?

Shemini

This important Parsha covers a number of crucial issues. It opens with an awe-inspiring description of the offerings that Aaron and his sons make to God on behalf of all the people of Israel. Later on, two of Aaron's sons offer sacrifices improperly, and die. Finally, this Parsha closes with a description of those animals that are kosher and not kosher.

Read Lev. 9.1–11.47.

1   What animals did Aaron and his sons offer on behalf of the people of Israel to atone for misdeeds? What did they offer on behalf of Israel to thank God?

2   What, if anything, do you think we can learn from Nadav and Avihu's fate?

3 What qualities make an animal kosher? What qualities make a fish kosher?

Tazria

The Parsha begins with a discussion about when women give offerings to God after giving birth. Most of the Parsha is concerned with ways of detecting a disease called "tzarat": a sickness resulting from the sin of gossip, which prevents sufferers from entering the Mishkan.

Read Lev. 12.1–13.44.

1 After giving birth, what sacrifices did a woman offer to God?
2 How could tzarat be diagnosed on clothing? What was the procedure for diagnosing tzarat on clothes?
3 What became of a person suffering from tzarat? What became of a garment suffering from tzarat?

Metzora

"Tzarat" is a specific disease, visited on the ancient Israelites in biblical times, signifying that the sufferer had gossiped. It is a visual reminder not to slander other people.

Read Lev. 14.1–15.33.

1 What offering to God did a person bring after they were cured of tzarat? When?
2 How could symptoms of tzarat be seen in a house?
3 How was a house cured of tzarat? What happened if it could not be cured of tzarat?

Acharei Mot

This Parsha is familiar to many Jews, because it is read each year in shul (synagogue) on Yom Kippur. It describes the preparations and activities of the Cohens (Temple workers) each Yom Kippur, as they ask for atonement for the sins of the Jewish people from God. This Parsha then discusses some of the most grievous sins that God warns us about: sins of idol worship, incest, and other sexual immorality.

Read Lev. 16.1–18.30.

1   On Yom Kippur, what did Aaron do before offering sacrifices on behalf of the Jewish people?

2   How did Aaron use the two goats to make atonement for the Jewish people on Yom Kippur?

3   How is Yom Kippur, the Jewish Day of Atonement, described in this Parsha?

Kedoshim

We are presented in this Parsha with many fundamental laws, including famous injunctions such as not to put a stumbling block before the blind, and the requirement to love a stranger as we love ourselves, "for we were strangers in the land of Egypt." "Kedoshim" means "Holinesses"; we gain insight here into how to maintain the holy state that God intended for us.

Read Lev. 19.1–20.27.

1   Why should the Jewish people be holy?

2   What two commandments does God single out, repeating them here, in this Parsha, immediately after His warning to be a holy nation? Which comes first?

3   Most of the time, in Judaism, it is our actions, not our thoughts, that count. We are almost always judged by what we do, not whether we did it grudgingly or not. Yet in this Parsha, we are warned against a sin that takes place in our minds. What is it?

Emor

As workers in the Mishkan (and later in the Beit Hamikdash, or Temple, in Jerusalem), Cohens are to have high standards of behavior. The middle section of Parshat Emor describes the six great Jewish holidays. Finally, we are warned about sins such as idol worship, murder, and injuring.

Read Lev. 21.1–24.23.

1   Whose funeral may a Cohen attend?

2   What sorts of animals were we instructed to offer to God as a sacrifice?

3   When this Parsha describes all the holy days the Jewish people are to

keep, which holiday is mentioned first? What other holidays are we instructed to keep in this Parsha?

Behar

God gives instructions about how the Jewish people will live once they are settled in the land of Israel. Each of the 12 tribes of Israel has their own ancestral lands. Although owners will be able to buy or sell their fields as fortunes increase and decline, every fiftieth year, the ancestral property lines will be restored. Also, every seven years will be a "Shabbat" for the land, when farms will lie fallow.

Read Lev. 25.1–26.2.

1   How can the land of Israel have a "Shabbat"?
2   Who can eat food that grows wild during the "Shabbat year" when fields in Israel rest?
3   Was property in walled cities included in the Yovel ("Jubilee") year?

Bechukotai

So long as the Jewish people adhere to God's Torah in the Land of Israel, we will enjoy security and abundance. If we turn away from God's commandments, we will have misfortune, poverty, and exile. Yet even in the midst of exile and degradation, God will never forget His people. The Parsha concludes with a discussion of how families calculate their donations for the Mishkan's (and later the Temple in Jerusalem's) upkeep.

Read Lev. 26.3–27.34.

1   What rewards does God promise the people of Israel if they keep His commandments?
2   What curses does God promise to bring if the Jewish people reject God's laws?
3   When does God say He will redeem the Jewish people?

The Book of Bemidbar (Numbers)

Bemidbar

We read a detailed tally of the 12 tribes of Israel. The Tribe of Levi is to live apart from the other tribes, dedicated to conducting services to God. When

the Jews break camp in the desert, Aaron and his helpers dismantle the Mishkan, wrapping its precious contents for the trip.

Read Num. 1.1–4.20.

1 We can deduce how many individual families there were among the people of Israel in the desert, as God tells Moses to count the number of first-born children. How many first-born children were there?

2 Each time the Jews moved camp in the desert, they packed up the Mishkan and all that was in it, and then set it up again in their new camp. In what did they pack the Ark, Menorah, and golden instruments for safekeeping during each move?

3 Who arranged the holy vessels inside the Mishkan?

Naso

Each family in the Tribe of Levi has a special job in transporting the Mishkan, the portable synagogue used in the desert. In the middle of this Parsha, there are two distinct legal discussions (applicable in biblical times only). One concerns a man who accuses his wife of adultery. The second concerns those who dedicate themselves to an extra-high level of holiness and become "Nazirim": people who take extra steps to try to come closer to God.

Read Num. 4.21–7.89.

1 Who of the Tribe of Levi performed the ritual functions connected with transporting the Mishkan from camp to camp?

2 Who could become a Nazir?

3 How was a Nazir supposed to behave? How did one become a Nazir? What did one do at the conclusion of one's period of being a Nazir?

Be-Ha-Alotecha

With a beautiful ceremony, the Tribe of Levi inaugurates their holy work in the Mishkan (synagogue). The 12 Tribes of Israel, hundreds of thousands strong, travel through the desert on their way to the land of Israel. Perhaps the best-known stories in this Parsha, however, are negative. In the first, a number of Jews turn against God, and pine for the meat they ate when they were slaves in Egypt. Later, Miriam and Aaron, living in the most holy surroundings imaginable, nevertheless sin by gossiping.

Read Num. 8.1–12.16.

1   In this Parsha, the Jewish people once more turn against God. What did they complain about? How did God answer their complaints?
2   How was Moses a greater prophet than any other? How do we know this?
3   Why was Miriam punished with the disease "tzarat"?

Shelach Lecha

Ready to enter the land of Israel, the Jewish people first send scouts to explore it. These scouts return with an enormous bunch of grapes, demonstrating Israel's fertility. But most of them are afraid, and warn their fellow Jews that the land is full of frightening giants. The Jews refuse to enter the Land of Israel, and Moses begs God not to forsake his people.

Read Num. 13.1–15.41.

1   What did Caleb and Joshua report? What praise did the remaining ten spies have for the Land of Israel, and what negative things did they say?
2   After hearing these reports, what did the Jews demand of one another?
3   For a second time (the first was after the Golden Calf incident at Mount Sinai) Moses persuaded God not to abandon His people. What did Moses say to God?

Korach

The Jewish people rise up against Moses, demanding an end to his leadership, proffering Korach, a leader of the Tribe of Levi, instead. God makes visible miracles occur, showing His support for Moses' rule. Yet no sooner has God finished these miracles than the Jewish people rebel once more.

Read Num. 16.1–18.32.

1   How many men allied themselves with Korach and his rebellion? Who were Korach's main supporters?
2   What did Moses say to God when he was challenged by Korach?
3   How did the Jewish people react when God showed that He did not accept the leadership of Korach?

Chukat

A ceremony involving the sacrifice of a red heifer is used to ritually cleanse people and objects after contact with a dead body. The Jewish people again rebel against the authority of Moses and Aaron, and Moses seems at last to lose his patience. The Jewish people begin to conquer territories at the eastern edge of ancient Israel. (We also learn an interesting story, which is the source of the universal medical insignia of a snake against a pole.)

Read Num. 19.1–22.1.

1 What were the requirements for the red heifer that was sacrificed in the Mishkan?
2 Why was Moses not allowed to enter the Land of Israel?
3 Where was the first territory the Jews conquered in the ancient land of Canaan?

Balak

Fearing the Israelites will conquer his land as they conquered the neighboring Amorites, Balak, King of Moav, summons the non-Jewish prophet Balam. Again and again, King Balak commands the prophet Balam to curse the Jewish people, and again and again, Balam blesses them instead.

1 Why did Balam's donkey refuse to walk? (Do you see any echoes in this episode of an earlier Parsha?)
2 What miracles did God make happen in connection with Balam's donkey?
3 How many times did Balam bless the people of Israel?

Pinchas

As the Jewish people approach the Land of Israel and prepare to enter it, they pause for an accounting. Afterwards, God reminds the Jewish people of the ritual sacrifices they are to bring on various festivals when they live in Israel.

Read Num. 25.10–30.1.

1 When the daughters of Tzelafchad came to Moses and asked to inherit their father's land, Moses conferred with God. What did God instruct?
2 What was Moses' last act on earth to be?

3   Who was to replace Moses as leader of the Jewish people?

Mattot

"Mattot" begins with a discussion of who may make a vow, and who may invalidate another person's vow. It then describes the war between the People of Israel and the Midianite nation. Two of the Jewish tribes choose to settle outside of the Land of Israel.

Read Num. 30.2–32.42.

1   Why did God instruct Moses to fight against the Midianites?
2   Who among the Midianites was saved?
3   Which tribes wished to settle outside of the land that God had promised to the Nation of Israel? Where did they want to settle? Why did Moses object? How did these tribes counter Moses' objections?

Massey

We learn places the people of Israel journeyed, from their starting place in Ramses, in Egypt, to the plains of Moav overlooking Israel from the east, in what today is Jordan. God gives detailed instructions about how and where the land of Israel is to be settled.

Read Num. 33.1–36.13.

1   What were the Jewish people to do first when they entered the land of Israel?
2   How were the Jewish tribes to determine where their land should be?
3   In some Middle Eastern cultures, there is a concept of blood money: a person guilty of a crime may pay money to avoid punishment. What does the Torah say about this concept?

The Book of Devarim (Deuteronomy)
Devarim

As the People of Israel prepare to enter their land, Moses begins a stirring speech, tracing the history of the Jewish people, their internal fighting and rebellions, and their military victories over the Amorite peoples. Moses cautions the Jewish people about which lands they may conquer, and promises God will watch over the people of Israel

and help them gain victories, and will eventually give them peace in their land.

1 Read Deut. 1.1–3.22.
2 Why does Moses say it was difficult to lead the Jewish people?
3 What rules governed Jewish judges when hearing cases involving a Jew and a non-Jew?
4 God did not allow anyone who was an adult at the time of the exodus from Egypt to enter the land of Israel — except for one man. Who? (Do you know why God allowed him to enter Israel?)

Ve-etchanan

Moses foretells the history of the Jewish people: we will be scattered among the nations and gravely weakened, but one day will return to Israel, our national home. Moses reviews the Ten Commandments, and exhorts the Jewish people to remember his words: to think of them always, to teach them to our children, to talk about them all the time, in our house, on the road, when we go to sleep and when we wake up. These timeless words form the first paragraph of the "Shema" prayer. Further sections in this Parsha form parts of the Passover Hagaddah.

Read Deut. 3.23–7.11.

1 In this discourse, Moses does not seek to aggrandize himself. As he recounts for the children of Israel their history in the desert, Moses includes some details about himself that are less than flattering. What prayer of Moses did God categorically deny?
2 For how long will God show His anger to those who rejected them? For how long will God show His mercy to those who love Him and keep His mitzvot?
3 How many other tribes were living in the land of Israel before the Jews entered it? How were the Jews instructed to relate to them?

Ekev

Moses continues to remind the Jewish people of all that befell them in the wilderness after they left Egypt, and foresees the prosperity they will enjoy in the land of Israel. Moses reminds the Jews of their past rebellions against

God, and warns them not to be tempted to turn away from God again, once they are living in Israel.

Read Deut. 7.12–11.25.

1   In Jewish tradition, the Land of Israel is associated with seven fruits. This tradition comes from Parshat Ekev. What specific riches does Moses tell the Jewish people await them in the land of Israel?

2   When does Moses warn the Jewish people that the temptation to forget God will come to them? Why might this happen?

3   Moses mentions an interesting difference in agriculture between Israel and Egypt. What is it? (Can you think of what different feelings would be engendered by the agricultural arrangements in Egypt and Israel?)

Re-eh

God places two possibilities before the Jewish people: a blessing and a curse. Which future we enjoy depends on whether we follow God's Torah. These fates are represented by actual mountains that stand side by side near Schechem (Nablus): Mount Gerizim, which is green and lush (representing blessing) and Mount Ebal, which is barren and rocky (representing the curse).

Read Deut. 11.26–16.17.

1   The Jews are not to follow the idolatrous ways of the other inhabitants of Israel. What particularly disturbing aspect of idolatry is mentioned in Parshat Re'eh?

2   Besides not emulating their idolatrous behavior, what does God forbid the Jewish people to do regarding the idolatrous rites of the tribes inhabiting Israel?

3   The Torah allowed indentured servitude in ancient Israel. How long was an indentured servant to be kept? What was to be given to them upon their release? Why? Could an indentured servant choose to remain enslaved?

Shoftim

"Shoftim" in Hebrew means "judges," and this Parsha reminds us to be evenhanded and honest in judgment, and provides numerous examples

of times when people have to determine guilt in difficult or unclear cases.

Read Deut. 6.18–21.9.

1   It is foretold in this Parsha that the Jewish people would one day appoint themselves a king, like all the other peoples. What restrictions does this Parsha give for the behavior of the kings of Israel? What was the king of Israel to do every day? Why?

2   What were the conditions under which a man was excused from going into battle?

3   What was to be done with fruit trees during battle?

Ki Tetze

This portion of Moses' final speech describes different commandments, many of which are beautiful in the extreme. The Jewish commandment not to plow with an ox and a donkey harnessed together, because this places undue strain on the weaker animal, is an example of the Torah's timeless beauty and sensitivity.

Read Deut. 11.10–25.19.

1   One mitzvah that is still very much stressed today is "Hashovas Aveida," or returning lost things. What should we do if we cannot find the owner of a lost item?

2   What are we required to do when constructing a new house? Why?

3   When may parents be punished for their children's sins?

Ki Tavo

In this section of Moses' final speech to the Jewish people, delivered just before they are to leave the wilderness and pass into the land of Israel, Moses warns that they will be either blessed or cursed in the future.

Read Deut. 16.1–19.8.

1   What were the Jews instructed to build immediately after entering the land of Israel?

2   The blessings the Jews will receive when they keep God's commandments will be great wealth and success within the land of Israel. Where will the curses occur?

3 After 40 years in the wilderness, what was the physical condition of the of the Jewish people? Why were they in this condition?

Nitzavim

Moses reiterates the choice God has given the Jewish people: to follow His Torah, and reap the rewards of plenty within the land of Israel; or to, God forbid, turn away from Him, and suffer poverty and exile.

Read Deut. 19.9–30.20.

1 What covenant did God make with the Jewish people?
2 Why will non-Jews one day say that God cast the Jews out of their land?
3 This Parsha contains an amazingly poetic, beautiful passage that discusses how close or far away the Torah is from the Jewish people. Where does God say the Torah is not? Where is it?

Vayelech

Moses concludes his great speech to the Jewish people. Later this day, the Jewish people will cross over the Jordan River and begin to take possession of the Land of Israel. Moses once again affirms that Joshua will take over from him after his death, leading the Jewish people into Israel.

Read Deut. 31.1–31.30.

1 What was Moses' advice to Joshua before he crossed the Jordan River into Israel?
2 What did God say the Jewish people will think one day when trouble comes upon them?
3 What did Moses write at the end of his life? Where was this document placed?

Hazinu

This Parsha is a beautiful, poetic song that God instructs Moses to sing at the side of the Jordan River just before the Jewish people pass into Israel. It describes the Jewish people's early cleaving to God, and warns that one day they will turn away from God and incur his anger. Throughout this history, however, God reassures the Jewish people that He will never forsake us.

Read Deut. 32.1–32.52.

1   Who does God call on to be his witnesses in this song?
2   Why will God not forsake the Jewish people?
3   Where did Moses die? Why there?

Vezot Ha-Berachah

"Vezot Ha-Berachah" means "And this is the blessing." This emotional final Parsha begins with the abundant blessings God showers on the Jewish people. The final section of this Parsha describes the ending of an era: the death of Moses, on the day that the children of Israel were about to enter into the land of Israel.

Read Deut. 32.1–34.12.

1   How are the people of Israel unique?
2   Where was Moses buried? Why is Moses' grave not a destination for Jews to come and pray?
3   How old was Moses when he died? What was his physical condition then?

Bereshit (Genesis)

Answers to Bereshit questions

1   In Gen. 1.27, the Torah says that God created man in His (God's) own image, male and female, implying that these are two sides of God's own likeness. In Gen. 2.18, God creates a complement to Adam: in Hebrew an "ezer kenegdo," which translates roughly as a "helpmate-against" him. In Gen. 2.21–22, God removes a side of Adam and creates Eve out of this material. In Gen. 4.1–2, the Torah says God created Adam male and female.
2   God told Adam and Eve not to eat the fruit of the tree; Eve told the serpent they were not allowed to even touch the tree.
3   Cain offered ordinary produce to God, while Abel offered God the first, best animals of his flock.

Answers to Noah questions

1 God told Noah He wanted to destroy all living creatures (animals as well as humans), because the world was violent and corrupt.
2 The rainbow is a sign of the covenant between God and the descendants of Noah, that God will never again destroy the earth.
3 Ham looked at his father while he was naked and drunk, while Shem and Jafet covered up their father and did not look at him.

Answers to Lech Lecha questions

1 Abraham himself refused all spoils of war, although he did allow the men who fought alongside him to take them.
2 God told Abraham his descendants would be slaves for 400 years.
3 God will bless the descendants of Ishmael by making them numerous and a great nation. With the descendants of Isaac, God promises to make a special covenant.

Answers to Vayera questions

1 Abraham hailed the angels as guests, and offered them shelter, food, and drinks.
2 God will not destroy Sodom and Gemorrah if ten righteous men can be found to be living there.
3 The angel had to call out to Abraham twice.

Answers to Chaye Sarah questions

1 Abraham insisted on buying the Cave of Machpelah for its full value: 400 silver shekels.
2 In present-day Hebron.
3 Eliezer stood by the town's well, waiting for a maiden to offer him and his camels water.

Answers to Toledot questions

1 Esau emerged first, with Jacob grasping his heel.
2 Esau was a cunning hunter, while Jacob was a quiet man, preferring the indoors.

3   Jacob covered himself with animal skins and Esau's clothes. His mother Rebecca prepared meat for him to offer his father.

Answers to Vayetze questions

1   God promised Jacob: that He would give Jacob and Jacob's descendants this land (Israel); that Jacob's descendants would be as numerous as the dust of the earth; that Jacob's descendants would be blessed through Jacob; that God would return Jacob's descendants to their Land; and that God would never leave Jacob's descendants.

2   Lavan promised Jacob that if he worked for seven years, he could marry Rachel. Instead, Lavan substituted Leah during the wedding, and Jacob married Leah.

3   Rachel took away Lavan's idols.

Answers to Veyishlach questions

1   Jacob sent a servant ahead to offer Esau gifts: 220 goats, 220 sheep, 30 camels, 50 cows, and 30 donkeys.

2   The angel changes Jacob's name to Israel. Note: the name "Jacob" in Hebrew comes from the word "deceit." The name "Israel" comes from the Hebrew words for "going straight towards" and "God." In the past, Jacob triumphed through trickery; henceforth, he would triumph through God's will alone.

3   Shimon and Levi avenged themselves on the inhabitants of Shechem, after the prince of Shechem attacked their sister Dinah.

Answers to Veyeshev questions

1   God caused everything in Potiphar's house to prosper because of Joseph.

2   Joseph says it would be unfair to Potiphar, and a sin against God.

3   The butler's dream signified that he would be released from prison and restored to office in three days. The baker's dream signified that he would be executed in three days.

Answers to Miketz questions

1 Egypt would enjoy seven years of abundance, followed by seven years of famine. Joseph recommended that Pharaoh store food to use during the famine.

2 His father, Jacob, was afraid of anything dangerous happening to Benjamin.

3 Joseph instructs one brother to remain in Egypt as a hostage, while the others return with Benjamin.

Answers to Vayigash questions

1 Judah explains that his father Jacob is already distraught that he lost Joseph, and he cannot bear to lose his youngest son, Benjamin, too. Joseph sent all the Egyptians out of the room, and revealed his identity to his brothers.

2 Joseph is not angry; he realizes that God sent him to Egypt for a purpose.

3 God tells Jacob that He will make Jacob's family a mighty nation in Egypt, and that He will go down to Egypt with Jacob's family, and that He will also bring Jacob's family out of Egypt again one day.

Answers to Vayechi questions

1 Joseph's brothers feared that Joseph would be angry with them now that their father was no longer alive. (They worried that Joseph had only forgiven them to please Jacob.)

2 Joseph assured his brothers he bore them no ill will, and would continue to protect them.

3 Joseph wished to be buried in the land of Israel.

Shemot (Exodus)

Answers to Shemot questions

1 Pharaoh decreed that all male Jewish babies be killed at birth, but the Jewish midwives refused to comply with this order, and instead lied to Pharaoh, saying that the Jewish women delivered their babies quickly, before a midwife could arrive.

2 Moses' own mother was hired as his nurse. Many traditional Jewish commentators have supposed that Moses was thus raised with the knowledge that he was Jewish, and with all the sensitivities that brought towards his fellow Jews.

3 Moses asked Pharaoh to allow the Jews to go into the wilderness for three days to hold a feast to God. Pharaoh refused, and said that if the Jews had time to worship God for three days, they obviously didn't have enough work to do, and demanded that henceforth the Jews had to gather the straw they used to make bricks.

Answers to Va-ayera questions

1 In Exodus 6.3, God tells Moses that He appeared to Moses' ancestors Abraham, Isaac, and Jacob, but only to Moses did God reveal his name (spelled in Hebrew Yod-Hey-Vav-Hey).

2 They didn't listen to him.

3 God wanted the Jews to sacrifice animals that the Egyptians worshipped; Moses and Aaron feared the Egyptians would kill the Jews if they saw this.

Answers to Bo questions

1 Each household was instructed to slaughter a lamb and daub its blood on the doorposts of their house. They were then instructed to roast and eat the lamb meat, along with unleavened bread and bitter herbs.

2 Jews lived in Egypt 430 years.

3 We don't know the exact number of Jews who left Egypt, but there were 600,000 men.

Answers to Beshalach questions

1 The Jews turned on Moses, and complained it would have been better to remain in Egypt.

2 The Jews complained to Moses that they had no water to drink and no food to eat. Yet God provided both water, from springs, and manna, for food.

3 Shabbat.

Answers to Yitro questions

1 Yitro advised Moses to appoint supervisors to adjudicate disputes among groups of ten people, then judges above them to enforce order over groups of 50 people, then managers above them to enforce order over groups of 100 people, and finally senior managers to be in charge of groups of 1,000.

2 God promises the Jewish people that they will be God's treasure from among all people: a nation of priests, and a holy nation.

3 Moses said God would make the Jews a holy, treasured nation, if they would accept His Law. The elders of the Jewish people replied: "All that the Lord has spoken we will do."

Answers to Mishpatim questions

1 One who deliberately kills another shall be put to death. One who accidentally causes another's death shall travel to a special city of sanctuary, and is not harmed.

2 If we receive an article of clothing to secure a loan, we are obliged to return the item to its owner each night so he can sleep under it.

3 The elders of Israel saw the sapphire stone under God's feet.

Answers to Terumah questions

1 The Aron ("Ark") had a cover of pure gold. Two figures of two golden angels faced each other on top: their wings stretched out to cover the golden top of the Aron.

2 God spoke from within the wings of the golden angels on top of the Aron ("Ark").

3 God instructed the Jews to build a table of acacia wood covered with gold; dishes and cups made of pure gold, and a seven-branched menorah (candelabra) of pure gold.

Answers to Tetzaveh questions

1 Moses' brother Aaron and Aaron's sons (Nadav, Abihu, Eleazar, and Itamar) were the original Cohens who led services in the Mishkan.

2 Blue, purple, and red pomegranates, interspersed with golden bells,

decorated the hems of Aaron's robes. The gold plate on Aaron's forehead was engraved "Holy to the Lord."

3   Bulls, rams, unleavened bread, unleavened cakes, oil, and unleavened wafers were offered to God to sanctify the Mishkan.

Answers to Ki Tisa questions

1   Moses levied a tax of half a shekel (today, about a dime) on each person.

2   God told Moses the Jewish people must keep Shabbat (this is mentioned twice), Passover, and the three festivals (Sukkot, Passover, and Shavuot).

3   Moses reminded God of his promises to Abraham, Isaac, and Jacob. Moses also said that the Egyptians would gloat that God rescued the Jews only to kill them later.

Answers to Vayakhel questions

1   They brought too much; Bezalel complained to Moses that he had too many materials, and Moses asked the people of Israel to stop bringing gifts to decorate the Mishkan.

2   The Aron ("Ark") was made of acacia wood, covered with pure gold, and decorated with gold statues of angels. It had a gold cover and gold rings for handles on its side.

3   They donated their mirrors. There are many rabbinic commentaries about this. It is said that Moses initially protested that mirrors were a symbol of vanity, but God Himself intervened, because using mirrors to make one's self attractive to one's husband is holy.

Answers to Pekuday questions

1   God Himself gave Moses the precise plans for the Mishkan and all that was in it. Moses relayed these instructions, and Bezalal, with the help of Oholiav, directed the building and decorating of the Mishkan and everything associated with it.

2   There were 603,550 men.

3   In Judaism, something that belongs to a person may be counted. (People

themselves are never counted.) Just as Moses counted the half shekels he received from each Jew, we can count belongings, such as shoes, or coats, etc., and deduce the number of people present from these items.

Vayikra (Leviticus)
Answers to Vayikra questions
1 Any Jew could bring a sacrifice to atone for a sin they committed, and restore their connection to God. They could also bring a "peace" offering, to thank God, if they liked.
2 Aaron and his sons emptied the blood from the animal and burned the animal as a sacrifice. Aaron and his sons offered some of the flour and oil offerings to God by burning them; the remainder they ate themselves.
3 No. Only unleavened breads, cakes, and wafers were offered to God.

Answers to Tzav questions
1 Never. The fire on which sacrifices were burned in the Mishkan never went out.
2 Aaron and his sons couldn't eat meat from animals whose blood entered the Mishkan.
3 Aaron and his sons remained inside the Mishkan seven days during the consecrating ceremony.

Answers to Shemini questions
1 For sin offerings, they offered a bull-calf, a ram, a male goat, a calf, and a lamb. For peace offerings, they offered an ox and a ram.
2 There is no one right answer to this question. This passage has drawn much anguished thought and comment over the years. One common lesson drawn from this incident by many Jewish commentators is that the higher one's level (and Nadav and Avihu, as workers in the Mishkan, were on an exceedingly high level), the higher and more refined are one's actions expected to be. Amid the many, many comments written by rabbis and others on this Parsha, I have always liked the words of Nechama Leibowitz: "Evidently, Nadav and Avihu did not offend against any ritual precepts but sinned by reaching for God

through the dictates of their own hearts rather than through the path set by God. Submission to the yoke of Heaven — the ultimate aim of the Torah — was here supplanted by unbridled religious ecstasy. Hence their punishment."

3 Kosher animals have cloven hooves and chew their cud. Kosher fish have fins and scales.

Answers to Tazria questions

1 After giving birth, a woman brought a lamb and young pigeon to sacrifice to God. (If she could not afford both a lamb and pigeon, she was allowed to bring two pigeons.)

2 Tzarat on garments manifested with red or green spots on white cloth. Suspected clothing was isolated for a week at a time, up to two weeks, before tzarat was diagnosed.

3 The sufferer was declared contaminated by tzarat, and was not allowed to come into the Mishkan to offer sacrifices to God. If tzarat did not spread, the garment was washed and then locked up for seven days and re-examined. If the tzarat remained or spread, the garment was burned. If the tzarat faded, its remains were picked out of the wool and the garment was cleared of tzarat.

Answers to Metzora questions

1 Eight days after becoming cured, one brought offerings for God to the Mishkan: three lambs, a mixture of flour and oil, and some oil.

2 A house could contract tzarat, too: it was manifest by green or red streaks on the wall.

3 The Cohen shut up an infected house for seven days, then checked it again. If the red or green streaks of tzarat were still there or had spread, he removed the affected stones. If the tzarat reappeared after that, the house was dismantled and all materials discarded.

Answers to Acharei Mot questions

1 Before Aaron offered sacrifices to God on behalf of the people of Israel, he first made a sin-offering of a bullock, to atone for himself. (To this

day, the person leading Yom Kippur services first recites a prayer, aton-
ing for himself.)
2   Aaron cast lots. One goat was chosen to be sacrificed to God in the
Mishkan. The second goat symbolically received the sins of the Jewish,
and was sent into the wilderness.
3   Yom Kippur is called "a Shabbat of solemn rest for you" (Lev. 16.31).
Indeed, many of the rules concerning Yom Kippur are identical to those
of Shabbat. We may not do any of the 39 types of work on Yom Kippur
that are prohibited on Shabbat.

Answers for Kedoshim questions

1   We should be holy because God is holy.
2   After telling us to be a holy people, God immediately commands us to
"fear" (i.e. respect) our parents, and then to keep Shabbat.
3   We are warned not to hate our brother in our heart (Lev. 19.17).
Indeed, Jewish tradition teaches that our Beit Hamikdash, our Temple
in Jerusalem, was destroyed because of the sin of baseless hatred.

Answers to Emor questions

1   A Cohen may attend only the funerals of his parents, children (God
forbid), brother, and unmarried sister.
2   Jews were told to bring animals that were healthy, not blind, broken,
maimed, sick, deformed or injured.
3   The first holiday mentioned in this Parsha is Shabbat. We are also
instructed to keep Passover, Shavuot, Rosh Hashana, Yom Kippur, and
Sukkot.

Answers to Behar questions

1   Every seven years, we do not sow or plow our fields. This timetable is
followed scrupulously in Israel today by religiously observant Jews.
2   People who are not Jewish can eat food that grew wild in Israel during
the "Shabbat" year. On a separate note, animals can also eat this food.
3   Only properties outside of walled towns were included in the Yovel
transactions.

Answers to Bechukotai questions

1 God promised rains in their seasons, bounteous crops, fruit harvests, and that harmful wild animals will not live in the land of Israel.

2 God promised to help Israel triumph over its enemies. God also promised to bless the people of Israel with children and to establish a covenant with them.

3 God will make the Jewish people fainthearted; their enemies will hate them and rule over them. (In a memorable passage, God says that the Jews will be afraid and think they are pursued even when they hear the sound of a driven leaf.) God will remember his covenant with Abraham, Isaac, and Jacob, however, when the Jews repent of their sins.

Bemidbar (Numbers)

Answers to Bemidbar questions

1 There were 22,273 first-born children among the people of Israel in the desert.

2 They wrapped these items in cloths of purple and blue, and in sealskin.

3 Aaron and his sons were responsible for arranging the interior of the Mishkan.

Answers to Naso questions

1 Men aged 30 to 50 helped to pack and move the Mishkan.

2 Any man or woman who desired could become a Nazir.

3 Nazirim vowed to abstain from: wine; other alcoholic beverages; vinegar made from wine or other alcoholic beverages; grape juice; grapes; raisins; any food made of grapes. A Nazir did not cut their hair nor go near a dead body, even that of a close relative. When their period of being a Nazir was fulfilled, they brought sacrifices to the Mishkan: two lambs (one male and one female); a basket of unleavened bread; cakes of fine flour mixed with oil; unleavened wafers spread with oil; and offerings of grain and of drinks.

Answers to Be-Ha-Alotecha questions

1 The Jewish people complained that they wanted meat, as they enjoyed in Egypt, and not the manna that God provided for them. God caused a great flock of birds to fly over the camp of the Jews, and the Jews who complained that they wanted meat ate them. As they were eating, God killed the people who were feasting on flesh.

2 God Himself told Miriam and Aaron: other prophets heard God's voice in a vision. Only Moses could speak with God: "with him do I (God) speak mouth to mouth, even manifestly, and not in dark speeches" (Num. 12.8).

3 Miriam spoke lashon ha'rah (gossip) about Moses and his Ethiopian wife, Tzipporah.

Answers to Shelach Lecha questions

1 Caleb and Joshua reported: "The land, which we passed through to spy it out, is an exceeding good land" (Num. 14.7); they also said that it was possible to conquer. The remaining ten spies said that the land was fruitful, and was a land flowing with milk and honey, but they warned that the people living there were "giants," and that next to them the Jews seemed as small as grasshoppers. They also said that the Land of Israel "ate" its inhabitants.

2 The Jews began to talk about electing a new leader to lead them back to Egypt.

3 Moses says that other nations will think that God was unable to bring the Jewish people into the land that He swore to give them.

Answers to Korach questions

1 Korach, along with Datan and Aviram, also of the Tribe of Levi, led the rebellion. They were joined by 250 prominent men, including the leaders of the families in each of the 12 Tribes of Israel.

2 Moses asked God to refuse Korach's and his allies' offerings, and said he'd been fair: "I have not taken one donkey from them, neither have I hurt one of them" (Num. 16.15).

3 The next day, after the death of Korach and Korach's followers, the

Jewish people started speaking against Moses and Aaron, accusing them of killing holy people such as Korach.

Answers to Chukat questions

1 The sacrifice was a red heifer (female cow) that had no other colors on her, no flaws, and had never been yoked.
2 God told Moses he couldn't enter the land of Israel because he "believed not in (God), to sanctify (God) in the eyes of the children of Israel" (Num. 20.12). Many Jewish commentators see this as a rebuke for striking, instead of speaking to (as God commanded), a rock to make it gush forth water. Moses' striking it diminished the impression of God's power in the eyes of the people of Israel.
3 The Jews first conquered the lands of the Amorites.

Answers to Balak questions

1 Balam's donkey refused to walk because a "malach," an angel, holding a fiery sword in his hand, blocked the way. At first it was only visible to Balam's donkey. (A similar malach was posted at the entrance to the Garden of Eden after Adam and Eve were expelled.)
2 The first miracle was that Balam's donkey could see the malach (angel) in his path. The second was that the donkey could talk, to rebuke Balam.
3 Balam blessed the people of Israel four times.

Answers to Pinchas questions

1 God decreed that when a man has no sons, his daughters inherit his land. If he has no children, his land should be inherited by his brothers. If he has no children and no brothers, his land will be inherited by his nearest relative.
2 Moses was to climb the mountain of Avarim. Jewish commentators traditionally explain that this was so Moses could see the Land of Israel, even though he could not enter it.
3 Joshua was appointed by God to succeed Moses as leader of the Jewish people.

Answers to Mattot questions

1   God instructed Moses to avenge the Jewish people against the Midianites, who had led them into idol worship.

2   Only the female children of Midian were saved.

3   The Tribes of Gad and Reuben requested that their inheritance be on the east side of the Jordan River, outside of the Land of Israel, because the grass was better there for their cattle. When Moses objected that it would be unfair to the other Ten Tribes if Gad and Reuben did not fight alongside them, the people of Gad and Reuben promised they would aid in conquering the Land of Israel, even though they did not want to live there.

Answers to Massey questions

1   The Jewish people were to drive out the inhabitants from the land, and destroy their idols and idolatrous altars.

2   The Tribes were to apportion land by casting lots.

3   The Torah says one may not pay to avoid punishment.

Devarim (Deuteronomy)

Answers to Devarim questions

1   Moses says it was difficult to lead the Jewish people because they were numerous, and fought with each other.

2   People were to be judged equally and fairly, with no regard for their differences in status.

3   Caleb was allowed to enter the land of Israel because he reported favorably after exploring it. (See Parshat Shelach Lecha.)

Answers to Ve-etchanan questions

1   Moses requested to be allowed to enter the land of Israel.

2   God will punish those who reject Him for four generations, and He will show mercy for one thousand generations to those who love Him and follow his commandments.

3   The Jewish people were instructed to destroy the seven nations in the land of Israel, not to make any covenant with them, not to

intermarry with them, and also to destroy their idolatrous images and altars.

Answers to Ekev questions

1 Moses said the Jews would find Israel a land of brooks, fountains, and pools, a land of honey and prosperity, a land rich in brass and iron. This Parsha also mentions the seven fruits in which Israel is rich: wheat, barley, grapes, figs, dates, pomegranates, and olives.
2 Moses warned that when the Jewish become prosperous and comfortable in Israel, they might believe they are responsible for their own wealth and ease, and forget that wealth and ease are gifts from God, and might forget all that God did for them in the desert.
3 In Egypt, people sowed and watered their seeds. In Israel, the land drinks rain as it comes down from the Heavens. (Jewish commentators, and the text here itself, imply that the latter arrangement engenders stronger feelings of thanks to God.)

Answers to Re-eh questions

1 Idolatrous residents in the land of Israel practiced child sacrifice.
2 God forbade the Jewish people from even asking about idolatrous rites.
3 Indentured servants were kept for six years. At that time, they were released and given gifts of livestock, grain, wine, and wealth. The Jewish people are commanded to be generous to servants because they were once slaves in Egypt, and God redeemed them. If an indentured servant chose not to be released, their ear was pierced as a sign of their continued servitude.

Answers to Shoftim questions

1 The King of Israel was not allowed to have many horses, silver, or gold. He couldn't have many wives, and he was never allowed to return the Jewish people to Egypt. He was also required to write a copy of the Torah and read it every day, to ensure he feared God and kept His commandments, and did not think himself greater than others.

2   A man is excused from going into battle the first year (the length of time is given in the Talmud) he has married, the first year he has built a house, and the first year he has planted a vineyard. A man who is afraid to fight is also excused.

3   Fruit trees are not to be cut down during battles.

Answers to Ki Tetze questions

1   If we cannot find a lost item's owner, we should keep it for them until we are able to return it.

2   We must build fences around rooftops, to prevent accidental falls.

3   Nobody may be punished for another's sin: everyone is responsible for their own actions.

Answers to Ki Tavo questions

1   The Jews were instructed to erect stone pillars covered with plaster, on which the words of the Torah were to be written. (The Talmud specifies that these were 12 in number.) The Jews were then instructed to build an altar on Mount Ebal for offerings to God.

2   The Jews would be cursed within the land of Israel, through poverty and oppression, and also outside the land of Israel, after they are scattered among the nations.

3   After 40 years in the wilderness, the Jewish people were still wearing new clothes and shoes. This taught them that God would take care of them.

Answers to Nitzavim questions

1   God made a covenant with the Jewish people to be their God; in return, the Jews would be "his people": the Jewish people have an obligation to follow the Torah in return.

2   Others will say that God cast the Jews out of their land because they (the Jews) turned away from God and worshipped idols.

3   The Torah is not in the Heavens ("that you should say 'who will go up for us to Heaven, and bring it to us' . . .") and it is not over the sea ("that you should say 'who shall go over the sea for us, and bring it to

us' . . ."). The Torah "is very close to you, in your mouth, and in your heart" (Deut. 30.12–14).

Answers to Vayelech questions

1 Moses told Joshua to be strong and courageous, because God would go with him into Israel.
2 The Jews would think that God was no longer with them.
3 Moses wrote down the entire Torah. This document was placed inside the Aron (Ark), beside the tablets on which God had carved the words of the Torah.

Answers to Hazinu questions

1 God called on the heavens and the earth to be his witnesses.
2 God will not forsake the Jewish people because He does not want Israel's enemies to rejoice at Israel's downfall.
3 Moses climbed Mount Avarim so that he could see the land of Israel from its high peak, and he died there, atop Mount Avarim.

Answers to Vezot Ha-Berachah questions

1 The people of Israel were saved by God, and God continues to protect them.
2 Moses was buried in the land of Moav, near Bet-Peor. The location of his grave is a secret.
3 Moses was 120 years old when he died. His vision and strength were undiminished.

12

Songs for Shabbat

For centuries, singing "zemirot" (the Hebrew word for songs) has been a major part of Shabbat. It is a mitzvah to be happy in Judaism. Our religion recognizes the central role that singing plays in creating happiness, therefore singing is a large part of traditional Jewish occasions, from weddings, to holiday celebrations, to festive meals, to Shabbat. Even if it seems strange at first, singing together creates a joyous feeling, and elevates the mood of any meal or gathering to a much higher, holier level. Zemirot are usually sung after Shabbat meals, while everyone is still sitting around the table, enjoying each other's company.

Short Jewish favorites

If you are lucky enough to have attended Jewish camp, or even just Jewish Sunday school, there are some short traditional songs that might be familiar to you. Some of these are part of the liturgy of Shabbat. Others are taken from the Jewish Bible. If you are not familiar with the catchy tunes that are traditional with these songs, you can easily look them up in Jewish CDs or on-line. For many of these songs, you can also experiment with adapting them to appealing tunes that you already know, from nursery rhymes to popular music to show tunes. I've given some examples of well-known melodies that go with many of these songs; you can experiment further with your own favorite melodies, as well.

David Melech Yisrael

This is a fun song. The words are simple: "David, King of Israel, lives forever." King David was the monarch who, acting on God's instructions and with God's aid, captured Jerusalem and made it the capital of Israel.

David, Melech Yisrael	David, King of Israel
Chai, Chai Vikayam	Lives, Lives Forever
David Melech Yisrael	David, King of Israel
Chai, Chai Vikayam.	Lives, Lives Forever
(repeat)	

Eretz Zavat Chalav

The words of this simple song are taken from the biblical description of the land of Israel: it is a land flowing with milk and honey. This song was popular with the Jewish "chilutzim," or pioneers, of the later 1800s and early 1900s, who liked to sing it with an energetic tune that is still popular today. If you are unfamiliar with this camp standard, or wish to sing it to a softer melody, it goes very well with "Twinkle Twinkle Little Star."

Eretz Zavat	A Land Flowing
Chalav U'Dvash	(with) Milk and Honey
Eretz Zavat	A Land Flowing
Chalav U'Dvash	(with) Milk and Honey
(repeat)	

Hiney Ma Tov

This song (taken from the opening of Psalm 133) is appropriate for any gathering or meal. There is a traditional tune for this song, but it also works well with "Row Row Row Your Boat" (particularly if you sing the last line twice) or "What a Wonderful World." If you use this tune, try it in a round. (A round is when one half of the singers starts the song first, then the second half of singers comes in mid-way, starting the song after the first group has completed the first verse, and finishing after them.)

Hiney ma tov u'ma nayim	Here, how good and how pleasant
Shevet, achim, gam yachad.	Sitting (together), brotherhood,
	and being together.

(repeat)

Am Yisrael Chai

I remember one extremely moving instance singing this. It was Purim, and there had just been a huge terrorist attack in Israel. At my shul (synagogue) Purim celebrations that night, the mood was a little more subdued than usual. Finally, at the end of the evening, our rabbi called for quiet. He asked us all to sing "Am Yisrael Chai," proclaiming "The People of Israel Still Live." No matter what, he said. Always. Everyone in the shul sang with gusto, and there was hardly a dry eye.

Am Yisrael chai!	The people of Israel lives!
Am Yisrael chai!	The people of Israel lives!
Am Yisrael chai!	The people of Israel lives!
(repeat)	
Od Avinu chai!	Still our Father (God) lives!
Od Avinu chai!	Still our Father (God) lives!
Od Avinu, Od Avinu,	Still our Father, still our Father,
Od Avinu chai!	still our Father lives!
(repeat)	

Chiri Biri Bim Bom

This is a fun song to sing, particularly if you don't know Hebrew. The traditional version of this song is actually in Yiddish, the language of many European Jews, but its refrain is a simple "Bim Bom Bim Bom Bim Bom" that anyone can sing. This is a funny nonsense song, and once you get the hang of it, you can make up your own words. (Try singing "When I say kugel you say broccoli — kugel! — broccoli! — kugel! — broccoli!" or "When I say 'go to bed' you say 'stay up'! — go to bed! — stay up! — go to bed! — stay up!" You get the point.) This song can easily be sung in English, too.

As ich vel zingen "lecha dodi"	When I sing "Come my beloved"
Zolzu zingen "chiri biri bim."	You sing "chiri biri bim."
As ich vel zingen "likras kala".	When I sing "To greet the bride"
Zolzu zingen "chiri biri bam"	You sing "chiri biri bam."
"Lecha dodi" — chiri biri bim	"Come my beloved" — chiri biri bim
"Likrat Kala" — chiri biri bam	"To greet the bride" — chiri biri bam
"Lecha dodi" "Likrat Kala"	"Come my beloved"
	"To greet the bride"
Chiri biri biri biri birir biri biri bam.	Chiri biri biri biri biri biri biri bam.
As ich vel zingen "Yom HaShabbos"	When I sing "The Shabbat Day"
Zolzu zingen "chiri biri bim."	You sing "chiri biri bim."
As ich vel zingen "Yom Menucha"	When you sing "A Day of Rest"
Zolzu zingen "chiri biri bam"	You sing "chiri biri bam."
"Yom HaShabbos" — chiri biri bim	"The Shabbat Day" — chiri biri bim
"Yom Menucha" — chiri biri bam	"A Day of Rest" — chiri biri bam
"Yom HaShabbos" "Yom Menucha"	"The Shabbat Day" "A Day of Rest"
Chiri biri biri biri birir biri biri bam.	Chiri biri biri biri biri biri biri bam.
As ich vel zingen "Yerushalayim"	When I sing "Yerushalayim (Jerusalem)"
Zolzu zingen "chiri biri bim."	You sing "chiri biri bim."
As ich vel zingen "Ir Ha-Kodesh"	When you sing "Ir Ha-Kodesh (the holy city)"
Zolzu zingen "chiri biri bam"	You sing "chiri biri bam."
"Yerushalayim" — chiri biri bim	"Yerushalayim (Jerusalem)" — chiri biri bim
"Ir Ha-Kodesh" — chiri biri bam	"Ir Ha-Kodesh (the holy city)" — chiri biri bam
"Yerushalayim" "Ir Ha-Kodesh"	"Yerushalayim" "Ir Ha-Kodesh"
Chiri biri biri biri birir biri biri bam.	Chiri biri biri biri biri biri biri bam.

Shabbat Shalom Hey

Everybody is able to sing this song. You can play with it, repeating it over and over if you like, or setting it to different tunes.

Shabbat Shalom, Hey!	A Good (literally, a "Complete") Shabbat, Hey!
Shabbat Shalom, Hey!	Good Shabbat, Hey!
Shabbat, Shabbat, Shabbat	Shabbat, Shabbat, Shabbat,
Shabbat Shalom, Hey!	A good Shabbat, Hey!
(repeat)	

Lo Yisah Goy

These words are found in the prophet Isaiah's vision of the perfect peace that will reign on earth in the time of the Messiah (Isaiah 2.4). "Lo Yisah Goy" is often sung as a round. If you are unfamiliar with the traditional melody, these words can be sung to virtually any tune. Try it with the tunes to "Yankee Doodle Dandy," "America the Beautiful," and "This Land is Your Land," among others.

Lo Yisah goy el goy cherev	Nation shall not lift up sword against nation
V'lo yilmadu od milchama.	And they shall not learn war any more.
(repeat many times)	

Kol Ha'Olam Kulo

I first heard this song in the Israeli city of Safed, which is famous as a center of Jewish mysticism. Many Jews who are drawn to the mystical side of Judaism live and study there, and Safed also attracts a number of New Age and alternative artists and visitors. When I arrived in Safed, a band was playing this song outdoors, and a group of women and girls were holding hands, dancing together through the streets. I joined them; I learned the words they were singing: this song of absolute trust in God.

Kol Ha'Olam Kulo	All of the entire world
Gesher tzar me'od	(Is a) very narrow bridge
Gesher tzar me'od	(Is a) very narrow bridge
(repeat several times)	
Ve'ha ikkar	And the central thing

Ve'ha ikkar	And the central thing
Lo Le'fahed klal.	(Is) Do not fear anything
	(because God is with you).

Haveinu Shalom Aleichem

This is another extremely easy song for everyone to sing, as it only has three words. Try singing it over and over, with a lot of energy, even tapping the table to keep an energetic beat.

Haveinu Shalom Aleichem.	Bring Peace to You.
Haveinu Shalom Aleichem.	Bring Peace to You.
Haveinu Shalom, Shalom,	Bring Peace, Peace
Shalom Aleichem.	Peace to You.
(repeat)	

Hava Nagilah

Many people know this song, a standard at Jewish weddings and bar mitzvah and bat mitzvah parties. Here are the full words. This is a great song to get a room full of people roused and happy, creating a real holiday atmosphere!

Hava Nagila	Here we will be happy
Hava Nagila	Here we will be happy
Hava Nagila	Here we will be happy
Ve'nismecha!	And we will rejoice!
Hava Naranana	Here we will be invigorated
Hava Naranana	Here we will be invigorated
Hava Naranana	Here we will be invigorated
Ve'nismecha!	And we will rejoice!
Uroo! Uroo!	Arise! Arise!
Uroo achim	Arise siblings
Be'lev sameach!	With a heart of joy!
Uroo achim	Arise siblings
Be'lev sameach!	With a heart of joy!

Uroo achim, Uroo achim	Arise siblings, Arise siblings
Be'lev sameach!	With a heart of joy!
(repeat whole song)	

Hatikvah

Many people know the beautiful, melodic national anthem of Israel. The words are by the Hebrew poet Naphtali Imber, who wrote them at the very dawn of modern Zionism, when he travelled in the 1880s to what was soon to become modern Israel. The music was drawn from traditional Moldavian folk music. (The famous Czech composer Bedrich Smetana used the same melody in his hauntingly beautiful composition "Die Moldau.")

Kol od be'levav penimah	Still in the innermost heart
Nefesh Yehudi homiyah	The Jewish soul yearns
U'lefa'atei Mizrach Kadimah	And goes forward to the East
Ayin le'Tzion tzofiyah.	The eye searches for Zion.
Od lo avdah Tikvateinu	We still have not lost our Hope
Hatikvah bat shenot alpayim.	The two thousand year old Hope.
Lehiyot am chofshi be'artzainu	To be a free people in our Land
Eretz Tzion v'Yerusahalayim.	The Land of Zion and Jerusalem.
(repeat last two lines)	

La-Shana Ha-Ba

This is a very easy, rousing song. It contains only four easily pronounceable words. The traditional tune for it is fast-paced and energetic. If you are unfamiliar with this song's traditional melody, however, you might try singing it to other simple, rousing tunes you might be familiar with. It works with kids' tunes like "The Bear Went over the Mountain," "The Wheels on the Bus," and "You are My Sunshine."

La-Shana Ha-Ba'ah	Next Year
Ba-Yerusahalayim	In Jerusalem
(repeat several times)	
La-Shana Ha-Ba'ah	Next Year

Ba-Yerusahalayim Ha-Bnuyah	In a Jerusalem that's Rebuilt (i.e. in Messianic times)

Zum Gali Gali

This is a catchy song that was popular in Israel with the "chalutzim," the pioneers who built the modern state. It works very well as a round.

Zum gali gali gali	Zum gali gali gali
Zum gali gali	Zum gali gali
(repeat)	
Ha-amim la'ma-an ha-shalom.	The peoples (of the world) are for peace.
Ha'shalom le'ma-an ha-amim.	Peace is for the peoples of the world.
(repeat)	

Anachnu Ma'aminim

"Anachnu Ma'aminim" ("We are Believers") is a short, intensely meaning-ful song. There are a number of tunes for these moving lyrics. One of the most popular modern versions is performed by the well-known Orthodox Jewish singer Mordechai ben David. (Fans of the book or movie *Schindler's List*, about the German industrialist who saved over a thousand Jews during the Holocaust by employing them as slave labor in his factory, might be interested to know that Mordechai ben David is the son of one of the Jews Oskar Schindler saved: a "chazzan," or cantor, from Cracow named David Werdyger.) Try the melodies from "The Yellow Rose of Texas" or "Sunrise Sunset."

Anachnu ma'aminim b'nei ma'aminim	We are believers, children of believers
V'ein lanu al mi le'hisha'en.	And we have no one (else) to rely on.
Ela ela al Avinu,	Only only on our Father (God),
Avinu she'ba'Shamayim.	Our Father in Heaven.
Yisrael, Yisrael	(People of) Israel, (People of) Israel
Betach b'Hashem	Believe in God

Ezram u'Meginam Hu.	He is your Help and your Protection.
(repeat)	

Ani Me'amin

"Ani Me'amin" ("I Believe") is widely sung, testifying to the central Jewish belief in the coming of the Messiah. There are many tunes for these words, from the somber to the extremely peppy. Two modern melodies that works (if you repeat the words over and over to make them fit the music) are "California Dreaming" and "If I Could Save Time in a Bottle."

Ani me'amin	I believe
Ani me'amin	I believe
Be'emunah shlaima	With perfect faith
Be'viat ha-Mashiach.	In the coming of the Messiah.
(repeat)	
Ve'af al pi she-yitmameh'ya	And even if he is delayed
Im kol ze achakeh lo,	Even with all this,
	I will still wait for him,
Be'kol yom she'yavo.	Every day until the day he comes.
(repeat)	

Siman Tov

Many people are familiar with this song from Jewish weddings, bar and bat mitzvahs, and other happy events. This positive song can make a fun addition to your Shabbat table, too.

Siman Tov u'Mazal Tov	Good portents and good luck
U'Mazal Tov v'Siman Tov	And good luck and good portents
Siman Tov u'Mazal Tov	Good portents and good luck
U'Mazal Tov v'Siman Tov	And good luck and good portents
Ye-hey lanu.	To us.
Ye-hey lanu, ye-hey lanu	To us, to us
U'lechol Yisrael	And to all Israel
Ye-hey lanu, ye-hey lanu	To us, to us

U'lechol Yisrael	And to all Israel.

Urah Vanim

This is an easy, traditional song that works very well with the tune "Row, Row, Row Your Boat."

Urah vanim l'vanecha	May you see your children and their children
Shalom al Yisrael	Peace to Israel
Shalom al Yisrael	Peace to Israel
(repeat)	

English songs

Eli Eli

This moving song was written (in Hebrew) by the Hungarian poet and partisan Hannah Senesh. Hannah Senesh left her home in Hungary for Mandatory Palestine (which later became modern Israel) on the eve of World War II. In Palestine, she trained with the British army, and eventually was sent on a top-secret mission: she parachuted into Nazi-occupied Europe, and made her way to Hungary, with the goal of warning the Jewish residents there of the Nazi extermination plans and helping form a resistance. Hannah Senesh was eventually caught by the Nazis, imprisoned, tortured, and executed in 1944. She was 21 years old. She left behind a body of beautiful poetry, as well as a diary, which is still in print and remains riveting reading today.

It is popular to sing this song first in Hebrew, then in English. (I'm including the popular English translation that people sing.)

Eli, Eli	My Lord, My God
Shelo Yigamer Le'olam.	I pray that these things never end.
Rishrush shel ha'mayim,	The rush of the waters,
Barak ha'shamayim,	The crash of the Heavens,

Tefillat ha'adam.	The prayers of man.
(repeat)	

Walking in the Path of Hashem (God)

This pretty song works with the tunes of "Row, Row, Row Your Boat" and "When Johnny Comes Marching Home Again." Try it as a round. (Note: Orthodox Jews say "Hashem," which means "the Name," rather than attempt to speak God's actual name.)

Don't walk in front of me; I may not follow.

Don't walk behind me; I may not lead.

Just walk beside me and be my friend, and together we will walk in the path of Hashem.

Traditional prayers

These traditional prayers are very well-known. They can add a lovely feeling of happiness and spirituality to your Shabbat table.

Adon Olam

"Adon Olam" can be sung to any tune. Go ahead and try it.

Adon Olam, Asher Malach	Lord of the World, Who Ruled
B'terem kol yetzir nivrah	Before each creature was created
L'eit na'a'sa v'cheftzo kol	When He created everything through His will
Azai melech shemo nikra	Then His name was called "King."
Ve'acha'ray kichlot hakol	And after everything has gone away
L'vado yimloch norah	He will rule alone, awesomely
Vehu haya vehu hoveh	He was and He is
Vehu yiheyeh beti-farah	And He will be — in Glory.
Vehu echada v'ain shainee	He is One and there is no second
Le'ham-shil lo lehachbirah	To compare to Him to be another

Beli rashit beli tachlit	Without beginning without end
Velo ha'oz vehamisra	And to Him is the strength and the ability.
Vehu kayli vechai go'ali	He is my God and my living redeemer
Vetzhur chevli b'et tzara	And my rock when I'm in pain or in trouble
Vehu nisi umanos li	He is my miracle and my deliverance
Menat kosi be'yom ekra	The portion in my cup on the day that I call.
Beyado afkid ruchee	I will place my soul into the safety of His hand
Be'ait ishan ve'a'eerah	In awe of Him I will go to sleep and I will wake up
Ve'im ruche geviyatee	And with my soul my body will remain
Hashem li velo irah	God is with me and I shall not be afraid.

Ein Keloheinu

Ein Ke-loheinu.	There is no one like our Lord.
Ein Ka-doneinu.	There is no one like our God.
Ein Ke-malkeinu.	There is no one like our King.
Ein Ke-moshi-einu.	There is no one like our Redeemer.
Mi Ke-loheinui?	Who is like our Lord?
Mi Ka-doneinu?	Who is like our God?
Mi Ke-malkeunu?	Who is like our King?
Mi Ke-moshi-einu?	Who is like our Redeemer?
Nodeh Le-loheinu.	We will thank our Lord.
Nodeh L-adoneinu.	We will thank our God.
Nodeh Le-malkeinu.	We will thank our King.
Nodeh Le-moshi-einu.	We will thank our Redeemer.
Baruch Keloheinu.	Blessed is our Lord.
Baruch Adoneinu.	Blessed is our God.
Baruch Malkeinu.	Blessed is our King.
Baruch Moshi-einu.	Blessed is our Redeemer.
Atah hu Keloheinu.	You are our Lord.

Atah hu Adoneinu.	You are your God.
Atah hu Malkeinu	You are our King.
Atah hu Moshi-einu.	You are your Redeemer.
Atah hu she-hiktiru avoteinu	You are the One our forefathers worshipped
Lefanecha et ketoret hasamim.	Before you with offerings of incense.

Etz Chaim He

Etz Chaim Hee	It is a Tree of Life
La'macha'zikim ba	To those who grasp it strongly
Vetom-checha me-ushar.	And who place themselves in Your care.
Deracheha darchei noam	All the paths of (the Torah) are pleasant paths
Vechol netivotecha	And all its ways are
Shalom.	Peace.
Hashiveinu Hashem.	Return us, God.
Kelecha Ve-nashuva.	To You and we will return.
Chadeish yimenu ki-kedem.	Renew our days as they used to be.

Sim Shalom

This line is taken from the "Shemoneh Esrei" prayer of the "Mussaf" ("Additional") service on Shabbat mornings. It can be made to fit many simple tunes such as "Twinkle Twinkle Little Star," "London Bridge is Falling Down," and "You are my Sunshine."

Sim shalom	Place peace,
Tovah u'vracha	Torah, and blessings,
Chein v'chesed	Favor, and kindness,
Ve'rachamim	And mercy
Aleinu ve'al kol	On us and on all
Yisrael amecha.	Israel, Your people.

Oseh Shalom Bimromav

This beautiful wish is said at the conclusion of the Shemoneh Esrei prayer.

Oseh Shalom Bimromav	The one who makes peace in His high places
Hu ya'aseh shalom aleinu	May He make peace upon us
V'al kol Yisrael,	And on all of Israel,
Ve'imru "Amen."	And we say "Amen."
(repeat)	

Shema Yisrael

The "Shema" prayer can be made to fit any simple melody if you repeat it enough, from national anthems to common children's songs to popular music. Try "America the Beautiful" or "Rule Britannia." (When singing prayers for enjoyment, rather than actually praying, it is common to use the name "Hashem," which means "The Name," instead of "Adonoy," which is a name Jews use for God.)

Shema Yisrael,	Listen Israel,
Hashem Keloheinu,	God is our Lord,
Hashem Echad!	God is One!

Ze Ha'Yom

This jubilant line, the final in Psalm 118, is sung on Jewish festivals as part of the morning service. It can be sung to many popular tunes.

Ze ha'Yom Asah Hashem	This is the day God has made
Nagila v'Nismecha Vo.	We will rejoice and be happy in it.

Traditional Shabbat songs

Over the centuries, several zemirot have become closely identified with Shabbat. Most of these songs speak to the centrality of Shabbat in the Jewish week, and our gratitude to God for giving us this day of holiness.

Yom Ze L'Yisrael

This song was written by Rabbi Yitzchak Luria (1534–72), a mystic rabbi and teacher in the Israeli city of Safed.

First verse:

Yom ze l'Yisrael	This is a day for Israel
Orah v'simcha,	Light and happiness,
Shabbat menucha.	Shabbat of rest.
Tzivita pikudim	You ordered us to be under Your care
B'ma-ah-mad Seenai.	When we were positioned at
	Mount Sinai.
Shabbat u-moadim	Shabbat and the festivals
Lishmor bechol-shana	To keep the whole year
La'aroch lifanai	To set before me
Masait ve-arucha,	Banquets and feasts,
Shabbat Menucha	A Shabbat of rest.

Ka Ribon

This song was written by another Safed rabbi who was influenced by Jewish mystical thought: Rabbi Yisrael Najara (1555–1625). It is written in Aramaic, a language closely related to Hebrew, which was spoken in ancient Babylonia.

First verse:

Ka Ribon Olam	God, Ruler of the World
V'almaya (2 x)	And all worlds
Ant hu malka	He is King who
Melech malchaya (2x)	Rules over all kings

Ovad G'vur'tach	Your works are strong
Ve'tim'haya (2x)	And beautiful.
Shefar kadamach	Before you I will declare
L'ha'ch'avaya (2x)	Your praise.

Menucha V'Simcha

It is not known who wrote this song or when. The only indication we have of its authorship is in the name embedded in the first letters of each verse, which spell "Moshe" (Moses). The earliest written copy of "Menucha V'Simcha" is from 1545.

First verse:

Menucha v'simcha	Rest and happiness
Or le-yehudim	Light for the Jews
Yom Shabbaton	Day of ceasing work
Yom Machamadim.	Day of loveliness
Shomrav ve'zochrav,	"Guard" and "Remember,"
Hayma me'idim,	Stand and proclaim,
Ki l'shisa kol	Because in six (days) everything
Bru'im v'omdim!	Was created, and still exists!

Ma Yedidut Menuchatecha

The authorship and date of this zemir (song) is unknown, but the theme it addresses is timeless: our extensive preparations for, and our enjoyment on, Shabbat.

First verse:

Ma yedidut menucha-techa	What preciousness is your rest
Et Shabbat hamalka	Shabbat the Queen
Bechain narutz likra-taych	In sincerity we will run close to you
Bo'ee kala n'sucha	Come, royal Queen!
Levush bigday chamudot	Wearing lovely clothes
Lehadlik nair bivracha	To light candles with the blessing
Ve'teichel kol ha'avodot	And we stop all our work

Lo ta'asu melacha.	"Thou shalt not work."
Refrain:	
Le-hit'aneg be-ta'anugim	To rejoice in our celebration:
Barburim uslav ve'dagim	(Eating) Swans and quails and fish.
(Repeat refrain.)	

Tsur Mishelo

This is a rousing zemir that is usually sung last on Friday night, right before Birkat HaMazon (the prayer recited after meals).

Refrain:	
Tzur mishalo achalnu	Rock, from which we have eaten
Barechu emunai	We, who have faith, will bless Him
Savanu ve'otarnu	We were satisfied, and even more than satisfied
Kidvar Hashem.	According to the word of God (as He promised).
First verse:	
Hazan, hazan, hazan	Provider, provider, provider
Hazan et olamo	Provider for His world
(Repeat)	
Ro'einu avinu	Our Shepherd, our Father
Achalnu et lachmo	We have eaten His bread
Ve'aino shateinu	And drunk His wine
Et kein nodeh lishmo	Therefore we will thank His Name
Un'halelo befinu	And praise Him with our mouths
Amarnu ve'aninu	We will say and we will sing
Ein kodesh ke-Hashem.	"There is no holiness like God!"
(Repeat refrain.)	

Dror Yikrah

Two popular tunes to this song are "Scarborough Fair" (as recorded by Simon and Garfunkel) and "Sloop John B" (as recorded by the Beach Boys).

First verse:

Dror yikra	Freedom He will call out
levein im bach	For the son and the daughter
Ve'yin'tzar'chem	And He will guard you
Ke'mo vavat.	Like the pupil of an eye.
Ne'im shim'chem	Pleasant will be your name
Ve'lo yushbat	And this will never cease.
Shevu venuchu	Stop and rest
Be'yom Shabbat!	On the day of Shabbat!

Baruch Ad-noy Yom Yom

This song was written by Rabbi Shimon HaGadol, who lived in Germany in the eleventh century. There is a fascinating story that Rabbi Shimon HaGadol's son was kidnapped and raised as a Christian, eventually becoming Pope. It is thought that Rabbi Shimon HaGadol, who was one of the leaders of his Jewish community, eventually met with the pope; father and son recognized each other, and Rabbi Shimon's son abandoned Christianity to return to Judaism. There is some speculation that this legend might be true: Pope Victor III served as Pope for 12 years in the late eleventh century, and then, according to some accounts, abruptly retired from public life; some think it is possible that he did so after meeting with his long-lost Jewish father, Rabbi Shimon HaGadol.

First verse:

Baruch Hashem yom yom	Blessed is God every day
Ya'a'mas lanu yesha ufid'yom	He carries us to salvation and redemption
Uvish'mo nagil kol ha'yom	And through His name we will rejoice all day
Uvish'u'ato narim rosh Kelyon.	And through His salvation we will lift our heads.
Ki hu ma'oz ladal,	Because He is strength for the weak,
U'ma'chaseh la'ev'yon.	And a shelter for the destitute.

Yom Shabbaton

This was written by the great Hebrew poet Yehudah HaLevi, who lived in twelfth-century Spain. Here, HaLevi compares the rest we experience on Shabbat to the rest experienced by the dove that Noah set free after the flood. After 40 days of rain, the dove finally found a solid piece of land on which to rest. Similarly, as we are tossed about on the rough seas of life, Shabbat provides us with our rest.

First verse:

Yom Shabbaton ein Lish'ko'ach	The Day of Shabbat is not forsaken
Zichru ke'ray'ach ha'ni'cho'ach.	We remember it like a fragrance.
Yonah ma'tze'a vo mano'ach	The dove found rest on it
Vesham ya'nu'chu ye'gi'ya koach.	And on it weary ones will find strength.

Refrain:

Yona matz'a vo mano'ach	The dove found rest on it
Vesham yanuchu ye'gi'ya koach.	And on it weary ones will find strength.

Zemirot for Shalosh Seudos
(the third meal on Saturday evening)

The third meal on Shabbat, eaten late on Saturday afternoon, often has a melancholy, wistful feel to it. As we prepare to say goodbye to this holy day, our "zemirot" (songs), and the melodies we sing them to, are a little mournful. Unlike the other Shabbat meals, when we pick and choose which zemirot to sing depending on our mood, it is generally customary at Shalosh Seudos to sing these specific songs.

Yedid Nefesh

"Yedid Nefesh" was written by the great sixteenth-century Safed mystic, Rabbi Eliezer Azikri. It is a poignant love song to God.

First verse:

Yedid nefesh	Soul's beloved

Av Ha'rachaman	Father of compassion,
Mishoch avdecha	Draw Your servant
El Ritzon'echa.	To Your will.
Yarutz avdecha	Your servant will run
Kemo ayal	Like a deer
Yish'ta'chaveh	To bow
El mul ha'darecha.	Facing your splendor.
Ye'erav lo	To him, your closeness,
Yedid'otecha	Your Friendship
Menofet tzuf	Conjures up nectar
Ve'chol ta'am.	And everything that is sweet.

Psalm 23

King David wrote a number of stunning psalms that were sung in the Beit Hamikdash, our holy Temple in Jerusalem in ancient times.

Psalm 23.

Mizmor l'Dovid:	A song of David:
Hashem ro'ee	God is my shepherd
Lo echsar.	I will not be lacking.
Binot desh'eh	In pleasant fields
Yar'bitzein'ee	He lays me down
Al mei menuchot	Next to restful water
Ye'naha'leinee	He leads me.
Nafshi yeshoveiv	My soul will be restored.
Yan'cheini	He leads me
Be'ma'aglei tzedek	On paths of righteousness
Le'ma'an shemo.	For the sake of His name.
Gam ki eleich	Even though I walk
Be'gei tzal'ma'vet	Through the valley of the shadow of death,
Lo ira ra	I will not be afraid of evil
Ki Ata imadi	Because you are with me.
Shiv'techa	Your rod
U'mish'antecha	And your staff

Heima yenacha'muni.	They are a comfort to me.
Ta'aroch lefanai shulchan	You set before me a table
Neget tzor-era	In front of those who torment me.
Dishanta veshem roshi	You anoint my head with oil
Kosi rev'aya.	My cup overflows.
Ach tov ve'chesed	Surely good and kindness
Yir'dif'uni kol yemai chaya	Will follow me all the days of my life.
Veshavti bevait Hashem	And I will sit in the house of God
Le'oreich ya'mim.	Until the end of days.

13

Activities on Shabbat

On Shabbat, we try to infuse everything we do with holiness. Everything becomes special. Our food is more appetizing than usual, we dress well, we invite guests, we fill our day with a formality it does not ordinarily have. Shabbat is a day to reach for a higher level of being. Besides enjoying festive meals, refraining from prohibited activities and reciting the special Shabbat services, however, what else can we do to distinguish our activities on Shabbat and make this day feel even more special? More pressing for many people, given the many rules about what we cannot do on Shabbat, how can we give ourselves the special joy this day merits? How can our activities on this special day elevate us? Crucially, with all the strictures on our behavior on Shabbat, how can we ensure that our day is spent in meaningful, interesting and fun pursuits?

It might sound counterintuitive, but even without the use of electrical gadgets or other prohibited items, it is indeed easier on Shabbat than other days to enjoy ourselves. This might take a little planning, but the activities that are open to us on Shabbat have the ability to satisfy us on a much deeper level than many of the items we spend our time on during the week. Here's a tiny quiz that can illustrate this pretty well: think for a moment of the last television show you watched. Can you remember it? If you're like most people, this was probably pretty recent, and you'll probably have to think for a moment to recall its content. What was it about? What were the memorable lines? In many cases, when we try to recall the program we last watched on television, it seems pretty vague and often a little uninteresting a day or so later. You can do the same thing with other screen-based activities:

how much of them do you recall, and what feelings do they elicit in you: satisfaction, or something less? Really, spend a moment trying to recall your last television program, your last Internet session, your last video game (if you play them).

Now contrast these memories with your recollections of the last time you saw your best friend. Not talked to them on the phone, but saw them face to face. Even if you met up for a quick coffee, I'm betting that the memory of the meeting and your conversation is a little sharper. Perhaps this is not fair; after all, it is always pretty special seeing our best friends. But even less momentous meetings feel more real and satisfying when they take place face to face, too. When was the last time you spoke with your next-door neighbor? What did you talk about? It might not have been a very interesting conversation, but in most cases the memory of it will be a little clearer and the feelings it elicits will be much more fulfilling than those from television shows, video games, or many other passive, electronic pastimes.

People crave "real" experiences. We also crave connection with other people. There have been a host of scientific studies that show heavy use of "virtual" media can make people feel socially isolated and depressed. Many of us will identify with the words of Dr. Patricia Greenfield, who directs the Children's Digital Media Center, a collaboration between UCLA and California State University, Los Angeles: "Human beings evolved for face-to-face communication. The presence of another person in the flesh triggers important human emotions such as empathy. We may be reducing such emotions in developing human beings by reducing face-to-face communication and augmenting electronic communication." While Dr. Greenfield (like many of us) acknowledges that modern inventions like the Internet have great uses and benefits as well as drawbacks, her words seem to capture something essential in social communication today. In our fast-paced world, we can do and learn so much, but so often these amazing new abilities do nothing to make us happier or more fulfilled. Frequently, in our modern world of instant connections, there is a feeling that something is missing: that some basic human need for connection with something solid and real is going unmet.

Shabbat gives us the opportunities to forgo the world of the "virtual." It gives us a chance each week to reconnect with other people face to face. It gives us the chance to engage in old-fashioned activities such as games, reading, conversation, and appreciating nature that we often don't have time for in our fast-paced modern lives. One aspect of Shabbat that has always appealed to me is the timelessness of it. The ways we observe Shabbat today have changed very, very little over the past thousands of years. I've seen a few movies over the years that show a person from the past coming to visit the present day; you can wring a lot of humor out of scenes in which William Shakespeare is flummoxed by a word processor, or a Victorian gentleman confronts a modern career woman. It is a cute film conceit. But occasionally on Shabbat, it has occurred to me that if a figure from the past were to be brought to the present day, on Shabbat there would be fewer differences. For thousands of years, people's greatest pleasures have been simple ones: conversation, reading, walking, learning new things, perhaps passing the time by playing classic games with others. On Shabbat, these are our activities. They are immensely satisfying.

Fostering meaningful conversations

There is a very funny scene in the 1983 Monty Python movie *The Meaning of Life* in which a man and a woman enter a restaurant and are handed menus that offer them not choices of food, but choices of possible conversational topics instead. As they gaze doubtfully at their menus, their pushy waiter harangues them, urging them to discuss various schools of philosophy. As they are offered ever more preposterous choices (Schopenhauer! The meaning of life!), the couple grows more and more uncomfortable, with less and less to say to one another.

I find that in many cases, trying to jump-start a good conversation is like that scene. Either the people sitting around a dining room table or a living room are in the mood to talk, or they aren't. Conversations either "click" or they don't. What makes for a good conversation is elusive: the product of everyone's individual moods and temperaments at a given moment. Years

ago, when my husband and I were first married, we received a striking lesson in how capricious good conversation can be. We had recently been introduced to a pleasant-seeming couple, and this couple very generously invited us over for Shabbat dinner. We went to their home, but the entire evening was subdued. We all spent the meal making small talk, and the atmosphere throughout our Shabbat evening was bland, even boring. When dinner concluded, my husband and I thanked our hosts and took our leave.

As soon as we left their house, though, the sky opened up and the biggest downpour I'd ever seen drenched us to the skin. We started walking slowly back to our apartment through the enormous thunderstorm, when our host ran out of his house after us, and invited us to sleep over. My husband and I lived a long couple of miles away, and we gratefully accepted this gracious offer. The next morning, we joined our hosts for breakfast, and started chatting. And chatting, and chatting. The conversation was so great, we never stopped! We went with them to shul (synagogue), and chatted with them for hours during Kiddush afterwards. We had the greatest time. Walking back to our apartment the next afternoon, my husband and I commented that our hosts (and maybe we, too) had obviously been tired from work on Friday evening, and that was why our conversation had been subdued. When we caught them refreshed on Saturday morning, we all hit it off beautifully. Today, nearly ten years later, they remain two of our closest friends, and a lingering reminder that mere time and circumstance can almost randomly determine whether conversations are good or bad.

How can you ensure that conversations will be sparkling around your Shabbat table? One secret is to invite guests. Families are often on their best behavior when there are guests present; it often prevents people from lapsing into old arguments or slinking off the second they finish eating. Another secret my husband and I have discovered over the years is to cultivate "buffer guests." These are people who can talk to anyone; once one of our "buffer guests" (who didn't know that's how we regarded her) boasted to us that she and her husband could "talk to a wall." Indeed; that's why we invited them. Some people are sparkling conversationalists under every circumstance. Get to know them, and invite them often.

Among your ordinary (non-buffer) guests, try to think creatively about what they'll bring out in each other. I remember one surprising Shabbat dinner when we invited my parents, along with another couple their age whom we barely knew. As soon as the other couple walked through my door, I started panicking about the evening ahead. My dad's pretty traditional, and this other guy sported a pony tail. Then he mentioned some political views that were the exact opposite of my father's. Help! Yet it turned out to be the biggest hit: my father and our other guest had grown up near each other, and they stayed at our house late into the night, reminiscing about what the North Side of Chicago used to be like, telling stories about the good old days, and trading anecdotes about colorful events and personalities from their childhoods. It was one of the most fun Shabbat dinners we'd ever had; I've never learned so much about Chicago history, and I've rarely seen my father so animated. (And I was reminded, once again, that people are complex and sometimes bring out surprising qualities in each other.)

What if you're sitting around your Shabbat table, though, and the conversation just is not flowing? We once invited over Shabbat guests who brought a cute hostess gift: a set of cards with conversational topics on each one, meant to stimulate discussions at the Shabbat table. I thought this was a great gift, but over the years, I've found it can be a little artificial-feeling to use. It is hard to ask questions that will stimulate discussion, and it is hard to phrase them in a non-leading way. (Too often they can wind up feeling like the conversation menu in that Monty Python movie.) Yet when the conversation is stuck, it can help to play one of those ice-breaker games that some people use at work conferences or teachers sometimes assign on the first day of school. Each person takes turns answering a question, in an attempt to stimulate some more natural-feeling discussion. Here is a list of questions that I've seen used, first-hand, with great success. If you're looking for a way to spark a more interesting talk among your family or your guests, these questions can help.

➤ If you have time to plan ahead (and guests or family members who are willing to do the work), choose a section of that week's Torah Parsha, and ask each guest to read about it in a different book or

website. There are so many books and Jewish websites geared towards children, it is easy for kids to be involved in this project, too. (Check out some of the suggestions at the end of this book for resources.) When you come together at the Shabbat table, take turns explaining what each person has learned about it, and what thoughts they have. (Note: this doesn't have to be a big, heavy assignment. In fact, if you do a little planning, you can assemble a few books and print off some materials from websites. Give everyone a page to read, and ten minutes to prepare before lunch or dinner, then once the meal begins — viola! You'll all be Parsha experts.)

➤ The old Thanksgiving standby of going around the table and each person saying what they are thankful for often works to start a meaningful conversation. You can give this game a Jewish twist by trying a couple of variations. Give each person present time to answer the question *"What are you most thankful for about being Jewish?"* This can prompt interesting discussions about how people feel about religious ritual and tradition. Another, slightly heavier, version is the question *"What do you feel are the greatest blessings that God has given to you?"* Going around the table answering this can encourage people to be introspective for a moment, and can elevate the feeling at your Shabbat table, as you and your guests are encouraged to reflect on the central Jewish belief that God is intimately involved with each of our lives.

➤ There's an old ice-breaking game that's popular with many teachers, who use it on the first day of school. This encourages people to really focus on one another, ask questions and listen to what others have to say. It is especially appropriate if not everyone around your Shabbat table knows each other yet. Pair up guests into groups of two and give everyone five or ten minutes to "interview" their partner. When time is up, each person around the table takes a turn to give a brief presentation about the person they interviewed.

➤ If you are enjoying a meal with friends or relatives you know very well, here's a fun way to foster a different kind of conversation to the one you might normally have. Go around the table, and give each person a turn to list five things they admire about each person

present. People often say surprising and touching compliments during this game; it is a great way to create a positive atmosphere.

➤ I was once at a meeting where everyone played a surprisingly successful getting-to-know-you game. Each person took turns to say three things about themselves. Two of these statements had to be false, and one had to be true. Everyone struggled to find something a little bizarre to say about themselves, so that it would fit in well with the lies. I think the secret of this mixer's success is that it forces people to delve a little deeper into their lives when describing themselves than they would normally do. You might have no problem telling other people you're a tax attorney (yawn to anyone but another tax attorney), but how many people do you confide in that you once won a wine-tasting tournament, fought off a mugger in Japan, or were offered a job in corporate espionage?

➤ Go around the table and ask people what has inspired them most, Jewishly. People often credit relatives (especially grandparents), books, classes in college, or meetings with charismatic rabbis or rebbetzins as sources of Jewish inspiration. It can be interesting to hear what people answer; even those you know well might surprise you with what has given them a positive feeling towards Judaism. This question is simple, but it can spark some great conversations because it is so open-ended and personal.

➤ When you plan your Shabbat meals, take a hint from your yearly Passover seder. Most Jews, even those who are not religiously observant, participate in this ritual every year, and find it meaningful. On Passover, we read the Hagaddah, and discuss the Passover story. Many people who lead seders spend time in advance finding and copying interesting commentaries and supporting materials, and the result is often a stimulating, engaging evening. Before Shabbat, select one or two simple Jewish texts. They can be on anything. Here is a short list to get your imagination started: the weekly Parsha; the concept of Shabbat; "tzedakah" (Jewish charity); choose a period of Jewish history (such as the Golden Age of Spain, or nineteenth-century Poland); Zionism; famous Jewish historical figures (consider

starting with Rav Kook, the first Chief Rabbi of modern Israel, or Rabbi Menachem Mendel Schneerson, the last Lubavicher Rebbe, or Golda Meir, the former prime minister of Israel). Spend some time at the library, or looking on-line for engaging articles or books. Your choice is virtually endless. Have a few short texts on hand during Shabbat. During your Shabbat meal, take turns reading your selections, and talking about what they mean.

➤ Another option to introduce Torah learning to your Shabbat meals is to examine a classic Jewish text, such as "Pirkei Avot" ("Sayings of the Fathers") or a familiar story from the Torah, such as the Book of Job, Esther or Ecclesiastes. If your crowd already has a high level of Jewish literacy, you might even want to tackle something more advanced, such as a section of the Talmud. Find a good English translation, and keep it handy. (If there are children at your meals, you can also select a children's version of these texts.) On Shabbat, take turns reading from your book, then discussing what it says. This whole process might sound very serious, but all it takes is a few minutes, and can become really engrossing when people get engaged. Plus, if you tackle a short section each week, in time you can progress through entire Jewish books, and gain a feeling of satisfaction and accomplishment.

➤ Nothing fosters a feeling of camaraderie like a shared goal. Collect articles about or appeal letters from Jewish causes or charities. On Shabbat, spend time examining these with your family or with a group of friends. Discuss the needs of different groups, and what they are asking for. Some Jewish community organizations are looking desperately for funding; others are in dire need of volunteers. Many religious Jewish organizations ask that people recite Tehillim (Psalms) or learn a portion of Torah in order to help those who are sick, or in memory of those who have passed away. Consider the requests, and discuss what you can do to help people and fulfill the needs of your local Jewish community. This can be a very moving, inspirational activity, as people resolve to take on new responsibilities to help people in the future. It can be particularly meaningful and stirring to include children in these important discussions.

➤ At your Shabbat table, try to establish a few "ground rules." In order to set this day apart from the ordinary work week, and to inspire it with some extra holiness, it helps to be mindful of what makes Shabbat special. Here are ten rules to try to follow when talking on Shabbat. See how many of them you can keep in the course of one day!

1 No "lashon ha'ra" (literally, "bad tongue"): Do not gossip!

2 See if you can avoid talking about work on Shabbat.

3 Try not to talk about money on Shabbat.

4 Attempt to include at least one "Torah" thought at each meal. (Keep some Jewish books handy to inspire you!)

5 Dare yourself not to yell or become angry on Shabbat. On a spiritual level, keep in mind that Judaism regards it as a mitzvah (commandment) to be happy. On a practical level, everyone will enjoy Shabbat more if it is celebrated with joy instead of anger.

6 Remember that you are a King or Queen on Shabbat. Try to act accordingly.

7 If you find yourself slipping, try to elevate the situation. A complaint-fest can be turned into a brainstorm about what is positive in your life; if you find yourself ranting about something, try to reframe it in your mind in a more positive way. ("My boss is so demanding" can be turned into "But at least I'm lucky enough to have a job I enjoy," for instance.)

8 Shabbat gives us an opportunity to remember that God is near to us. It can be easier to remember this on this holy day. Use Shabbat to turn to Him, to speak with God, and to try to act in such a way that reflects our closeness with Him.

9 Try not to engage in mean humor on Shabbat; try to limit sarcasm. It can seem funny at first, but sarcasm also packs a dose of negativity that can lower the tone of our conversation.

10 Make an effort to listen to other people. Ask their views and really listen to their concerns.

➤ Finally, if all else fails and the conversation at your Shabbat table remains listless, you can try to ask a few slightly controversial questions of everyone present. You don't want to go overboard and

ignite a shouting match. (For this reason, I'd advise not to talk about politics!) But you might ask your guests to go around the table and each say a few words about what they think regarding issues on which people have a wide range of opinions. Try some of these.

1 "Have you ever personally seen a miracle?"
2 "What do you think God expects or wants from you?"
3 "What does it mean to be a 'good Jew'?"
4 "What do you think is the greatest accomplishment of your local Jewish community?"
5 "What do you think is the greatest threat to the Jewish people today?"
6 "What can we do to safeguard Jewish continuity?"
7 "Who do you think is the greatest Jewish figure alive today?"
8 "Who do you think has been the greatest figure in Jewish history?"
9 "Is there a Jewish future in the Diaspora?"
10 "When faced with need and want, should we choose to help our fellow Jews first?"

If you think you can ask these or other contentious questions without sparking World War III, go for it. They'll at least get people talking.

Shabbat games

One of the first pieces of advice I would give to anyone embarking upon traditional Shabbat observance is to visit a local store with a toy aisle, or a garage sale or resale shop, and browse the board games. There are so many wonderful games that conform to the requirements of Shabbat: that don't require electricity, drawing, or writing. Try to stock up on some of the classics, such as chess, checkers, backgammon, Chinese checkers, Chutes and Ladders and Go. There are also many newer board games for all ages that are loads of fun to play on Shabbat. We can even add a little extra Jewish spirit to Shabbat by buying Jewish-themed board games (found in Judaica stores and websites) and keeping them for use on Shabbat. Many

of us don't have the time during our busy weeks to enjoy the slower pace of board games; Shabbat offers a chance to sit with our friends and family and take the time to play them.

Word games

You don't need to purchase games or any equipment for these word games. They're fun to play in the house, or also as you walk.

Complete the Story

This is fun with several people. One person begins telling a story; after a few minutes, the next player yells "Stop!," then continues telling the story in their own way. After a few minutes, the next player interrupts and continues the story, and so on. Go around a few times, if you can. It can get very funny listening as the story line jerks around and the tale changes tone from player to player.

Telephone

This is an old game, best played with lots of people. The first player whispers a word or phrase into the ear of the next player, who then whispers it into the ear of the next player, and so on, until the end of the line. When the final player has been told the word (in a whisper), they say it out loud. Almost always, the word or phrase has changed out of all recognition since the first whisper!

Genius

Select a short poem, story, or Torah passage. (To give this game a Shabbat feel, try to keep your selections within a Jewish theme.) Who can memorize the most in five minutes? Prepare for five minutes: then have a contest to see who can repeat verbatim the most text, with the fewest mistakes.

Invent a Story

Did you know that Mary Shelly wrote her famous novel *Frankenstein* as the result of a bet? The year was 1816, and Mary was on vacation in Switzerland with her good friends, the poets Lord Byron and Percy Shelly.

(Mary Shelly was Mary Godwin at the time; she married Percy Shelly later that year.) These three amazing writers decided to have a contest to see who could write the best horror story during their trip. (*Frankenstein* won.)

Writing things down is of course prohibited on Shabbat, but telling long stories is a fun way to enjoy spending time with others. Take turns. Try giving each person ten minutes to make up a story. Have a vote at the end to determine which was the funniest, the scariest, the saddest, the happiest, etc.

Song Title Challenge

Take turns challenging each other to think of a song about a particular topic. (You can only make a challenge if you yourself can think of one.) For instance, one person might challenge the other players to think of a song about sunshine ("You are my Sunshine") or King David ("David Melech Yisrael"). Try to get obscure to stump the other players. (Do keep in mind, though, as you play this that Shabbat is a day to elevate ourselves. Try to choose songs that are uplifting and wholesome, rather than the opposite!)

Shopping List

This is a well-known children's game, but is lots of fun for everybody to play, no matter their age. One player starts, saying, "I went to the store, and I bought . . ." They then choose a food that starts with A, for instance "apples." The next player then says "I went to the store and I bought apples and . . ." They then choose a food that starts with B, for instance "bananas." The third player says, "I went to the store and I bought apples and bananas and . . ." They then choose a food that starts with C, for instance "carrots." Keep going around and around, and adding one new food item each time. This game quickly gets challenging as each player struggles to remember the growing list of food.

Botticelli

Botticelli was a favorite game in my family when I was a kid. To play, one person thinks of a well-known figure. The figure can be alive or dead, real, or fictional. The other players each take turns asking yes/no questions,

trying to find out who the figure is. Set a limit on the number of questions allowed, either ten or (to make the game easier) a higher number such as 15 or 20.

I Spy

To play this classic game, players take turns thinking of an object that is clearly visible to everyone in the game. One says, "I spy with my little eye something beginning with the letter . . ." and say what letter it starts with. The other players take turns guessing what it can be. Set a limit on the number of guesses allowed, say five or ten, before a player is out.

To play this game with the pre-literacy set, substitute colors for first letters. For instance, if somebody is thinking of the red fire hydrant outside the window, they would say, "I spy with my little eye something that is RED!" I've found that kids love this game, and can play it for ages.

"Shimon Omer"

"Shimon omer" means "Simon says" in Hebrew. On Shabbat, it can be fun to play this well-known children's game with a little Hebrew thrown in. The leader gives the players instructions, but players can only follow them if they are preceded by "Shimon omer." Thus, "Shimon omer touch your heads" means that all players should touch their heads. "Shimon omer clap your hands" means all players clap their hands.

If you want to include more Hebrew, here is a quick glossary:

Einayim	=	eyes
Af	=	nose
Peh	=	mouth
Shechem	=	shoulder
Yadayim	=	hands
Berech	=	knee
Regel	=	foot
Gav	=	back
Hikfitz	=	jump

| Tafach | = | clap |
| Nagah | = | touch |

The leader tries to trick the players into doing something that "Shimon" (Simon) didn't "omer" (say). When a player makes the mistake of doing something without "Shimon omer" before it, they are out.

Card games

Gin

This game is usually played by two players, although it can be stretched to include three or even four players. Deal one player 11 cards. The other player(s) receives ten cards. Place the remaining stack of cards face down on a table. The player with 11 cards goes first. He or she opens play by discarding one card from their hand, placing it face up on the table.

The object of Gin is to collect either runs or sets of cards. To win, you need either one "run" or one "set" of four cards, and two "runs" or "sets" of three cards each. A run is cards of the same suite that go in sequential order. (Ace can be counted either as a "one," or as the highest value card, above a king.) A set is a group of three or four cards each of the same value, from different suites.

A winning hand could look like this: a "set" of four cards (say seven of spades, seven of hearts, seven of clubs, and seven of diamonds); a "run" of three cards (say ace of hearts, two of hearts, and three of hearts); and a "set" of three cards (say king of diamonds, king of spades, and king of clubs.) Keep in mind: you need one group of four cards, and two groups of three cards each.

Players take turns. On a turn, a player chooses a card, either from the discard pile (which is face up on the table) or the deck (which is face down on the table) and adds it to their hand. The player then completes his or her turn by selecting a card from their hand to discard. Discards go face up in the discard pile on the table.

This is a game partly of luck, and partly of skill as you try to rearrange your hand with each turn to maximize your chances of amassing one either

"set" or "run" of four cards, and two either "sets" or "runs" of three cards each.

When a player has won, they indicate this by placing their final discard card face down on top of the discard pile, and saying, "Gin."

Old Maid

This is a great game to play: the rules are simple, the action is fast-paced, and you can play with any number of people. People often play Old Maid with special, dedicated decks of cards. The game, however, was originally played with ordinary playing cards, and they work just fine.

First, remove one of the Queens from your deck. (I actually hate the name Old Maid — it is so sexist. Perhaps we'd be better off calling it "Ultimate Queen" or something more complimentary.)

Deal the entire deck of cards. Some players will have an extra card; that doesn't matter. Everyone looks at their hand of cards and selects out all the pairs. A pair is any two cards of the same value — for instance, two "twos" or two kings.

Choose a player to start the play. They will turn to their right and proffer their hand to their neighbor (keeping the value of their cards hidden). Their neighbor selects a card at random and adds it to their hand. If this new card results in a pair, the neighbor can discard the new pair. Otherwise, they just keep their new card in their hand. The neighbor then offers *their* hand (again, with the value of the cards kept hidden) to *their* right-hand neighbor, who chooses a card. Again, if this results in a pair for the next neighbor, the pair of cards can be discarded. Otherwise, this neighbor offers their hand to the next player along, and so on.

You can end this card in two ways: by finding a winner, or by finding a loser. If you want to play until you find a winner, then the first person to discard all of their cards wins!

If you want to play this game to the bitter end, until you have found the loser (the person holding the last, unmatched queen: the old maid), keep playing until all the cards except the losing queen are left. (Or reverse the concept: for "Ultimate Queen," declare the player left with the sole remaining queen the winner!)

War

This is a fast-paced game for two players. Shuffle a deck of cards and deal it out between two players. Each player keeps their stack of cards face down in front of them. Simultaneously, each player turns over a card. If they are of different values, the player with the higher value card takes them both.

Play keeps going in this way, the players turning over card after card, until they each turn over a card of the same value — say, two "threes" or two "fours." When they see they have matching cards, they yell out "War!"

This is a "War": the players each place two more cards face down, then a third card face-up. The person whose face-up card has the higher value takes all eight of the cards played during the "War." (If the second cards are also of matching values, proceed with another "War," with the winner again taking all.)

When a player has exhausted their deck, they shuffle their cards and resume play. The player to amass all the cards wins.

Snap

This is a game for two players. Shuffle a deck of cards and place it face down on a table. The players each take a card and place them face up, near each other, on the table. If the cards are of different values (say, a "seven" and a "three"), they each turn over another card from the deck, and place these face up on top of the previously selected cards.

Play continues this way, each player taking cards and placing them face up on the growing face-up pile, until they draw matching cards (for example, two "sevens" or two Jacks). When this happens, it is a "Snap" and the first player to call out "SNAP!" gets all of the face-up cards on the table.

Play resumes until all of the face-down cards have been drawn. The player who has amassed the greatest number of cards wins.

Crazy Eights

Shuffle a deck and deal five cards to each player. Place the remaining cards face down on a table. Select a player to begin. They choose one of their cards and place it face up on the table; this is now the discard pile.

The next player (go in a clockwise circle) can discard a card, too, provided it matches either the suite (e.g. spades, hearts, diamonds, or clubs) of the top card in the discard pile, or the value (e.g. ace, two, three, etc.) of the top card in the discard pile. If they cannot discard any of their cards, they draw a new card from the upside-down pile.

This game is called "Crazy Eights" because Eights can represent anything: any suite or any number. A player can put down an eight on top of anything in the discard pile; when they do so, they must specify the value and suite they want their Eight to represent.

The first player to discard all their cards wins.

Creative games

Mancala

I first learned this game as a "Shabbat" game, and found out later on that it is played, in various, forms, throughout Africa and in parts of the Middle East. It is a wonderfully absorbing game for two players. You can buy beautiful Mancala sets in the store, or else you can make your own with a few simple items from your kitchen.

You will need an empty (dozen) egg carton, two small shallow bowls (or jar lids), and 60 dried beans.

Place five beans in each hole in the egg carton. Place the egg-carton lengthwise between two players (so each player is facing the long end of the carton). Place a bowl at each end of the egg carton (to the left and right of the players).

The six holes — and all the beans in them — facing you are yours. The bowl to your right, at the end of the egg carton, is your Home. Every bean that lands in your Home is yours; your opponent can never touch them. (You want lots of beans in your Home, as amassing the most in your Home is how you win the game.)

To play, select a hole on your side of the egg carton, and scoop out all the beans from it. Moving leftwards (clockwise), distribute one bean in each subsequent hole. (In some countries, Mancala is called "The Sowing Game," because this action is akin to sowing seeds, dropping one in each hole.) If you have enough holes to reach the bowl to your right — your Home

— then drop one in there, too. If you still have beans in your hand, then you continue around the egg carton, and drop one bean into each of your opponent's holes, too, until you have used up the beans in your hand. At this point, it becomes your opponent's turn.

The only major rule in Mancala is this: if you have an empty hole on your side of the egg carton, and you drop the last bean from one of your turns into it, then you get to take both it and all of the beans from your opponent's hole opposite, and place these beans in your Home.

Thus, the strategy becomes to empty one of your holes, then work it so you have enough beans to scoop out of another hole, and drop around the egg carton, so that you can finish up by dropping the last bean into your empty hole. At the same time, you must try to prevent your opponent from doing the same.

This game seems easy at first, but as it is a game entirely of skill, not of luck, once you and your playing partner get the hang of it, it can become incredibly difficult. (I had to stop playing with my husband once he began to approach Mancala like chess: each game started to take hours, and of course after taking the time to think through dozens of moves ahead, he always won. Now I much prefer playing with my children, who are still too young — for now — to learn how to play as painstakingly as their dad!)

Who am I?

This is best played with a lot of people. One person is selected to leave the room for a few minutes. While they are absent, the remaining players agree on a famous person. (You can try putting a Jewish spin on this game, by keeping your selections to well-known figures in Jewish history or Jewish life.)

When the player who left the room returns, they have five minutes to guess the identity of the famous person, asking only yes or no questions. If they can successfully identify the famous person in that time limit, they win.

Charades

Divide into teams, or play as individuals. To start, think of a category. You can choose anything: books, adages, movies, songs, activities, countries,

hobbies, subjects in school. The more creative the better.

One team or individual goes first, and spends a few moments acting out something in the chosen category. The person or people doing the acting are not allowed to talk, only to mime.

In addition to miming the action, they can give clues by cupping their ear (which means "sounds like") and then miming something that sounds like what they want to convey. They can also hold up their fingers to show the number of words in the title of what they are acting out, and then holding up a finger to indicate they are showing you one particular word first.

Members of the audience try to guess what is being acted out by calling out ideas. When the players acting out a charade hear a correct guess, they point to the person who said it, then touch their own noses, signifying "on the nose" (correct). When the entire title of the thing being acted out is guessed, the players who were miming take their seats, and another team or individual gets a turn to select and act their own item.

Memory

This game takes a while to set up (and it involves some clean-up afterwards), but it can be lots of fun.

You can play this with a minimum of two people, but it is better with more. If you have more than two players, divide into teams.

One team leaves the room of play, while the second team sets up a tableau on a table or the floor. Select a dozen or so ordinary, everyday objects, and group them together. (It is best to use very humdrum things in this game, as they are harder to remember.)

When everything is ready, invite the first team back into the room. They have one minute to look at the tableau. (If you're playing with kids, or using many objects, you can make the time frame longer: three minutes, or even five.)

When time is up, the first team must leave the room again. Wait a minute, then quiz them to identify as many items as they can from the tableau.

Clean up, and reverse. The individual or team who is able to remember the most items wins.

Hide and Seek

There are two fun versions. In one, lots of people hide while the "seeker" counts to 20, with his or her eyes closed. Afterwards, the seeker calls out "Ready or not, here I come!" and embarks on a search to find all the hiders. The game ends when the last hider is found.

In a second version, only one person hides while lots of seekers count to 20. Then, all the seekers fan out, looking for the hider. Whenever one of the seekers finds the hider, they get into the hiding place with them. As play progresses, the number of seekers diminishes, and the number of hiders grows. By the end, there is only one seeker left; when they find the hiding place, the game is over.

Dark Box

My kids love this game. Place a long blanket or other cloth over a small table, so the area under the table is completely obscured. Take turns selecting an object to place under the table. The other players then reach their hand under the cloth (no peeking!), feel the object, and try to guess what it is. This game can be surprisingly original and fun, as each player schemes to find puzzling or unexpected objects to hide on their turn.

Children's projects

Town

Encourage your children to set up a town throughout your home. (Yes, there will be a lot of clean-up afterwards, but this is a fun way for children to spend Shabbat afternoon — or, sometimes in my home, the hours from 5 to 8 a.m.) Use toy trains or cars to connect the rooms. Get as creative as you can. Where's the library? The school? The playground? Dolls or the kids themselves can use the toy town when it is finished.

Hospital

My brother and I used to spend rainy days playing this when we were kids. Our mother would unfold the spare sofa bed, we'd set out each of our stuffed animals and dolls, and get to work.

Act out the Parsha

My kids and their guests love acting out the stories from that week's Parsha in grand plays they organize on Shabbat. Use costumes, puppets (for supporting characters), and props.

Put on a show!

This is a fun activity for Shabbat. Encourage your children to put on a play, or a musical, or a puppet show. Kids often love magic; assemble a few tricks (or borrow a book on magic tricks from the library), and keep them especially for Shabbat. Give your kids and any guest children who are over an hour to practice and set up a "stage," then promise that all the grown-ups will come and watch.

This is always a big activity for my kids and their friends on Shabbat, and the resulting Shabbat shows are always really wonderful to watch.

Doll's house

Many children love doll's houses. I'd encourage any family that is becoming Shabbat-observant to buy or make a lovely doll's house, and keep it for use on Shabbat only. That will ensure that it remains special, and your kids will associate it with Shabbat and look forward to playing with it.

If you don't have a dedicated doll's house, Shabbat is a fun time to assemble lots of odds and ends and set up one together with your kids. Choose the size doll you'd like to use, then scour the house looking for beds, chairs, tables, etc. to furnish it. (Think of tissue boxes for chairs, saucers for plates, scarves for blankets and rugs, cushions for beds . . .)

Nature walk

My husband and I rely on this one so much on Shabbat. At times, everyone just needs to get outside and get some fresh air. When boredom looms, have

everyone head outdoors. Even a walk around the block — sometimes just a few minutes in the backyard — is often enough to find a few birds, insects, or interesting plants.

Take the time to look at the nature you encounter. My husband even bought a book about local birds, so that he and the kids could identify the birds we see around our house. Even very common birds and plants are still interesting, when you take the time to read up on them. If you have time, borrow a book or print out something from the Internet about some things you know you'll see on a nature walk — robins or sparrows, or even dandelions — and discuss it on Shabbat. You'll see that even a ho-hum walk will quickly become fascinating and meaningful.

Obstacle course

This is a lifesaver in our backyard or at the playground on Shabbat. When my kids get bored with the swings and the slide, I give them obstacle course assignments to complete.

"Okay," I'll call out. "Here's what you have to do: go down a slide! Then run and touch three different trees! Then do the monkey bars. Swing on all the swings! Smell two different flowers, hop around the playground on one leg, then walk to me backwards!" Then I time them: they love trying to beat their previous bests. (This is so popular that often, the other children playing in playgrounds will beg me to make up courses for them, too!)

Hebrew School

Kids of all ages love teaching others: on Shabbat, why not tap into this universal desire, and get into the spirit of the day by making a Hebrew School?

For younger kids, stock some simple Jewish books in your home; the older ones can read them to the young, or can explain some simple Jewish concepts to their guests or siblings.

For older kids (and adults, too) you can be more ambitious. Encourage older children or adults to spend 20 or 30 minutes preparing a topic, then present it to the others. This is a great activity for the whole family. It gets people in the spirit of learning Torah, which is a very appropriate Shabbat

activity, and it also empowers people, as they become the family "expert" on a particular topic.

Choose any Jewish-related topic or text that interests you. Even if all you do is parrot back to your family what you just read, you will be teaching others and ensuring that you yourself enjoy a deeper understanding of the material.

14

Easy, traditional Shabbat recipes

There once was a king who took a journey. He travelled through many lands and met many different people. One Friday night, as darkness approached, he stopped at the modest house of a humble Jewish family. "The king is here!" the king's guards announced. The Jewish family came outside and the guards said, "It is time for the king's evening meal! We request that you share your meal with us!" The Jewish family gladly welcomed the king and invited his entourage in to share their Shabbat dinner.

It was the best meal the king had ever tasted. He ate with relish, and afterwards the king thanked the family and left them gold coins for their trouble. The king returned to his palace, but the memory of the fantastic meal he had eaten lingered with him. He craved the wonderful soup, the tasty bread, the savory meat and the sweet desserts he had eaten that night.

The king ordered his cooks to recreate the dishes he had sampled, and they tried, mimicking every detail the king recalled. But though the food seemed similar, it was never as good. The king sent away for new cooks, famous cooks from other lands, and of each cook he asked the same thing: could they make the simple dishes the king had tasted at the home of the humble Jewish family, and make them taste as mouth-watering as they had been the first time? Alas, no cook was successful.

Finally, the king decided there was nothing to do but return to the home of the family to see if there was some secret ingredient he had not known about that made their food so mouthwatering. He rode to their obscure home, and the king himself knocked on the door. "What," he asked, "did you put into the food the night I ate with you? What secret ingredient do you possess? I have

had legions of cooks make the same simple dishes I ate here, but the food I ate in my palace was never as good as the food I ate here with you!"

"Yes, your royal highness," the mother replied. "There was a secret ingredient in the food you ate in our home, but I cannot give it to you. You see," she continued, "the night you ate with us the sun had recently set, and it was Shabbat. The Torah teaches us that every Shabbat, angels come into our home and sprinkle a magic ingredient over our food, rendering it especially delicious, giving us a taste of the riches awaiting us in next world. The secret ingredient you tasted in our food was the taste of Shabbat."

Unfortunately, while the Shabbat angels improve the taste of our foods, we still have to cook them first. This chapter provides simple, traditional recipes for all the Shabbat meals. It can be fun to experiment with more unusual, elaborate cooking at times, but if you're like me, you'll also appreciate some quick, easy, fail-proof recipes for your Shabbat table. Here they are, honed by years and years of practice, and tasted week after week by my husband, kids, and guests. Enjoy, and bon appétit or, as we say in Hebrew, *bitay-avon*!

A note on measurements

t	=	teaspoon	=	5 ml
T	=	tablespoon	=	15 ml
oz	=	ounce	=	30 ml
1 cup	=	8 oz	=	236 ml
1 quart	=	4 cups	=	(nearly) 1 liter
350°F	=	177°C		
375°F	=	190°C		

Golden traditional challah

2 cups warm water

2 T dry yeast

½ cup sugar

3 eggs

1 t salt

½ cup oil

8 cups flour (approx.)

For glaze, choose one: 1 egg, 2 T honey, ¼ cup apple juice. Optional: sesame or poppy seeds.

Step one: Start the yeast. Pour water into a mixing bowl, and sprinkle yeast and sugar on top. Let this sit about ten minutes, until bubbly.

Step two: Add the eggs, salt, oil, and half the flour to the mixing bowl with the bubbling yeast mixture in it.

Step three: Mix the dough. An electric mixer with a bread hook is the easiest way to do this. If you are mixing by hand, start out with a large spoon and switch to kneading by hand when the dough starts to get stiff. The dough will start out wet and sticky; add around 2–4 cups more flour, a little at a time, until dough is smooth, soft, and not sticky any more. Many factors, including the source and type of your flour, humidity, and altitude, will affect the amounts of flour your dough will absorb, so rely on your sense of touch: good challah dough should look and feel like baby's skin. Some people work in about ½ cup raisins at this point. It is also very nice to add a dash of cinnamon.

Step four: Place the kneaded dough in an oiled bowl and cover with a towel. Let it rise anywhere between 45 minutes and two or three hours. (Bread is a lot more forgiving than many people realize; it can accommodate to your schedule.)

Step five: It is unusual to use an enormous amount of flour, but if you do ever find yourself tripling or more this recipe and using 5 lbs. or more of flour, you will need to tear off a piece of dough the size of a small egg at this point and set it aside to burn later. This recalls the practice of separating out some of our produce and sacrificing it to God during Biblical times.

Before the egg-sized piece is torn off and set aside, the following blessing is recited:

Baruch Atah Adonoi, Eloheinu Melech HaOlam, Asher Kidishanu be'Mitzvotav ve'Tzivanu le'hafrish min ha'isah.

"Blessed are You O Lord our God, King of the Universe, Who Has Commanded us to separate (challah) from the dough."

Step six: Punch down the risen dough and knead it briefly. Replace in its bowl, cover, and let rise again, a minimum of 45 minutes.

Step seven: Briefly knead the dough again and prepare its baking shape. This recipe is enough to yield three or four small loaves. (I always make a few, because we need two loaves for Friday dinner and two loaves for Saturday lunch.)

Usually, challah is braided. You can make braids with three strands or with five or six. Roll out lengths of dough and pinch together at the top. For three strands, alternate crossing over the right and left strands so they are in the middle. For five or six strands, alternate crossing the right strand over the two strands to its left, then crossing the left strand over the two strands to its right, etc. Braided challah can be baked on an ungreased baking sheet or in loaf pans. (I usually line the baking sheet or loaf pans, as the glaze you'll brush on the top often dribbles down and sticks.)

From Rosh Hashana, the Jewish New Year, through Simchat Torah, the holiday that celebrates the yearly completion of reading the Torah in synagogue, about a month later, it is customary to have round challah loaves. To make a round loaf, roll out long strands, and coil each strand around like a sleeping snake, tucking the two ends under the loaf. Round challah can be baked on an ungreased baking sheet or in round baking pans.

No matter what shape you make your challah loaves, they have to rise a third time, covered, in their baking sheets or pans, for another minimum of 45 minutes.

Step eight: Before baking, glaze your loaves by painting the tops. You can use a beaten egg, honey, or apple juice. A pastry brush helps in this step, but if you don't have one you can use some paper towel, plastic wrap, or even your fingers. The glaze will ensure your challah looks shiny and brown. You can sprinkle some sesame or poppy seeds on top for decoration.

Preheat the oven to 375°F. Bake your challah for approximately 30 minutes. You will know when your loaves are done when they appear

golden brown on top and — this is crucial — when they sound hollow when tapped on the bottom.

Makes 3–4 loaves.

Miraculous one-hour homemade challah

Prepare the bread dough as above, but instead of letting it rise, braid it immediately. Place braided, un-risen loaves in bread pans or on baking sheets, then cover with a towel and allow to rise for 30 minutes. Glaze the tops and bake at 370°F for approximately half an hour, until loaves are a golden color and sound hollow when tapped on the bottom.

This method results in a slightly less chewy, more cake-y bread, but when you're in a hurry — who cares? It is so close to the flavor and texture of traditional challah no one will believe it only took an hour to make!

Gefilte fish dishes

Many Jews remember gefilte fish as tasteless beige slabs fished out of jelly. These recipes rely on the frozen loaves of gefilte fish that are widely available in kosher sections of supermarkets today, and taste nothing at all like the jelly-in-a-jar version.

Gefilte fish kugel

    1 frozen gefilte fish loaf, defrosted
    10 oz package frozen spinach, defrosted
    2 carrots, grated
    1 egg

Mix ingredients and pat into an 8-inch × 8-inch pan. Bake at 350°F for approximately 1 hour, until set and slightly browned on top.

Serves 6–8.

Janet's honey baked gefilte fish

    1 frozen gefilte fish loaf
    1 carrot
    ¼ cup honey (approx.)

Place gefilte fish and carrot in a baking dish. Drizzle fish with honey. Cover and bake at 350°F for 1 hour, until fish is cooked through. Serve fish sliced, garnished with carrot slices, and accompanied by horseradish.

Serves 6–8.

Mediterranean gefilte fish

1 onion, diced

1 T oil

1 green pepper, diced

28 oz can of crushed tomatoes

1 frozen gefilte fish loaf

Fry onion in oil over medium heat until soft, about 10 minutes. Add green pepper and cook 5 minutes more. Add tomatoes and cook, stirring frequently, until tomato mixture is thickened, about 15 minutes. Slice frozen gefilte fish loaf and place slices in baking pan. Pour the tomato mixture over the fish slices, cover, and bake at 350°F for 1 hour. Refrigerate after cooking, and serve cold.

Serves 6–8.

Easy herring appetizer

1 cup pickled herring (sold in the kosher or kosher-style aisle in many supermarkets)

1 apple (cored and peeled)

1 small yellow onion

Optional: 2 hard boiled eggs, peeled and chopped finely

Combine first three ingredients in food processor and process until finely chopped and blended. If you want a mild version, omit the onion. For another variation, stir in eggs after processing other ingredients. This looks lovely served on lettuce leaves.

Serves 4.

Great-aunt Cissie's "sees und zour" (sweet and sour) fish

Jewish history can be traced in the traditional dishes of Jewish cuisine. Jews were persecuted during the Spanish Inquisition, and eventually exiled in 1492. Many of these Spanish Jews settled in the Netherlands, which was for many years part of the Spanish Empire, bringing their Mediterranean cuisine with them.

Jews were likewise barred from living in England from 1290 until the year 1651, when Oliver Cromwell invited Dutch Jews to settle there. These immigrants brought their "Sephardi" ("Spanish") cuisine with them. Thus, certain Mediterranean dishes, such as egg-lemon sauces, became closely identified with British Jews.

My own family in Britain came from Eastern Europe, yet when they settled in London, they adopted the Sephardi favorites of other British Jews. My great-aunt Cissie, may her memory be for a blessing, used to make this sweet and sour fish.

> 1 lb. firm white fish (my aunt used halibut, but you can use any type of firm fish fillet)
> 1 lemon
> 1 egg
> 1 T sugar (approx.)
> ½ cup flour

Simmer fish in a saucepan in enough water to cover. When the fish is cooked through, remove pan from heat, and let cool.

Meanwhile, squeeze lemon. Beat together egg, lemon juice, sugar, and flour.

Remove fish from dish. Add egg mixture to the water in pan. Return the pan to medium heat, and stir occasionally until slightly thickened. Add more sugar if necessary.

Pour egg-lemon sauce over the fish and let it cool in the refrigerator. The sauce will thicken as it cools. Serve chilled.

Serves 2–3.

Chicken soup

Two variables make a good chicken soup: chicken, and cooking time. The more of each, the better your soup will be.

1–1½ lb. bone-in chicken pieces (you can use any part of the chicken, so long as you include bones)

1 onion

4–5 carrots

Large dash of salt

Large dash of pepper (I prefer white, but black will do)

3 quarts water (approx.)

Optional ingredients can include:

2–3 celery stalks

1–2 parsnips

1 zucchini

½ beetroot

bunch dill

bunch cilantro

1 beef bone

Combine ingredients, bring to a boil, and simmer for as long as you can, at least 5 hours. I sometimes make mine in a crockpot, and let it cook all day long — up to 12 hours. Strain soup.

If you have lots of time and want to make a truly memorable soup, do what French cooks do, and cook your soup twice. Make a chicken soup, then the next day, take that soup and use it instead of water, and cook this recipe a second time. (That results in an incredibly rich soup.)

Makes 8–10 servings.

Matzah balls, kreplach, and meatballs

Once you make your soup, you can serve it alone, with the chicken and carrots it was cooked with, or with additions such as cooked noodles, matzah balls, kreplach, or meatballs.

Cook these "floaters," as my husband calls them, in a large pot of salted

water. (Don't cook them in your good chicken soup, as they make their cooking liquid thick and oily.)

Matzah balls
> 1 quart salted water
> 3 eggs
> ¼ cup oil (or schmaltz)
> Large dash each of salt and pepper
> 1 cup matzah meal (approx.)

Bring salted water to a boil. While you are waiting for water to heat, mix matzah ball dough.

Combine eggs, oil, salt, and pepper. Then mix in matzah meal, a little at at a time, until the mixture is thickened but still sticky. Matzah meal absorbs lots of water, so wait 10 minutes or so to see if you need more. Aim for your batter to feel like modeling clay. (If it is too dry, you'll have heavy, gummy balls; if it is too wet, your matzah balls will disintegrate.)

Wet your hands and roll batter into balls; for large balls, roll them into the size of a small egg. For smaller balls, aim for walnut-sized. Drop balls into the boiling water, then reduce heat and simmer for at least 30 minutes.

(My mother's grandparents came from Poland, and to this day my mum cooks her matzah balls in an old-fashioned Jewish-Polish manner, adding a couple drops of almond extract to matzah ball dough. If you do this, you might also want to form each ball around a single skinless almond: it is a fancy, nice touch.)

Makes approximately 12 matzah balls.

Kreplach
Traditionally, kreplach are made with chopped brisket meat. Here is a recipe full of shortcuts, which makes about two dozen kreplach.

For dough:
> 4 eggs
> 2 cups flour

For filling:

½ pound ground beef, chicken, or turkey

Large dash each: salt, pepper, and onion powder

For cooking:

2 quarts salted water

Fry meat, with spices, until cooked through.

For the dough, mix together eggs and flour. Roll until thin on a floured board, and cut out rounds with a small cup. Gather scraps together and re-roll until all dough is used up. Note: the dough will thicken as it cooks, so try to get it as thin as you can and still work with it.

To assemble kreplach, place a small amount of meat on each dough round, moisten edges with water, and fold to make a half-circle.

Boil a pot of the salted water. Drop filled kreplach into boiling water, cover pot, turn heat to low, and simmer for 20 minutes. Drain kreplach and add to chicken soup.

Makes approximately 20 kreplach.

Meatballs

The Jews of Iran make small fragrant meatballs called gondi to eat in soup. I've adapted this concept to make small meatballs for my family to eat in chicken soup on Friday nights.

2 quarts boiling water, salted

1 lb. ground beef, chicken, or turkey

Optional: 2 T instant chicken soup powder

Bring water to boil. (For extra flavor, add the instant chicken soup powder to the boiling water.)

With wet hands, form meat mixture into small balls, no more than one inch across, and drop into boiling water. Turn heat to low and simmer for at least 30 minutes.

Makes approximately 20 meatballs.

Cold soups

Cold soups are particularly useful on Shabbat day, when we are not able to heat up liquids. Here are three fantastic cold soups that you can serve for any meal.

Cold fruit soup

    1 lb. fruit (fresh, frozen or canned), skin and pits removed

    1 cup organge juice

    ½ cup sugar

    1 cup soy milk (or, if making with a dairy meal, milk)

Combine all ingredients. You can use any type of fruit such as berries, apricots, peaches, nectarines, cherries, or a combination of different fruits. Then blend. I use an immersion blender for this soup, and purée it right in its serving bowl, but you can also purée this soup in a blender.

You can serve the soup as is, or experiment with different seasonings. Try adding a dash of a spice such as ginger, allspice, nutmeg, cardamom, mint or cinnamon, or the zest of an orange or lemon.

A particularly beautiful way to serve this soup is to make two different soups, in contrasting colors, and spoon a little of each into each person's bowl. This soup is slightly thick, and the colors will remain separate, which looks nice, or else you can swirl them together, which also looks very attractive.

Makes approximately 12 servings.

Grandma's cold zucchini soup

    1 onion, finely chopped

    1 T olive oil

    1½ cups chicken broth

    1½ lbs. unpeeled, chopped (about 1-inch pieces) zucchini

    Salt, pepper, and garlic powder to taste

Saute onion in oil until golden. Add chicken broth and zucchini. Cover and simmer about 15 minutes. Pour all contents into a blender and purée.

(I prefer to use a hand-held immersion blender, and purée it right in the pot.) Add seasonings.

Optional: garnish with chopped chives or green onions.

Variation: to make this soup dairy, substitute butter instead of margarine, and vegetable or parve-"chicken" flavored broth instead of chicken broth. If this soup is dairy, it can be garnished with sour cream.

Serves 8.

Cold yogurt soup

2 cups plain yogurt

2 cups whole milk

3 cloves of garlic, finely minced

1 cucumber, peeled, seeded, cut in half lengthwise, and finely sliced

¼ cup fresh mint, finely chopped

Large dash of salt

Mix ingredients together. Let this soup sit in the refrigerator for at least one day to give the flavors time to mingle.

Makes approx. 12 servings.

Kugel

Kugels are great for Shabbat. They call for inexpensive ingredients, can serve a few people or a large crowd, and taste good hot, cold, or room temperature.

Onion kugel

2 onions, finely chopped

½ cup plus 1 t sugar

¼ cup oil

10 oz fine egg noodles

2 quarts boiling water

3 eggs

⅓ cup raisins

1–2 T salt

1 T ground black pepper

Carmelize onion by sprinkling with salt and (1 t) sugar, and frying in oil, over medium heat, about 20 minutes, stirring occasionally, until dark brown.

Cook noodles 10 minutes in boiling water and drain. Mix together with the fried onion, eggs, remaining sugar, raisins, and salt and pepper.

Pour into an 8-inch baking pan and cook at 350°F for 45 minutes, until lightly browned on top. Serve cut into small squares.

Serves 8.

Sweet noodle kugel

½ lb. egg noodles

2 quarts boiling water

4 eggs

2 T oil

1 cup sugar

Boil noodles until soft. Drain and let cool, then mix together with remaining ingredients. Pour into a 9-inch baking pan and cook at about 350°F for 30 minutes, until browned on top.

Variations: before baking, add any of the following to the kugel mixture:

½ cup raisins

1–2 peeled and diced apples or pears

1–2 diced peaches, nectarines, plums, or 3–4 diced apricots

1 15 oz can crushed pineapple, drained

1 15 oz can fruit cocktail, drained

Serve cut into small squares.

Serves 8.

Sara's amazing no-mix noodle kugel

    6¾ cups water

    4 T oil

    4 T brown sugar

    ½ cup white sugar

    ½ cup apple sauce

    1 t salt

    Dash of pepper

    3 eggs

    24 oz fine egg noodles

Combine first seven ingredients and bring to a boil. When boiling, add eggs and noodles. Mix to combine. Turn off heat and allow this mixture to stand for 10 minutes. (Do not drain the water; the noodles will absorb it.) Pour mixture into a deep 9-inch by 13-inch greased pan. Bake at 350°F for 1 hour.

This is great for a crowd; it makes about 16 servings.

Broccoli kugel

    4 large stalks broccoli

    1 cup mayonnaise

    2 T onion soup mix

    4 eggs

    Dash of white pepper (or black pepper if you don't have white)

Boil broccoli until very soft. Drain, cool, and mash with a fork in a bowl. Add remaining ingredients and mix until well blended. Pour in lined 8-inch or 9-inch baking pan and bake uncovered at 350°F for 1 hour.

Let cool, then cut into squares. Serve hot or cold.

Serves 8.

Carrot kugel

    4–5 large carrots, peeled and grated

    ¾ cup sugar

¼ cup oil

¼ cup matzah meal or flour

1 t salt

3 eggs

Combine ingredients and mix well. Pour into a greased 8-inch pan and bake for 30 minutes at 350°F.

Serves 8.

Cauliflower kugel

1 head cauliflower

2 quarts boiling water (to cook cauliflower)

1 onion, chopped

1 T salt

¼ cup oil

1 t pepper

3 eggs

Boil cauliflower until tender. While cauliflower is cooking, sprinkle onion with salt, and fry it in oil for about 20 minutes, until dark brown. Mash cauli-flower and mix it with remaining ingredients. Pour into a greased 8-inch pan and bake for 30 minutes at 350°F.

Serves 8.

Apple kugel

2 cups apple sauce

1 cup flour

1 t baking powder

Dash of salt

1 cup sugar

3 eggs

(Optional: dash of cinnamon, and one peeled, cored, and finely chopped apple)

Mix together ingredients. Pour into a greased 8-inch pan and bake for 40 minutes at 350°F, until set and light brown on top.

Serves 8.

Rebbetzin Berger's kishka

Kishka is traditionally a spicy, breaded stuffing encased in cow intestine. As with much of Jewish food, old-fashioned dishes have remained popular in traditional communities, but often in healthier forms. This is an easy vegetarian version.

1 cup water
½ cup oil
¼ cup corn meal
1½ cups flour
1 t paprika
1 t sugar
Dash each salt and pepper

Optional:
1 grated onion
1 grated carrot
Large bunch of minced parsley

Boil together water and oil. Remove from heat and stir in remaining ingredients. Form into a cylinder and bake, covered with foil, for 45 minutes at 350°F. Uncover kishka, and bake for a further 10 minutes.

For an onion and carrot variation: add onion, carrot, and parsley to the oil and water mixture, and simmer for 10 minutes. Then follow the recipe as above.

My mother often makes these kishkas, and cooks them in loaf pans or baking tins, which gives them a less traditional shape, more like a kugel or cornbread.

Serves 8.

Chicken

Chicken seems to be one of the most commonly served main courses for Shabbat dinner. Here are nine incredibly easy, no-fail recipes.

Easiest roast chicken

> 1 whole raw chicken
>
> 2 T olive oil
>
> Large dash each: salt, pepper, and garlic powder
>
> 1–2 onions, sliced
>
> Optional: 4–5 cloves of garlic, sliced
>
> Optional: ¼ cup fresh herbs (for example, sage, rosemary, tarragon, etc.)

Optional rub:

> 1 lemon (zest and juice)
>
> 2 T extra virgin olive oil
>
> 1 T paprika
>
> 1 t cumin
>
> Large dash each of salt and pepper

Place a chicken in a pan, feet-side down. Sprinkle with oil, then salt, pepper, and garlic powder. Scatter onion slices around the chicken; place a few onion slices in cavity and under skin. (Optional: place garlic and/or herbs under skin, too.) Lightly cover chicken with foil (leave an opening between the foil and the pan), place in oven and bake at 400°F for 1–2 hours, until skin is crispy and golden brown and juices run clear when you prick the chicken just above the thigh.

To make rub, zest the lemon (grate the lemon's shiny yellow surface), and combine the zest of the lemon with its juice and remaining rub ingredients. Spread the rub on chicken skin before roasting.

Serves 6.

Great-aunt Cissie's roast chicken

When I lived in London, I spent many Shabbat lunches with my great-aunt Cissie, of blessed memory. She grew up in a Yiddish-speaking community

in London's East End, and cooked the same recipes she learned from her mother and grandmother, whose cooking reflected the shtetls of Eastern Europe. Her roast chicken with "helzel" stuffing was my favorite dish.

"Helzel" originally was a stuffed chicken neck. I remember going to the last kosher butcher in the London's East End for my great-aunt, to buy her a chicken; even in the 1990s, it was an old-fashioned store with sawdust on the floor, like something out of the nineteenth century. When that butcher closed, we found one of the newer kosher markets in North London that would deliver. Unfortunately, the newer butcher couldn't supply my great-aunt with chicken necks, so she started making this delicious dish instead.

For stuffing:
1 onion finely diced
1 cup matzah meal (approx.)
Large dash each salt and pepper
½ cup shmaltz (chicken fat) or margarine

For chicken:
1 small onion, thinly sliced
1 small raw chicken
1 cup water
Dash of salt

First, make a stuffing by mixing the first four ingredients until they achieve a paste-like consistency. (Adjust matzah meal if it is too dry or wet.) Stuff this paste under chicken skin.

Line a baking pan with thinly sliced onion. Place stuffed chicken in pan, feet side down. Slowly pour water into pan around the chicken. Sprinkle chicken with salt. Cover loosely with foil or a pot lid (not one that is airtight). Bake at 300°F for 2–3 hours, until skin is browned and chicken is cooked through and tender. Add more water if pan becomes dry.

Serves 6.

Mediterranean chicken
2 lbs. cut-up raw chicken (skin removed)

1 cup white wine

1 cup orange juice

3 cloves garlic, finely minced

1 cup pitted olives

1 cup prunes

½ cup capers

½ cup brown sugar

2 T dried thyme (or oregano if you do not have thyme)

Place chicken in a baking pan. Mix next eight ingredients together and pour over chicken. Cover, and marinade in the refrigerator for several hours or overnight.

Bake the chicken in its marinade at 350°F for approximately 1 hour. Uncover and cook until chicken is browned, another 30 minutes to 1 hour.

Serve hot or room-temperature, with sauce. This is particularly good served over rice.

Serves 8–10.

Baked chicken with onions and carrots

5 carrots, peeled and cut into fours

5 potatoes, peeled and cut into fours

2 quarts of boiling water (to cook carrots and potatoes)

1 cut-up raw chicken

Dash each of salt and white pepper (use black if you do not have white)

½ cup cold water

Parboil the vegetables by letting them simmer for about 10 minutes in boiling water. Drain.

Place chicken in a baking pan, skin side up, and arrange parboiled vegetables around pieces. Sprinkle liberally with salt and white ground pepper (if you don't have white, use black pepper). Pour cold water into pan.

Put in oven and bake uncovered at 400°F for 1–2 hours, until chicken and potatoes are crispy and golden. (If they are not yet crispy and golden, bake for up to 30 minutes more.)

Note: if you are pressed for time, don't parboil the vegetables; just dice them finely, and place them in the baking pan. Serves 4–6.

Chicken with apples and prunes

1 cut-up raw chicken
2 apples, peeled, cored and sliced
½ cup prunes
1 cup white wine or orange juice

Remove skin from chicken, place in a baking pan, and sprinkle it with the apples and prunes. Pour wine or orange juice around chicken into pan. Cover and bake at 350°F for 2 hours, until chicken is golden brown and cooked through. If it is not browning, uncover and cook for an additional 20–30 minutes.

Serves 4–6.

Oven-fried chicken

½ cup oil
2 eggs
1 raw cut-up chicken
3 cups flour
Large dash each of salt and pepper

Preheat oven to 375°F. Pour ½ cup oil into a wide baking pan, and place in the oven to warm up while you prepare the chicken.

Beat eggs and pour them into a plastic bag. Place chicken in the bag and shake so that chicken is coated with beaten egg. In a second plastic bag, pour flour, salt and pepper. Shake to mix. Working in batches, place the chicken pieces in the flour bag, and shake to coat. Remove heated pan from the oven, and place chicken pieces in it, skin-side down. Bake one hour, until lightly browned. Flip pieces, and bake another 30–40 minutes, until browned on both sides.

Variation: Instead of coating the chicken pieces with egg, place them in a bag that contains 2 cups barbecue sauce and shake to coat. Then put them

in the flour bag for a coating of flour. This is messy, but delicious!
Serves 4–6.

Easy broiled chicken

1 raw cut-up chicken (or any chicken parts you desire — legs, wings, etc.)
Dash each of salt, black pepper, and garlic powder

Place chicken pieces in a shallow roasting pan and sprinkle *very* liberally with salt, pepper, and garlic powder.

Place pan in broiler rack in oven, and broil until skin is crispy, about 20–30 minutes. Flip chicken pieces, sprinkle with spices again, and broil for a further 20–30 minutes. Check to make sure chicken is cooked through before serving. Serves 4–6.

Simple slow-cooker chicken

If you simply don't have the time to prepare a main course for Shabbat, and you don't want to spend the money buying a main course from a deli, try using a slow cooker. It is a great way to make meat flavorful and tender. These recipes generate a lot of sauce; they're nice served over rice or noodles.

Place a cut-up chicken (or approx. 2 lbs. of chicken pieces, such as breasts or thighs) in your slow cooker.

Variation one. Add:

5 carrots (peeled and cut in half)
5 potatoes (peeled and cut in half or quarters)
1 small onion (peeled and roughly chopped)
2 cups water
Salt and pepper
Optional: 2 T instant soup powder

Variation two. Add:

1 jar of prepared Marinara sauce

Variations three. Add:

   1–2 cups dried fruits (such as prunes, apricots, or raisins)

   2–3 cups of orange juice, wine, chicken stock or water

In all cases, cook on low all day.

   Serves 6.

Chicken shnitzel

My grandmother, may her memory be for a blessing, grew up in Vienna, and was schooled in the traditional, formal cooking of Viennese haute cuisine. I remember going over to her house for her special wiener schnitzel dinners: she used to pound the cutlets so thin she said she could read a newspaper through them. (Intrigued, I once tried, and found I could actually read the paper through the pounded meat.) Here is a simplified version that tastes divine.

   2 eggs

   2 cups flour

   2 cups seasoned breadcrumbs

   6 raw boneless chicken breasts or thighs

   ½ cup oil (or more, if needed)

Beat eggs in one bowl. Place flour in a second bowl, and seasoned breadcrumbs in a third.

   Slice chicken pieces in half. (Large breasts might need to be cut into quarters.) Dip each piece first in flour, then in egg, then in breadcrumbs.

   Fry in oil, in small batches, over medium heat, until browned on one side, approximately 8 minutes. Turn chicken, and brown on other side, another approximately 8 minutes. (Add more oil if pan becomes dry.) Make sure chicken is cooked through.

   This is good served hot or cold. Cold schnitzel pieces can even be served in sandwiches with ketchup and mustard.

   Serves 6.

Meatballs

Old-fashioned meatballs

My mother remembers her Bubbe (Grandmother) Yitta, who was born in the little shtetl of Dobra, Poland, making this dish. Nothing could be simpler — or more tasty.

> 2 carrots
>
> 1 onion
>
> 1 lb. raw ground beef
>
> (you can also use chicken or turkey)

Finely grate carrots and onion. (This is easiest with a food processor.) Mix half the vegetable mixture with the ground beef. Place the other half of the vegetable mixture on the bottom of a small baking pan. Form the ground meat mixture into 1–2 inch balls and place in pan. Bake, uncovered, at 350°F for 1 hour, until meatballs are dark brown and slightly crisp on top.

Serves 6.

Easy Middle-Eastern "Kibbeh" meatballs

Here's a faux version of the Middle Eastern meatballs called Kibbeh. The meatballs turn out crispy and spicy, and are great with a cool salad or relish.

> 1½ pounds of raw ground meat (beef, lamb, chicken, turkey, or a mixture of any of these)
>
> Large dash each: salt, black pepper, and cayenne pepper

Form meat into six large, oblong meatballs. The shape you are going for looks like a football.

Place the meatballs on a baking pan and sprinkle very liberally with the spices. Place under a very hot broiler, or grill and cook until slightly charred on the outside. Flip, sprinkle with salt and the two peppers again, and cook until the other side is slightly charred as well. Be sure to check that the meat is cooked thoroughly through before serving.

Serves 6.

Beef stew

Stew is a great way to make meat go further, especially when you are entertaining a crowd. Beef stews can also be kept hot overnight on Shabbat in a slow cooker, which makes them nice for Shabbat lunch. Here are two versions I like to make, which are always hits.

For a marinade:

2 cups dry red wine (or orange juice)

1 sliced onion

2 chopped garlic cloves

1 bay leaf

For the stew:

2 lbs. beef, cut into 1-inch pieces

¼ cup oil

2 sliced onions

For both versions, if you have time, mix first five ingredients, place in a large plastic food bag and marinate the beef in it several hours or overnight.

Remove beef from marinade (if using) and pat dry with a paper towel. Heat oil in a heavy pan on medium-high heat. Working in small batches, sear beef cubes on all sides until each side is browned. Remove beef and add onion to pan; cook until onion starts to turn brown (about 15 minutes).

If you are making this dish in a slow cooker, transfer all ingredients to slow cooker at this point, and turn cooker on "low." If you are making this dish on the stove, continue to use the pan in which you browned the beef and onions.

Beef daube

This is a quick, easy version of the classic French stew.

Add the following to the beef and onions:

15 oz can diced tomatoes

Dash each of salt and pepper

½ cup dry red wine

½ cup orange juice

5 large carrots, peeled and cut into 1-inch pieces

Sweet and sour tzimmes

Tzimmes is a traditional Eastern European Jewish dish incorporating meat and sweet stewed fruit. Here is a foolproof version.

Add the following to the beef and onions:

3 cups orange juice

Juice of 1 lemon

4 carrots, peeled and cut into 1-inch pieces

1 large sweet potato, peeled and cut into 1-inch pieces

1 cup dried apricots

1 cup prunes

Dash each of salt and pepper

In both versions, cover and cook over low heat (or in slow cooker) for at least 4 hours.

Serves 8.

Shabbat breakfasts

On Shabbat, we traditionally do not eat anything requiring a "hamotzi" blessing (the blessing made over bread) before the festive Shabbat lunch on Saturday afternoon. Here are a few ideas I make for my own children that are festive and easy to prepare.

Museli

2 apples, peeled, cored, and grated

½ cup raisins

1 cup quick-cooking raw oats

2 cups plain or vanilla yogurt

Combine ingredients, and let sit overnight in the refrigerator. Once you get the hang of museli, you can add anything you like to it: bananas, dried cranberries, nuts, peaches, plums, pears, etc. Find the version you like best!

Serves 4.

Peanut butter and jelly muffins

    2 cups flour
    2 eggs
    ⅓ cup sugar
    ⅓ cup oil
    1 cup orange juice
    1 cup peanut butter
    1 t salt
    1 t baking soda
    ¼ cup jam (approx.)

Combine first eight ingredients and blend until smooth. Spoon batter into a muffin baking tin lined with paper cupcake holders. Place a small spoonful of jam in the center of each. Bake at 350°F for 25 minutes.

(Variation: you can try this recipe with chocolate instead of jam.)

Makes 12 muffins.

Liptauer cheese spread

This recipe was a favorite of my grandmother. It is from her native Vienna, and I have never seen it elsewhere. If you like sharp, piquant tastes, this is a great breakfast, spread on crackers.

    8 oz cream cheese
    ½ T mustard
    1 T capers
    2 anchovies (or an inch of anchovy paste)
    1 green onion, finely chopped (use a small white onion if you don't have green)
    1 t black pepper
    1 t paprika

Using a fork, mash ingredients together until well blended. My grandmother used to add a stick of margarine, too, which made it creamier and richer, though in these health-conscious times I usually omit the margarine. This spread is delicious either way.

Makes about 1½ cups of cheese spread.

Easy oatmeal casserole

½ cup oil

2 eggs

1 cup milk

½ cup sugar

2 t baking powder

½ t salt

1 t cinnamon

3 cups quick-cooking raw oats

1 apple, peeled, cored, and chopped

1 cup raisins

1 cup dried cranberries

Beat together oil and eggs until smooth. Mix in (in this order, stirring well after each addition): milk, sugar, baking powder, salt, cinnamon, oats, apple, raisins, and cranberries. Pour into a greased 8-inch baking pan and bake at 350°F for approximately 30 minutes, until top is golden.

(Variation: if you don't have an apple, a large diced peach makes a great substitute.)

Serves 6.

Apple crisp

6 apples, peeled, cored, and chopped

¾ cup sugar

8 T butter

2 cups raw oats

Dash of cinnamon

Place apples in a wide baking pan, and swirl in cinnamon and ¼ cup of the sugar.

For the topping, mix together butter, oats, and ½ cup sugar. Press this down across the top of the apples. Bake at 350°F for 45 minutes, until apples are soft and top is lightly browned.

Variations: this crisp is delicious made with any other fruit; I sometimes

use peaches, nectarines, cherries, rhubarb, strawberries, or blueberries.
Serves 6.

Stuffed cabbage

This quintessential Eastern European Jewish dish makes an economical
main course.

> 1 large head of green cabbage

> **For stuffing:**
> ¼ dry rice
> ½ cup water
> 1 onion, chopped
> 2 T oil
> 1 lb. raw ground beef
> Dash each of salt and pepper

> **For sauce:**
> 28 oz can of tomato sauce
> Juice of 1 lemon
> 2 T sugar
> ¼ cup raisins

One or two days before you make this dish, place one large head of cabbage
in your freezer. Several hours before you want to assemble the dish, remove
the cabbage from your freezer and let it thaw. This will make the leaves soft
enough to remove easily. (If you don't have time to freeze your cabbage,
dip it into boiling water to make the leaves limp enough to remove easily:
you will have to keep dipping as you remove the outer leaves.)

Using a paring knife to cut the bottom of the leaves, carefully remove
the leaves from the cabbage head. Make one stack of all the whole leaves
and another of ripped leaves and scraps.

In a saucepan, combine dry rice with the water. Simmer, covered, on a
low flame for 20–25 minutes until rice is cooked.

In a separate saucepan, cook onion in oil until soft. Add beef and cook,
stirring, until brown. Add rice to meat mixture and stir to incorporate.
Season with salt and pepper to taste.

To stuff the cabbage, first line the bottom of a baking dish with cabbage scraps and torn leaves. Then place a dollop of about 1 T beef mixture on a whole cabbage leaf, and roll up, tucking the sides in, to make a packet. (First fold the bottom side up, then the right and left sides in like an envelope, then roll up the packet the rest of the way to the top.) Repeat with remaining leaves.

Place completed packets in the baking pan. You can stack packets on top of each other. When all the leaves are filled and rolled, mix the sauce ingredients together and pour over cabbage rolls into baking pan. Cover and bake at 350°F for 1 hour.

This dish is very durable, and can be easily reheated. In fact, it gets better with each reheating! It can also be frozen.

Serves 8–10.

Meat pie

For the crust:
½ cup oil
½ cup water
Dash of salt
2½–3 cups flour (approx.)

Mix the oil and water together. Add a dash of salt, then 2 cups flour. Add more flour as you mix, until it forms a soft dough. Knead the dough, and roll it out to ¼-inch thickness on a floured surface. Using a 9-inch round pie pan as a guide, cut out two circles: one slightly larger than 9 inches and one 9 inches. Line the pie pan with the larger circle.

For basic meat filling:
1 onion
1 T oil
1 lb. ground beef (you can use chicken, turkey, or lamb instead if you prefer)
Dash each: cinnamon, salt, and pepper
(Optional: ¼ toasted pine nuts and 2 chopped hard-boiled eggs)

Fry the onion in the oil until soft. Add meat and stir, breaking up the meat, until cooked through. Season meat with cinnamon, salt, and pepper. Turn off meat and stir in the pine nuts and hard-boiled eggs, if using.

For sweet and spicy meat filling:

1 onion

1 T oil

1 ground beef (you can use chicken, turkey, or lamb instead if you prefer)

⅓ cup raisins

½ cup chopped roasted red peppers

2 T capers

1 T sugar

Dash of salt

Dash of chili powder

Fry onion in oil until soft, then add the meat, stirring until meat is broken up and cooked through. Stir last six ingredients into meat mixure.

For the glaze:

1 egg, beaten

Spoon the meat into the pie pan. Cover with the second dough circle. Crimp the dough edges together and, using a sharp knife, cut out four decorative holes in the top sheet of dough to form air vents. Paint the top dough circle with beaten egg. Bake at 350°F for 45 minutes, until crust is golden brown.

Serves 6–8.

Cholent

Every family has their own favorite cholent recipe. Some of the rules for cooking for Shabbat are discussed in Chapter 2 but, briefly, the cholent must be edible once the sun sets and Shabbat begins. After Shabbat commences, it can't be stirred or adjusted in any way. Because cholent stews slowly for many hours, it calls for hardy ingredients, such as beans, barley, and potatoes. Here is the recipe that my favorite rebbetzin, Rebbetzin Berger,

makes, and serves each Shabbat in shul (synagogue).

Line a 5–6 quart slow cooker with a slow cooker bag. Place in slow cooker:

    1 lb. short ribs
    1 cup barley
    1 cup mixed beans (kidney, lima, northern, pinto)
    1 envelope (about 2 T) onion soup mix
    5–6 medium potatoes (often Yukon Gold), cubed
    1 large onion, quartered
    ¼ cup honey
    ¼ cup ketchup
    1 kishke
    Water to cover

Combine first 8 ingredients in slow cooker. Add enough water to cover ingredients. Place kishke (unwrapped, if it is not home-made) on top of ingredients. Close bag with a twist tie, cover crock pot, and cook on slow until Shabbat lunch.

Make this recipe once, then adjust the seasonings to your taste. You may like to add salt, pepper, garlic, cayenne pepper, or even barbecue sauce.

Salad
Israeli Salad

    4 tomatoes, diced
    1 onion, diced
    1 cucumber, diced
    Juice of one lemon
    (Optional: minced garlic, salt, and the Israeli spice zaatar, available in kosher super-
        market aisles.)

Combine ingredients and toss.

Serves 4–6.

Sweet salad

  1 head lettuce, torn into bite-sized pieces

  1 pear, cored, quartered and finely sliced

  ¼ cup raisins (or dried cranberries)

  ¼ cup chopped walnuts (or pecans), toasted (or even fried in a little oil and sugar).

For the dressing:

  Juice of 1 lemon

  2 T vegetable oil

  2 T sugar

Whisk dressing ingredients together, and pour over salad.

  Serves 6.

Sweet carrot salad

  5 carrots, peeled and grated

  ¼ cup raisins

  ¼ cup orange juice

Combine ingredients and mix well.

  Serves 4–6.

Orange and fennel salad

  2 large oranges, peeled and sliced

  1 fennel bulb, thinly sliced

For the dressing:

  Juice of one lemon

  2 T vegetable oil

  2 T sugar

Mix oranges and fennel. Whisk together dressing ingredients, and pour over salad. Toss to coat.

  Serves 4–6.

Oriental cabbage salad

   1 head cabbage, finely sliced

   1 package kosher instant ramen noodle soup mix

   ¼ cup sliced almonds (toasted if you have time)

   2 T toasted sesame oil

   2 T rice wine vinegar

Crush the noodles from ramen noodle soup mix and add to cabbage. Lightly toast the sliced almonds and add to cabbage mixture. For dressing, mix together toasted sesame oil, rice wine vinegar, and powder from the soup packet contained in the ramen noodle soup package. Pour over cabbage mixture and toss.

   Serves 8.

Coleslaw

   1 head cabbage, finely sliced

   2 carrots, peeled and grated

For dressing:

   ¼ cup mayonnaise

   Juice of 1 lemon (or 2 T of prepared lemon juice)

   1 T fennel seeds

Combine grated vegetables. Whisk together dressing ingredients, pour over salad, and mix.

   Serves 8.

Rice

Rice salad

   ½ cup dry white rice

   1 cup water

   ½ diced onion

   1 diced pepper

   2 diced celery stalks

For the dressing:
Juice of 1 lemon
¼ cup olive oil
1 t mustard

Place dry rice in a saucepan with the water. Cover, bring to a boil, then simmer on a low flame for 20 minutes.

Mix onion, pepper, and celery into the rice. (Optional: you can add anything else you like, such as olives, deli meat cut into pieces, cooked carrots or broccoli, capers, leftover chicken or meat cut into small pieces, marinated artichoke hearts, etc.)

Whisk dressing ingredients together, and add to rice. Stir well.

Sephardi rice and chickpeas
½ cup dry white rice (preferably basmati)
¼ cup oil
15 oz can chickpeas
½ cup water (approx.)
Dash each salt and pepper

Rinse dry rice until the water runs clear. Place it in a saucepan with oil, and heat over a low flame until rice is golden brown. Drain the can of chickpeaas, reserving the water chickpeas were packed in. Add chickpeas to rice. Add tap water to chickpea water until you have one cup water, and add to rice. Simmer, covered, for 20 minutes. Toss with salt and pepper to taste.

Variation: when you add the chickpeas and water to the rice, also add ¼ cup dried fruit. (You can use raisins, dates, cranberries, etc., or a mixture.)

Vegetables
Ratatouille
2 T oil
1 onion, diced

1 clove garlic, minced

1 eggplant, diced

1 red or green pepper, diced

1 zucchini, diced

3–5 tomatoes, diced (or a 28 oz can of chopped tomatoes)

Dash of salt and pepper

1 T thyme

Optional:

15 oz can chickpeas

1 cup tofu

Heat oil on medium heat, then add onion and cook until soft. Add garlic, and cook for a minute more. Then add eggplant, green pepper, and zucchini. Cook until soft, about 10 minutes, then add tomatoes. Season with salt, pepper, and thyme. Cook, covered, until vegetables are soft, about 15 minutes.

Variation: to make this dish more substantial, add a can of rinsed chickpeas or a package of diced tofu. With these additions, ratatouille can be a vegetarian main course, excellent served over couscous or rice.

Serves 6–8.

Green beans with almonds

1 lb. green beans

1 T oil

¼ cup sliced almonds

Wash and trim the beans. Heat oil in a pan and sauté green beans on medium flame until slightly cooked, about 5 minutes. Add almonds and sauté for 5 minutes more.

For an Asian-accented variation, use toasted sesame oil, and sauté one clove of chopped garlic with the beans. After you add the almonds, stir in a large dash (about 1 T) of soy sauce.

Serves 6.

Mum's English roast potatoes:
In this classic English dish, potatoes become crispy and salty on the outside, and stay creamy on the inside.

    8 potatoes
    2 pints boiling water
    ¼ cup oil
    1–2 T salt (approx.)

Peel potatoes and cut into quarters. Place in boiling water and parboil (boil until half-cooked) on medium heat, about 10 minutes. Drain potatoes well.

Meanwhile, preheat oven to 375°F. Pour oil into a shallow baking pan. Put pan in the oven and heat until the oil is hot. When potatoes are done, remove the pan from the oven and put parboiled potatoes in, turning them so that they are coated with oil on all sides. Sprinkle potatoes liberally with salt and return pan to the oven. (Do not crowd the potatoes. If you need more room, use two pans.)

Bake about 40 minutes, until tops of potatoes are golden brown. Turn potatoes and return pan to oven, baking another 40 minutes, until potatoes are browned all over. Serve hot.

Serves 6–8.

Crispy diced potatoes:

    8 potatoes
    ¼ cup oil
    1 T season salt (or use plain salt if you don't have season salt)

Peel potatoes and dice into small pieces (about ½ inch across). Put potato pieces in a plastic bag with oil and season salt. Shake to coat well, then place potatoes in a single layer on a baking sheet or in a shallow baking pan. Bake at 350°F for 40–60 minutes or until potatoes are crispy. Stir once or twice during cooking, to make sure all sides of potato pieces get browned. Serve hot.

Serves 6–8.

Carrot tzimmes

This classic Eastern European Jewish dish is delicious, popular with everyone (including children), and is very easy to make. It is similar to the French dish "Vichy Carrots."

> 6 carrots
> 3 oz butter or margarine
> ¼ cup water
> ¼ cup sugar

Peel and slice carrots. Cut them into thin "coins" (about ¼-inch thick), and place them in a pan with butter or margarine. Add water, and simmer over a low flame, stirring occasionally, until the carrots begin to soften, about 15 minutes. If the pan seems like it is getting too dry, add more water.

When carrots are cooked, add sugar. (French cooks use powdered sugar for a lighter texture.) Stir to coat. Serve warm or at room temperature.

Serves 6.

Easy cranberry relish

> 2 cups raw cranberries
> 1 whole orange (unpeeled, and cut into quarters)
> 1 cup sugar

Place all ingredients in a food processor, and process until finely chopped and mixed.

Serves 6–8.

Quick broiled fruit

> 3 peaches (or nectarines or plums)
> ¼ cup sugar

In the summer, when I'm broiling chicken, I often broil fruit alongside: the result is an instant dinner. Slice fruit, remove the pit, place in a pan cut side up, sprinkle with sugar, and broil (or grill) them until slightly charred.

Serves 6.

Desserts

Easiest, quickest, best brownies

  1 cup oil

  2 cups sugar

  3 eggs

  1 t vanilla extract

  ½ t baking soda

  1 t salt

  1 cup cocoa powder

  1 cup flour

In a mixing bowl, mix oil and sugar until well blended. Add eggs, vanilla extract, baking soda, salt, cocoa powder, and flour. Beat until smooth. Spread in a greased 9-inch pan and bake at 350°F for 40 minutes. Allow to cool before cutting.

Optional: before baking, scatter some multi-colored ice cream sprinkles on the top of these brownies. It is quicker and easier than icing them, and makes the brownies look fun and festive. Makes 12 brownies.

Grandma's bishopsbrot

This is another Austrian treat. It is easy to prepare, and is always popular.

  4 eggs

  1 cup sugar

  2 cups flour

  1 cup chopped walnuts

  ½ lb chopped candied fruit

  1 cup chocolate chips

Beat together the first three ingredients until smooth and glossy. Then stir in walnuts, fruit, and chocolate. Pour into a greased bread loaf pan and bake at 350°F for 1 hour. Test "doneness" by inserting a knife or toothpick into the center; if it does not come out clean, bake for a further 20 minutes.

Makes one loaf.

Amazing gooey chocolate pie

For the crust:
½ cup margarine

2 cups flour

1 t salt

½ cup sugar

½ cup water (approx.)

Mix together first four ingredients, then add water, a little at a time, until dough is soft: not so dry that it is crumbly, and not so wet that it is sticky. Pat into an 8-inch or 9-inch round baking pan, and bake at 350°F for 20 minutes, until crust is a very light golden brown.

For the filling:
3 eggs

¼ cup oil

½ cup sugar

⅓ cup flour

1 t salt

1½ cups choclolate chips

1 cup chopped walnuts

Mix first five ingredients together until well blended, then fold in chocolate and nuts. Pour into pie crust and bake, uncovered, at 350°F for 45 minutes. Serve warm.

Serves 6–8.

Honey cake

This is a great cake to make if you must do some of your Shabbat cooking early in the week, as honey cake improves significantly with age.

½ cup sugar

¼ cup oil

1 egg

¼ cup orange juice

¼ cup honey

½ t baking powder

½ t baking soda

½ t salt

2 T cinnamon

1¼ cups flour

¼ cup hot coffee

In the bowl of an electric mixer, place ingredients in the order above, mixing well after each addition. (Tip: measure the honey in the same measuring cup you used for the oil; the honey will slide right out.)

Pour into a lined, greased 8-inch by 4-inch bread loaf pan and bake at 350°F for 30 minutes. A knife inserted in the center should come out clean when this cake is done.

Makes one small loaf.

Tasty Shalosh Seudos ("third meal") recipes

Sushi

In Japan, "sushi" refers to a special mixture of sticky rice. Anything at all can be wrapped in this rice, and it can be a very fun Shalosh Seudos meal to provide different choices of fillings, so everyone can pick and choose and make their own sushi rolls.

For the rice:

1 cup dry white rice (try to find sushi rice, but plain white rice also works)

2¼ cups water

2 T rice wine vinegar

2 T sugar

Combine rice and water in a pot with a tight-fitting lid. Bring rice to a boil, then lower heat to a very low simmer, and cook for 15 minutes. Turn off heat and let rice stand an additional 10 minutes in uncovered pot. When the rice is cool, pour it into a bowl and mix in the vinegar and sugar.

For the fillings: To serve sushi, set out dishes of julienned meats, fish or vegetables. Try using three or four of the following:

Avocado

Cucumber

Scallion

Omelet

Cooked asparagus

Pepper

Cooked eggplant

Smoked salmon

Cooked chicken or beef

To make the rolls:

16 sheets of kosher seaweed sheets

1 cup soy sauce

Cut the seaweed sheets into smaller squares, about 4 inches × 4 inches. Give each person a few squares of seaweed. Place a spoonful of rice in the middle, then select two or three items to place on top of the rice. Fold over the seaweed to make a bite-sized roll, and dip your seaweed in a dish of soy sauce. (It is a nice touch to provide everyone with their own little bowl of soy sauce for dipping.)

Traditional accompaniments (if you can find them) include a green mustard-like condiment called wasabi, to mix into your soy sauce, and pickled ginger, to munch on between sushi rolls.

Serves 8.

Korean pancakes

This is absolutely delicious, and is also a good way to use up leftover vegetables or meat. It is great warm or cold.

3 eggs

2 cups water (or soy milk)

2 cups flour

½ t salt

2 T oil (approx.)

2 cups very finely diced vegetables or cooked meat (or a combination of both)

Some ideas to try:

Broccoli

Peas

Green onions

Asparagus

Peppers

Kale

Cooked chicken, beef, turkey, or lamb

For dipping sauce:

2 T rice wine vinegar

2 T soy sauce

Beat eggs together with water. Add flour and salt and mix well. Add the vegtetables and/or meat and stir well.

Heat 1 T vegetable oil in a frying pan over low heat. Ladle about ½ cup of pancake batter into pan and cook until lightly browned on the bottom, about 1 or 2 minutes. Using a spatula, flip pancake and cook until lightly browned on other side. Continue with the remaining batter (adding more oil if the pan becomes dry). Drain cooked pancakes on a paper towel.

To serve, cut pancakes into wedges once they are cooled. Dip into dipping sauce.

Makes approximately 8 pancakes.

English tea sandwiches

This is a popular Shalosh Seudos with my kids. Thinly slice soft white bread (or challah), and cut off the crusts. Spread bread with liberal amounts of butter. Try any of these fillings:

➤ Thinly sliced, peeled cucumber (sprinkled with salt)

➤ Chopped watercress (sprinkled with salt)

➤ Mashed sardines (sprinkled with lemon juice)

➤ Jam

To make the "afternoon tea" theme of your Shalosh Seudos even stronger, serve these sandwiches on attractive plates, with tea to drink.

Hearty Mexican vegetarian casserole

- 2 cups frozen corn
- 2 cups canned black beans (drained and rinsed)
- 15 oz can green chillies
- 1 small onion, finely chopped
- 1 cup sour cream
- 1 cup salsa sauce
- 3 cups grated cheddar cheese
- 2 cups cooked rice
- 15 oz can sliced olives
- 1 t cayenne pepper

Combine all ingredients except for olives and 1 cup of the cheese. Spread mixture in a baking dish. Sprinkle with olives and remaining cheese. Bake at 350°F for 45 minutes.

Serves 8.

15

"Birkat HaMazon": the blessings after a meal

Introductory blessings

On Shabbat, it is customary to sing Psalm 126, followed by other words of praise, before reciting "Birkat HaMazon."

Psalm 126

A Song of Ascents.

When God will return the captivity of Zion, we will be like dreamers. Then our mouth will be filled with laughter and our tongue with glad song. Then they will declare among the nations, "God has done greatly with these." God has done greatly with us, we were gladdened. O God — return our captivity like springs in the desert. Those who tearfully sow will reap in glad song. He who bears the measure of seeds walks along weeping, but will return in exultation, a bearer of his sheaves.

May my mouth declare the praise of God and may all flesh bless His Holy Name forever. (Psalms 145:21)

We will bless God from this time and forever, Halleluyah! (Psalms 115:18)

Give thanks to God for He is good, His kindness endures forever. (Psalms 118:1)

Who can express the mighty acts of God? Who can declare all His praise? (Psalms 106:2)

Invitation

If three or more bar mitzvahs (males 13 years or older) have eaten together, it is customary to ask one of them to lead a formal "invitation" to recite the blessings after the meal.

Leader says:	Sirs, let us bless.
Others respond:	Blessed be the Name of God from this time and forever!
Leader says:	Blessed be the Name of God from this time and forever! With the permission of the distinguished people present, let us bless . . .

(if more than ten bar mitzvahs have eaten together, add "our God")

	. . . He of Whose (food) we have eaten.
Others respond:	Blessed is . . .

(if more than ten bar mitzvahs have eaten together, add "our God")

	. . . He of Whose (food) we have eaten and through Whose goodness we live. Blessed is He and Blessed is His Name.

First blessing: For the nourishment

This paragraph has been recited by Jews for millennia; it was written by Moses, and gives voice to our most basic link with God: that, like a loving parent, God ensures we have the food we need to live.

Blessed are You, God our Lord, King of the universe, Who nourishes the entire world, in His goodness — with grace, with kindness, and with mercy. He gives nourishment to all flesh, for His kindness is eternal. And through His great goodness, we have never lacked, and may we never lack, nourishment, for all

eternity. For the sake of His Great Name, because He is God Who nourishes and sustains all, and benefits all, and He prepares food for all of His creatures which He has created. Blessed are You, God, Who nourishes all.

Second blessing: For the land

In this section, we thank God for setting us up as a free people, in our Land (the Land of Israel). (On the holidays of Chanukah and Purim, we also thank God here for the miracles He made on those holidays to allow us to continue existing as a nation.)

We thank You, God, our Lord, because You have given to our forefathers as a heritage a desirable, good and spacious land; becaue You removed us, God, our Lord, from the land of Egypt and You redeemed us from the house of bondage; for Your covenant which you sealed in our flesh; for Your Torah which You taught us and for Your statutes which You made known to us; for life, grace, and loving kindness which You granted us; and for the provision of food with which You nourish and sustain us constantly, in every day, in every season, and in every hour. (Extra blessings are added here on Chanukah[1] and Purim.[2])

---

1 On Chanukah say: And for the miracles, and for the salvation, and for the mighty deeds, and for the victories, and for the battles which You performed for our forefathers in those days, at this time. In the days of Mattisyahu, the son of Yochanan, the High Priest, the Hasmonean, and his sons — when the wicked Greek kingdom rose up against Your people Israel to make them forget Your Torah and compel them to stray from the statutes of Your Will — You in Your great mercy stood up for them in the time of their distress. You took up their grievance, judged their claim, and avenged their wrong. You delivered the strong into the hands of the weak, the many into the hands of the few, the impure into the hands of the pure, the wicked into the hands of the righteous, and the wanton into the hands of the diligent students of Your Torah. For Yourself You made a great and holy Name in Your world, and for Your people Israel you worked a great victory and salvation as this very day. Thereafter, your children came to the Holy of Holies of Your House, cleansed Your Temple, purified the site of Your Holiness and kindled lights in the Courtyards of Your sanctuary; and they established these eight days of Chanukah to express thanks and praise to Your great name

2 On Purim say: And for the miracles, and for the salvation, and for the mighty deeds, and for the victories, and for the battles which You performed for our forefathers in those days, at this time. In the days of Mordechai and Esther, in Shushan, the capital, when Haman, the wicked, rose up against them and sought to destroy, to slay, and to exterminate all the Jews, young and old, infants and women, on the same day, on the thirteenth of the twelfth month which is the month of Adar, and to plunder their possessions. But You, in Your abundant

For all, God, our Lord, we thank You and bless You. May Your Name be blessed by the mouth of all the living, continuously for all eternity. As it is written: "And you shall eat and you shall be satisfied and you shall bless God, your God, for the good land which He gave you." (Deut. 8.10) Blessed are You, God, for the land and for the nourishment.

Third blessing: For Jerusalem

In this section, we thank God for giving us Jerusalem, where our ancient holy Temple once stood. On Shabbat and other major Jewish holidays — when our ancestors used to bring special sacrifices to God at our Temple — we recite extra paragraphs in this section.

Have mercy God, our Lord, on Israel Your people; on Jerusalem, Your city, on Zion, the resting place of Your Glory; on the monarchy of the house of David, Your anointed; and on the great and holy House upon which Your Name is called. Our God, our Father — tend us, nourish us, sustain us, support us, relieve us; God, our Lord, grant a speedy relief from all our troubles. Please, make us not needful — God, our Lord — of the gifts of human hands nor of their loans, but only of Your Hand that is full, open, holy, and generous, that we not feel inner shame nor be humiliated for ever and ever.

(On Shabbat, say:) May it please You, God, our Lord — give us rest through Your commandments and through the commandment of the seventh day, this great and holy Shabbat. For this day is great and holy before You to rest on it and be content on it in love, as ordained by Your will. May it be Your will, God, our Lord, that there be no distress, grief, or lament on this day of our contentment. And show us, God, our Lord, that there be no distress, grief, or lament on this day of our contentment. And show us, God, our Lord, the consolation of Zion, Your city, and the rebuilding of Jerusalem, City of Your holiness, for You are the Master of salvations and Master of consolations.

---

mercy, nullified his counsel and frustrated his intention and caused his design to return upon his own head and they hanged him and his sons on the gallows.

(Extra blessings are added here on the major Jewish holidays.[3])

Rebuild Jerusalem, the Holy City, soon in our days. Blessed are You, God, Who rebuilds Jerusalem in His mercy. Amen.

Fourth blessing: For God's goodness

In this final section of Birkat HaMazon, we thank God for the goodness He showers upon us every day. On Shabbat and other Jewish holidays, we add extra passages asking God for good fortune and extra blessings. Also, in these concluding paragraphs, we take a moment to ask for blessings for ourselves, our families, and — if we are guests at someone else's table — for our hosts.

Blessed are You, God, our Lord, King of the universe, the Almighty, our Father, our King, our Sovereign, our Creator, our Redeemer, our Maker, our Holy One, Holy One of Jacob, our Shepherd, the Shepherd of Israel, the King Who is good and Who does good for all. For every single day He did good, He does good, and He will do good to us. He was bountiful with us, He is bountiful with us, and He will forever be bountiful with us — with grace and with kindness and with mercy, with relief, salvation, success, blessing, help, consolation, sustenance, support, mercy, life, peace, and all good; and of all good things may He never deprive us.

The compassionate One! May He reign over us forever. The compassionate

---

3 Our God and God of our forefathers, may there rise, come, reach, be noted, be favored, be heard, be considered, and be remembered — the remembrance and consideration of ourselves; the remembrance of our forefathers; the remembrance of Messiah, son of David, Your servant; the remembrance of Jerusalem, the City of Your Holiness; the remembrance of Your entire people the Family of Israel — before You for deliverance, for goodness, for grace, for kindness, and for compassion, for life, and for peace on this day of (On Rosh Hashanah say "Remembrance." On Passover say "the Festival of Matzos." On Succot say "the Succos Festival." On Shavuot say "the Shavuos Festival." On Shemini Atzeres say "the Shemini Atzeres Festival." On Rosh Chodesh say "Rosh Chodesh.") Remember us on it, God, our Lord, for goodness; consider us on it for blessing; and help us on it for life. In the matter of salvation and compassion, pity, be gracious and compassionate with us and help us, for our eyes are turned to You, because You are God, the gracious, and compassionate (On Rosh Hashanah add: "King").

One! May He be blessed in heaven and on earth. The compassionate One! May He be praised throughout all generations, may He be glorified through us forever to the ultimate ends, and be honored through us forever and for all eternity. The compassionate One! May He sustain us in honor. The compassionate One! May He break the yoke of oppression from our necks and guide us erect to our Land. The compassionate One! May He sends us abundant blessing to this house and upon this table at which we have eaten. The compassionate One! May he send us Elijah, the Prophet — he is remembered for good — to proclaim to us good tidings, salvations, and consolations.

Those eating at their own table recite (including the words in parentheses that apply):

The compassionate One! May He bless me (my wife/husband and my children and all that is mine).

Guests recite the following (children at their parents' table include the words in parentheses):

The compassionate One! May He bless (my father, my teacher) the master of this house, and (my mother, my teacher) lady of this house, them, their house, their family, and all that is theirs.

Ours and all that is ours — just as our forefathers Abraham, Isaac, and Jacob were blessed in everything, from everything, with everything. So may He bless us all together with a perfect blessing. And let us say: Amen!

On high, may merit be pleaded upon them and upon us, for a safeguard of peace. May we receive a blessing from God and just kindness from the God of our salvation, and find favor and good understanding in the eyes of God and man.

On Shabbat say: "The compassionate One! May He cause us to inherit the day which will be completely a Shabbat and rest day for eternal life."

On other Jewish holidays, we recite an extra line here.[4]

The compassionate One! May He make us worthy of the days of Messiah and the life of the World to Come . . .

([On Shabbat say] "He Who is a tower of salvations to His king"

[On weekdays say instead] "He Who makes great the salvations of His king")

and does kindness for His anointed, to David and to his descendants forever. He Who makes peace in His heights, may He make peace upon us and upon all Israel. Now respond: Amen!

Fear God, you — His holy ones — for there is no deprivation for His reverent ones. Young lions may want and hunger, but those who seek God will not lack any good. Give thanks to God for He is good; His kindness endures forever. You open Your hand and satisfy the desire of every living thing. Blessed is the man who trusts in God, then God will be his security. I was a youth and also have aged, and I have not seen a righteous man forsaken with his children begging for bread. God will give might to His people; God will bless His people with peace.

---

4 On Rosh Hashana say,
   "The compassionate One! May He inaugurate this year upon us for goodness and for blessing."
   On holidays (Rosh Hashana, Yom Kippur, Succot, Passover, Shavuot, Shemini Atzeres, and Rosh Chodesh) say "The compassionate One! May He cause us to inherit the day which is completely good."
   On Succot add: "The compassionate One! May He erect for us David's fallen booth."
   On Rosh Chodesh say, "The compassionate One! May He inaugurate this month upon us for goodness and for blessing."

Appendix

Ideas for further reading

As you begin to explore different Jewish topics and learn new aspects of Jewish tradition and Torah, you will soon find your own favorite authors and approaches. It is said that the Torah is a sea: we can sail in it our entire lives, and never hope to know all its vast riches. To study it, though, is fascinating and fun. If one book, author or topic fails to interest you, "dip your toe" into another part of this vast body of knowledge. There is something for everyone in the ocean of Torah learning. Here is a highly personal list of a few books that I have greatly enjoyed. Use these as a starting-off point as you begin navigating the mighty Sea of Torah yourself. It will take some reading and experimenting to find which Torah topics grab you the most. This is an incredibly rewarding journey. I wish you luck in getting started!

Classic Jewish commentaries

I find that often people don't know where to begin in learning Torah: it all seems so bewildering and confusing. Simply put, the Torah is not meant to be merely read. In order to understand all its many layers and components, we read it along with commentaries on its text. Commentaries turn what can otherwise seem like a simple story into a deep, meaningful tale, full of interesting lessons and hidden meanings. A commentary on the Torah is called a "peirush" in Hebrew, and many men and women have written their own

"peirush" on various parts of the Torah (and continue to do so today).

Rashi

The most basic, famous commentator on the Torah and the Talmud is a rabbi known as Rashi. This is an acronym for his full name, Rabbi Shlomo Yitzchaki. Rashi lived in northern France in the eleventh century CE, and wrote the most perceptive, authoritative peirush on the entire Torah, including the Talmud. Today, no traditional Jew would ever begin learning Torah without referring to Rashi, and "Torah with Rashi" is considered the most fundamental way to read the Torah. If you wish to begin studying Torah, you might acquire your own books of Torah with Rashi's commentary as a place to begin. Given Rashi's ubiquity, there are many, many editions of Torah with Rashi on the market. One you might like to start with is:

➤ The *Sapirstein Edition Rashi*, edited by Rabbi Yisrael Herczeg

Ramban

A second major classical commentator on the Torah — who is very accessible to beginner-level students — was Rabbi Moshe ben Nachman (also known by his acronym "Ramban," or his secular name, "Nachmonides"), who lived in Spain and Israel in the thirteenth century CE. Once you acquire and begin studying Torah with Rashi, you might want to learn Torah with Ramban's (more lengthy and detailed) commentaries to guide you, as well. There are several excellent editions of Ramban's commentaries on the Hebrew Bible. Two possible editions you might like to start with are:

➤ *Ramban*, edited by Yehuda Bulman and Avi Gold
➤ *Torah with Ramban's Commentary Translated, Annotated and Elucidated* (Mesorah Publications Ltd.)

Modern Jewish commentaries

Nechama Leibowitz

Rashi and Ramban are two of the most central Jewish commentators on the Torah, but there are myriad commentators from the modern age, as well.

My own favorite has always been Nechama Leibowitz, who taught about the "Chumash" (as the Hebrew Bible is called in Hebrew) in Israel from the 1930s until her death in 1997. In 1942, when she was 37, Nechama Leibowitz started sending out weekly sheets of Torah commentaries and questions on the weekly Parsha to Jewish individuals throughout Israel and abroad. On these sheets, she cited many of the major traditional commentaries on various passages, added her own thoughts and comments, posed thought-provoking questions on the text, and asked her readers to send in their various replies. Eventually, Dr. Leibowitz developed a written dialogue with thousands of students, and their questions and comments informed the five volumes she eventually published:

➤ *Studies in Bereshit (Genesis)*
➤ *Studies in Shemot (Exodus)*
➤ *Studies in Vayikra (Leviticus)*
➤ *Studies in Bemidbar (Numbers)*
➤ *Studies in Devarim (Deuteronomy)*

(These books are, sadly, out of print, but I find that many Jewish bookstores and on-line book and Judaica websites stock old copies of this excellent series.)

I'm always extremely touched when I read Nechama Leibowitz's thanks in her Introduction to her first book, *Studies in Bereshit (Genesis)*. She recalls:

There were regulars who wrote dutifully week by week, year in year out. . . . I wish here to pay tribute to those who contacted me under difficult conditions after a hard day's work, in the burning sun during a break in the field; to the streetsweeper who wrote in the height of a rainstorm after doing his day's stint, to the machinist dropping me a line during the lunch-break amidst the noise of the factory, to the nurse using her precious hours of rest after a back-breaking night shift. . . . There were soldiers who wrote to me under conditions defying description: coastguards, World War II volunteers in the Libyan desert and the Jewish Brigade, fighters in the War of Liberation delivering their notes to me personally from a forward position during a chance

lull in the Capital's shelling when the postal service was at a standstill, correspondents from the Suez Canal during the War of Attrition, from ambushes in the Golan and from all those guarding the borders of our homeland. . . . I am enthralled by this vast army of old and young, mothers and girls, teachers male and female, clerks and laborers, veterans and newcomers of all communities, hundreds of thousands, literally, studying Torah for its own sake. For our joint studies involved no certificates, examinations, marks, prizes; no credits, scholarships, income-tax rebates but simply the joy so deep of the one who studies Torah.

These words never fail to stir me, and inspire me to a similar dedication to learning Torah. In traditional Judaism, the ideal of learning Torah is to learn it "lishmah," for its own sake — not because one expects any sort of reward. When I think of the nurses and factory workers and street sweepers and soldiers studying Nechama Leibowitz's weekly lessons, I thank God that I can read her books in the comfort of my own living room. Leibowitz's discussions and questions on each week's Parsha are so thought-provoking that even though it is many years since she sent out her weekly Torah lessons, I still feel like I'm part of a vast network of people all studying Torah with her each week.

Rabbi Yehuda Nachshoni
Another major modern commentary, wonderful for beginners, is
➤ *Studies in the Weekly Parashah* by Rabbi Yehuda Nachshoni

Rabbi Moshe Weissman
➤ *The Midrash Says* by Rabbi Moshe Weissman

This series is also an excellent, thorough commentary on the weekly Parsha, incorporating commentaries from classical Jewish texts.

Rabbi Lord Jonathan Sacks
➤ *Covenant and Conversation* by Rabbi Lord Jonathan Sacks

This offers a modern perspective on each week's Parsha written by the Chief Rabbi of Great Britain.

Aviva Gottlieb Zorenberg

➤ *The Beginnings of Desire* by Aviva Gottlieb Zorenberg

Prof. Zorenberg blends modern psychotherapy insights with traditional biblical analysis.

Other commentaries

I'd advise anyone interested in learning the weekly Parsha with a commentary to browse a Jewish bookstore, the library of a local Orthodox shul or rabbi, or, at the very least, a Jewish book website such as www.feldheim.com, www.targum.com, www.judaicapress.com, www.ktav.com, or www. artscroll.com to get a sense of the many, many Torah commentaries out there, and select one or two with which to start your own Torah learning and library.

Commentaries on the Internet

For those who prefer a lighter approach, there are many "bite-sized" comments available on the weekly Parsha. Many Jewish websites contain numerous "divrei Torah" ("words of Torah") that you can download about each week's Parsha for study on Shabbat. A few of the most basic of these websites, suitable for beginners, are www.chabad.org, www.aish.org, www. arachimusa.org, and www.ou.org. For more advanced weekly divrei Torah, you might want to look at sites such as: http://parsha.net, which contains comments by many prominent modern rabbis; www.webyeshiva.org, an Israeli-based website founded by the distinguished Israel-based educator Rabbi Chaim Brovender; www.jewishstudies.org, a Jerusalem-based "Jewish Interactive Studies" website; www.ohr.edu, the excellent website

of the Israeli yeshiva (rabbinical academy) Ohr Somayach; and www.vbm-torah.org, the excellent Israel Koschitzky Virtual Beit Midrash ("house of study"). All of these sites, and others, provide numerous articles and sheets you can download for study on Shabbat.

Other classic Jewish texts

Pirkei Avot

Pirkei Avot (literally "Words of the Fathers") is a collection of profound words of advice for living taken from the part of the Talmud called the Mishnah. It was compiled in the third century CE, and is a thoughtful, inspiring work, full of beautiful and quotable insights. I have particularly enjoyed learning this work using the beautiful, inspiring commentary of the great twelfth-century Jewish philosopher Rabbi Moshe Ben Maimon. A wonderful version aimed at beginners is:

➤ *Maimonides' Commentary on Pirkey Avoth* edited by Paul Forchheimer

Given *Pirkei Avot*'s enduring popularity, there are many modern commentaries on the market which help explain this central Jewish work. One nice modern version is:

➤ *Pirkei Avot* by Rabbi Meir Zlotowitz.

Check out your favorite Jewish bookstore or website to find commentaries on *Pirkei Avot* you feel comfortable with.

Books of the Torah

You might also want to examine other, lesser-known books of the Torah such as the Books of Mishlei ("Proverbs"), Iyov ("Job"), Esther, Shir Hashirim ("Song of Songs"), and Kohelet ("Ecclesiastes"). In studying any of these, I'd recommend using modern translations and commentaries. Many current books contain commentaries and discussions that draw on many different traditional Jewish commentaries of these books, and serve as introductions to the topics that can be particularly useful to people with

little background in traditional Jewish study. Again, a good place to start is local Jewish bookstores, libraries, or the websites of major Jewish publishing houses.

Other Jewish-themed books

When people talk about learning Torah they often mean learning other Jewish-themed texts besides the weekly Parsha, as well. There are literally thousands of quality books on Jewish themes written from an Orthodox perspective. Going to a Jewish library or bookstore, or trawling Jewish publisher's websites can be a wonderful experience. Some of my particular favorites that I have enjoyed learning from include the following:

➤ I have greatly enjoyed learning the Jewish laws about gossip and proper speech from the book *Chofetz Chaim: A Lesson a Day* by Rabbi Shimon Finkelman; perhaps nothing else has changed my life so profoundly as learning what types of harmful speech and gossip Judaism forbids.

➤ I have also spent many rewarding Shabbats learning the rules of various mitzvot, such as keeping kosher, Shabbat, and the holidays. Three of my favorite books on these topics are:

    1 *How to Run a Traditional Jewish Household* by Blu Greenberg

    2 *The Laws of Kashrus* (which means the rules of keeping kosher in Hebrew) by Rabbi Binyomin Forst

    3 *Book of Our Heritage* by Eliyahu Kitov, a major work, originally published in Hebrew, which discusses the meanings and mitzvot of the different Jewish holidays

➤ Years ago, I was practically forced to buy the *Collected Letters by the Lubavitcher Rebbe* from a very insistent shopkeeper in Jerusalem who adhered to the Lubavitcher movement (a Chassidic Jewish group), who told me they would change my life. She was right, to an extent, and I have drawn spiritual and intellectual sustenance from these volumes, which address issues and concerns of Jews throughout the year, commenting on various seasons and holidays and the challenges

they pose for Jewish communities today.

➤ Other Jewish writers whose books have taught me a great deal over the years, and who appeal to beginners as well as "intermediate" Jewish learners include:

1 Esther Jungreis (my favorite is *The Committed Life* about accepting life's obligations)

2 Miriam Adahan (I really love *It's all a Gift*, about choosing to be happy)

3 Rabbi Abraham Twerski (my particular favorite is *Living Each Day*, which offers brief divrei Torah, or words of Torah, on diverse topics)

4 Rabbi Adin Steinsaltz (his *The Thirteen Petalled Rose*, about the nature of God, is a classic)

5 Norman Lamm (*Torah Umadda* a more advanced work about the relationship between Jewish and secular knowledge)

6 Rebbetzin Tziporah Heller (*More Precious Than Pearls* is an inspiring analysis of the Jewish Shabbat prayer "Eishet Chayil"; *Battle Plans* addresses how to resist temptation and live on a higher plane).

Jewish children's books

I love Jewish children's books that are aimed at an Orthodox readership. They don't take too much knowledge for granted, and they explain things in a clear and understandable way. For learning about the Jewish holidays, my favorite is the ten-volume

➤ *Bina and Benny* series by Yaffa Ganz.

There are some great children's books that explain the weekly Torah Parsha, too.

➤ *Let's Learn Parshas Ha-Shavua* by B. Heller is basic but informative.

➤ *The Parsha with Rabbi Juravel* by Rabbi Juravel is fantastic, though as of this writing his series was not yet finished.

➤ *The Little Midrash Says* by S. Forst is a classic, and includes many stories to illustrate its points.

➤ *A World of Midos* ("midos" are character traits) is a tape series, so unsuitable for Shabbat itself, but these tapes contain great information about the weekly Parshas and lovely Shabbat stories that can be listened to before Shabbat starts. They are written and narrated by Rabbis Fishel Schachter and Yonasan Schwartz.

Finally, children's translations and commentaries of the Books of Jonah and Esther, the Passover Haggadah, and especially the children's Siddur by Shmuel Blitz that are published by Artscroll (www.artscroll.com) are beautiful and informative. (*The Children's Siddur* by Shmuel Blitz is the siddur my businesswoman friend was talking about in Chapter 9.)

It is my hope for you that the beauty, wisdom, tradition, and truth that I have attempted to describe in these pages propel you towards the incredible, transcendent joy of a traditional Shabbat. May God bless you and keep watch over you. May God make His presence enlighten you and grant you grace. May God direct His providence towards you and grant you peace. May God's name thus be linked with yours, and may God bless you. Amen.

Index

Acknowledgements

No Jew wishes, nor can he, sever himself from God.
—The Alter Rebbe, 1745–1812

This is a beautiful quote, and one I've had cause to consider many times over the years. As my family and I have grown in Torah observance, I have found our lives enriched: our relationships strengthened, and our individual peace and sense of self enhanced. Of course, the purpose of Torah observance is not merely to boost our self-esteem; it is to engage in the incredible privilege of serving God. Yet, here too, I have always found traditional, Orthodox Judaism to be enormously empowering. By following God's laws, we increase holiness in the world. Not only is the Torah a blueprint for greater personal and family harmony, but by following the path that God has laid out for us as Jews, we can forge a powerful connection with God, and increase God's presence on earth.

Over the years, many Jewish friends and acquaintances have turned to me with questions about traditional Judaism. Often, the conversations that ensued have led to deep friendships. Frequently, these conversations led my husband and me to invite many of our non-Orthodox Jewish friends to share Shabbat meals with our family, and the conversations and questions continued at our Shabbat table. It would be folly for me to hold myself up as the possessor of one "right" answer to all the many Jewish questions I've been asked. Clearly, Jewish tradition is wide and varied, and I am a seeker within it, along with my friends.

Yet the more conversations about Jewish life in which I engaged, the more often friends who were interested in experiencing a traditional Shabbat

shared meals with my family, the more I began to formulate a plan in my mind. As the years have gone by, I became more and more certain of two things that I wish to convey to people who had come to me to help them gain a deeper understanding of Judaism. One idea is expressed in the daily morning service: "My God, the soul that you placed in me is pure." Unlike in some conceptions of modern Judaism, "Jewish guilt" has no place in traditional, Orthodox Judaism. Our religion is not a faith of misery and blame, but of spirituality and joy. The second thought I became certain that I wanted to share was that so much of the beauty of traditional, authentic Judaism is found in Shabbat, and that despite the common fallacy that Shabbat is too difficult, an Orthodox Shabbat is well within every Jew's grasp.

These twin ideas — of Jewish joy, and the accessibility of Shabbat — percolated in my mind for a long time. I began to draw the outlines of this book in my imagination at around the time I became pregnant with my son Natan. For nine months, I thought about it, and then, within days of Natan's birth, I began writing this book. "Natan" means "gave", in the sense that God gave us His Torah and Shabbat, and I hope that this book helps you to claim this heritage yourself. I wrote this book during Natan's many naps in his first year of life, and my greatest thanks are to Hakodesh Baruch Hu, the Holy One, Blessed be He, for giving me the strength to somehow persevere through extreme sleep deprivation. (I have very vivid memories of trying to take some naps myself during that busy first year, but of being too excited about whichever chapter I was then working on to sleep!)

This book owes its existence to Caroline Chartres of Continuum Books, who believed in its message and shepherded it to publication. I am indebted to her for her tireless work on behalf of this book, and for her wise advice on all aspects of its completion.

Early in the writing process, Miriam Zakon's encouragement and advice were invaluable. I am indebted to Rabbi Hershel Berger for reading through this book in manuscript form and providing comments and guidance. (Though, it should be stressed, any errors in this text are entirely my own.) I also benefited from the advice on some portions of Rabbi Shlomo Levin. (Again, all errors are my own.) In the early stages of this work, Rabbi Akiva Tatz, Rabbi Daniel Moskowitz, and Rabbi Eliyahu Karsh all offered

encouragement and support; their belief in this book was heartening and gave me the courage to proceed.

My family was also enormously loyal, kind and sympathetic while I completed this project. My husband, Jeremy Miller, my parents, Maureen and George Alt, and my brother Jonathan Alt all offered both moral and practical support as I wrote this, and were great sounding boards for ideas. My children, Jacob, Simi, Gideon and Natan have been patient and inspirational as well. (I'd like to thank them for being uncomplaining while Mommy worked on her book!)

Hebrew translations for several prayers are adapted from *The Complete Artscroll Siddur* by Yvette Alt Miller with permission of the copyright holders, Artscroll/Mesorah Publications, Ltd. These prayers are: Asher Yatzar, Eishet Chayil, Kiddush for Shabbat (Friday night and Saturday morning versions), Yehi Ratzon, Havdolah, and Birkat HaMazon.